Teaching in Further Education

An Outline of Principles and Practice

L.B. Curzon

Third Edition

Cassell

Cassell Educational Ltd: Artillery House, Artillery Row,
London SW1P 1RT

British Library Cataloguing in Publication Data

Curzon, L.B.
　Teaching in further education: an outline
　of principles and practice.—3rd ed.
　1. College teaching—Great Britain
　I. Title
　374'.02　　　LB2331

ISBN 0–304–31447–1

Typeset by Cotswold Typesetting Ltd, Cheltenham
Printed and bound in Great Britain by
Biddles Ltd, Guildford and King's Lynn

Last digit is print no: 9 8 7 6 5 4

TEACHING IN FURTHER EDUCATION

'What would we say of an architect who, in putting up a new building, could not tell you what he was building, whether it was a temple dedicated to the god of truth, love and right, a simple house in which it would be comfortable to live, a handsome though useless ceremonial gateway that those driving through would admire, a gilded hotel for fleecing improvident travellers, a kitchen for cooking victuals, a museum for the custody of rarities, or finally a shed for storing old junk that one no longer needed? You should say the same, too, about an educator who does not know how to define the ends of his educational work for you clearly and precisely.'

K. D. Ushinsky: *Man as the Object of Education* (1868)

'How to live?—that is the essential question for us. Not how to live in the mere material sense only, but in the widest sense. The general problem which comprehends every special problem is—the right ruling of conduct in all directions under all circumstances. In what way to treat the body; in what way to treat the mind; in what way to manage our affairs; in what way to bring up a family; in what way to behave as a citizen; in what way to utilise those sources of happiness which nature supplies—how to use all our faculties to the greatest advantage of ourselves and others—how to live completely? And this being the great thing needful for us to learn, is, by consequence, the great thing which education has to teach. To prepare us for complete living is the function which education has to discharge; and the only rational mode of judging of an educational course is to judge in what degree it discharges such function.'

Herbert Spencer: *Education* (1861)

Foreword

By E.I. Baker, CBE, MA
formerly one of Her Majesty's
Staff Inspectors of Schools

Teaching in Further Education covers a wide field and this new edition brings it fully up to date. It is written by an expert who has had a lifetime's experience in further education. He has served as a principal both in this country and abroad, he is a well-known author of textbooks on law and economics, he is a first-rate lecturer and teacher, and he is an experienced examiner.

This book, written in a direct and lucid style, has already enjoyed considerable success. The new matter included in this third edition—how to study with or without the use of computers, hints on the maintenance of class discipline, student counselling, and computer-aided learning—will make it an indispensable aid for practising teachers as well as a standard textbook for those preparing to teach. Having read this third edition with critical admiration and pleasure, I recommend it not only as a reliable guide to the latest theories in education but also as a handbook for the solution of practical problems in the classroom.

Contents

Introduction to the third edition

This book originated and took shape in the belief that there was a need for a text which would outline some of the principles and practices involved in formal teaching in the colleges of further education. It is intended specifically for those who are preparing for the various further education teachers' certificate examinations, whether they be full-time students attending teacher training courses or teachers engaged in part-time study, and for practising teachers who are interested in an analysis of the nature of their professional activities.

An attempt has been made throughout the text to combine principles and practice, to outline some of the theory behind classroom activities and to examine some of the techniques of formal instruction. The first part of the book notes some of the more important contributions of psychology to the theory of learning; it is hoped that this will whet the appetite of the reader for the rich and fascinating literature of experimental psychology. The second part deals with the techniques of communication and control as applied to the teacher's tasks, and with the concept and taxonomies of teaching objectives. The third part outlines some of the tasks of management which have to be carried out by the teacher and considers in detail the principal modes of formal instruction which are in common use in the colleges of further education.

Throughout the text the terms 'teacher', 'tutor', 'lecturer', 'instructor', are used synonymously (as they tend to be used in practice in the colleges) unless the context suggests a specialised meaning. This applies also to 'teaching' and 'instructing', and to 'classroom' and 'lecture room'.

A number of important changes have been made in this third edition, several of which are in response to valuable and constructive criticisms voiced by readers of the previous edition. Part One of the text has been enlarged and now includes sections dealing with the link between the theory and practice of teaching, and the concepts of teaching as science and art. Part Two has been enlarged and rewritten in part so as to include an extended treatment of communication and motivation theory. Part Three includes new chapters on teaching students how to study, and teaching the older student. The chapter on class discipline has been revised and now contains a section on student counselling. Tutorial groups and computer-aided learning are also covered. The formation of the Business and Technician Education Council and its impact on further education are noted. Material previously found in the reference notes has been embodied in the text, and an extensive bibliography, intended to assist teachers who are interested in further study, appears at the end of the book.

I am grateful to: the Royal Institution for permission to quote from Michael Faraday's *Advice to a Lecturer;* Macdonald & Evans for permission to use examples from my *Objective Tests in Economics* and *Objective Tests in Commerce;* Penguin for permission to use an extract from my *Test Your Economics;* and the City & Guilds of London Institute for permission to use an example of objective test items taken from the booklet, *Objective Testing.*

I express my thanks to: Mr A. Matten, of the Associated Examining Board, who permitted me to cite his taxonomy of educational objectives; and Mr E.I. Baker CBE, formerly one of Her Majesty's Staff Inspectors of Schools and Principal of the Uganda College of Commerce, for advice and encouragement.

The essential features of this book may best be summed up in the precise words of Marcus Fabius Quintilianus, writing in his *Institutio Oratoria,* in AD 100:

> I have presented in plain and simple terms, for the instruction of those who wished to learn, such lessons as I have gained from my own experience, and all else that I have been able to discover for the purposes of this work. And it is enough for a good man to have taught what he knows.

LBC

PART ONE

ASPECTS OF THE NATURE OF LEARNING

1
A view of the teaching-learning process

It is time, perhaps, to view theory and practice in education as two sides of the same coin, or maybe, more like a Möbius strip (Williams 1982).

The human activity which we call 'education' is largely based in our society on the related processes known as 'teaching' and 'learning'. The formalisation of these processes, so that they are carried out within schools, colleges and similar institutions, results basically from society's conscious responses to fundamental problems of adaptation and survival. Education in our society is generally concerned with the handing on of beliefs and moral standards, knowledge and skills. It may be viewed as 'the nurture of the human personality' *and* as 'investment in human capital'. In its essence it is a recognition of the fact that society's mode of life must be *learned*—since an understanding of it is not inherited—by each individual. The assimilation of earlier generations' experience is at the basis of this task. Education assists the younger generation in that process of assimilation. Learning depends on the individual's experiences within, for example, his family, his social environment and, more specifically, the educational institutions he attends. It is the processes of learning and teaching within some of those institutions that we consider in this book. In this chapter we examine the meaning of 'learning' and 'teaching'.

Teaching: art or science?

Discussion with almost any group of teachers will reveal fundamental differences of opinion on the classification of teaching as an art or a

3

science. Some will insist that teaching is the scientific application of tested theory; some will argue that it is essentially a 'performance' that can be characterised as aesthetic, so that it has to be considered as a form of art; some will maintain that it is a hybrid, an art with a scientific basis, or a science with overtones of artistic impression; some will deny art and science any place in the 'purely practical, day-to-day activity in the classroom'. Others will be amazed to learn that their teaching activities can be classified as partaking of the nature of either a science or an art—rather like Molière's M. Jourdain who was amazed to find that he had been 'speaking prose' all his life!

Observation of a series of teaching activities in a typical college of further education will reveal a variety of approaches. One successful lesson may have been prepared carefully on the basis of an analysis of student needs, culminating in a listing of instructional objectives. Teaching strategy and tactics will have played their part in a planned utilisation of class time. Another successful lesson may have been characterised by a seemingly casual approach in which the teacher has employed his skills in a deliberate attempt to discover 'ends through action'; his activities would bring to mind the description of the artist as 'one who plays hide-and-seek but does not know what he seeks until he finds it'.

The distinction between teaching as art and science is typified in the approaches of Eisner (1979) and Skinner (1938 and 1968). Eisner enumerates four senses in which teaching should be considered an art. First, it is an art in the sense that the teacher 'can perform with such skill and grace' that for teacher and student alike the performance provides an intrinsic form of expression—the lesson has the overtones of an 'aesthetic experience'. Secondly, it is an art in the sense that teachers, in their work, must exercise qualitative judgements in the interest of achieving qualitative ends. Thirdly, teaching, 'like any other art', involves a tension between 'automaticity and inventiveness'. Finally, teaching is an art in the sense that many of its ends are 'emergent'—they are not preconceived; they emerge in the course of an interaction (with students).

Skinner argues that 'successful teaching' must be the result of the conscious application of scientifically-validated theory to classroom situations. Successful teaching does not happen fortuitously; it emerges when the teacher has made, and understood, a correct analysis of student behaviour in terms of 'the complex interplay of elementary concepts and principles'. When behaviour is understood, an appropriate instructional methodology must be sought in order that it might be modified on the basis of desired ends. On the practising teacher and the scientist investigating classroom behaviour will fall the joint tasks of observing fact, formulating theory, applying it and then reinterpreting both fact and theory.

Fundamental to this book is the belief that the practice of teaching ought to move to a position in which it is based consciously on an application of theory abstracted from the full reality of the classroom and its environment, and that such theory and practice ought to be subjected to continuous, severe criticism. The critical, methodical appraisal of teaching principles and practice would seem to be a pre-requisite for the construction of a comprehensive theory of teaching, whether it be considered as science or art. One thing, however, is certain: teaching, because of its very nature, can never be an *exact* science. In any event, it is well to remember Solow's comment:

> All theory depends on assumptions which are not quite true. That is what makes it theory (Solow 1956).

The relevance and utility of theory

The relevance of theory to teaching practice is not immediately apparent to many teachers. The young teacher, fresh from his training course, overwhelmed by new experiences, is often unable to link the reality of the classroom with the theories he has learned. The experienced teacher, hard-pressed to maintain standards in the face of unimaginative administrative decisions, may feel that he has 'no time for theory conceived at a far, comfortable distance from the chalk face'. Both epitomise those teachers for whom difficulties in accepting theory make impossible its reception and translation into practice. Set out below are some frequently-posed questions on this topic.

'"Principles", "axioms", "theorems", "theories" . . . What exactly do these terms mean?'

These words are often used conterminously in books dealing with teaching theory. They can be differentiated, however. A *principle* is a generalisation that provides a guide to conduct or procedure, e.g. the principle that effective teaching demands control of the classroom situation. An *axiom* is a self-evident principle that is, apparently, not open to dispute, e.g. the axiom that lack of motivation makes for learning difficulties. A *theorem* is a proposition admitting of rational proof which is usually necessary to succeeding steps in some structure of reasoning, e.g. the theorem that it is possible to test and assess the level of a student's intelligence. A *theory* is a system of ideas attempting to explain a group of phenomena, such as the process of learning.

'Why do teaching theoreticians employ so much jargon? Why can't they use everyday language?'

A specialised body of knowledge tends to generate and use its own technical terminology. Consider, for example, the use of words such as 'energy' in physics, 'market' in economics, 'duty' in jurisprudence. The knowledge on which teaching theory rests is of a highly-specialised nature. Psychology, neurology, biology—all have contributed to teaching–learning theory. It is not easy to substitute 'everyday language' for technical terms and yet maintain acceptable standards of precision. As an example, attempt to replace with everyday language terms such as 'conditioning', 'encoding', 'channels of communication'.

'Why is there so much disagreement among teaching–learning theoreticians? They don't agree even on the meaning of basic terms, such as "education"!'

Teaching is a complex activity, varying outwardly from one situation to another, so that it is not easy to explain or define its nature with precision, hence much of the disagreement. (Try, as an exercise in definition, to bring under one conceptual heading the modes of instruction involved in showing a child how to tie her shoelaces, teaching an adolescent the use of a typewriter, explaining to an adult the concept of idiom in a foreign language. Attempt, further, to recall how you 'learned' to tell the time, to use logarithms, to drive a car.) Not all theoreticians and practising teachers perceive events in the same way; hence, interpretations of events differ. Disagreement is not necessarily a sign of an ineffective body of knowledge: difference in the interpretation of quantum theory have not prevented advances in physics. Terms such as 'education' overlap several areas, such as the 'inexact sciences' of sociology and politics, hence the disagreement as to precise meaning. Jurists continue to dispute the meaning of 'law', economists often disagree as to the meaning of 'economics'. Lack of agreement on definitions does not imply total uncertainty within a discipline; it may indicate, rather, the existence of a number of approaches to the areas of knowledge embraced by that discipline.

'Much teaching–learning theory seems to be based on the work of writers who lived centuries ago. Plato, Aristotle, Locke . . . what possible relevance have their views for education in an age which they could not have envisaged?'

> He who would confine his thought to present time will not understand present reality (Michelet).

Educational theory did not spring into existence, fully-armed with principles and axioms, in the 1960s or 1970s! Today, we, as teachers and theoreticians, see as sharply as we do, not because of any inherently superior acuity of vision, and not because we are wiser than our ancestors, but because in many areas of theory and practice we stand on their shoulders. What and how they perceived is often interwoven with our thought patterns, even though we may be unaware of the debt. Today's practice and burgeoning theory in education cannot be understood fully without reference to ideas rooted in the past.

'Do practical people, such as teachers, need theory?'

Substitute for the word 'teachers', the word 'surgeons' or 'airline pilots'—who are also 'practical people' involved in an important job—and the restricted nature of the argument becomes more apparent. If practice is the 'how', theory is the 'why'. Successful practitioners in any field will be the better equipped for their task if they understand both the 'how' and the 'why'. Theory and practice often go hand in hand; indeed, theory is generally 'distilled practice'. Fontenelle reminds us that 'to despise theory is to have the excessively vain pretension to do without knowing what one does, and to speak without knowing what one says.' Keynes, who was an outstanding example of a theoretician and man of action, warned in emphatic terms of the self-styled 'practical men' who, while affecting to abhor theory, are unconsciously guided by the ideas of defunct scribblers. How many generations of unacknowledged theoreticians, one wonders, have fashioned the views of the 'practical teacher' who declares that 'carrot and stick' is the only real answer to problems of classroom motivation? Indeed, the practical teacher, like all other professional workers, cannot escape the pervasive nature of theory. Popper reminds us clearly of this:

> All observations (and, even more, all experiments) are theory-impregnated: they are interpretations in the light of theories (Popper 1979).

'If a teacher's actions succeed in practice, why bother to theorise? Isn't there some truth in the jibe that educational theoreticians are people who say: "I agree that it works in practice, but I wonder if it works in theory"?'

Without knowing *why* a course of action is successful, without understanding the significance of its content and context, one may make mistakes in the future when the actions are performed, for example in a fundamentally different environment. Polanyi, commenting on the history of science, has made trenchant observations on the 'practice-is-all-you-need' school:

> Almost every major systematic error which has deluded men for thousands of years relied on practical experience . . . Horoscopes . . . the cures of witch doctors and of medical practitioners before the advent of modern medicine, were all firmly established through the centuries in the eyes of the public by their supposed practical success. The scientific method was devised precisely for the purpose of elucidating the nature of things under more carefully controlled conditions and by more rigorous criteria than are present in the situations created by practical problems (Polanyi 1958).

'Teachers are born, not made. Theory can never help those who can't teach.'

This argument, often presented in apodictic style, has been used in its time to downgrade and devalue the work of teacher-training institutions, industrial training boards, seminars aimed at the improvement of teaching practice—and books on teaching! There is, however, much evidence to suggest that improved understanding and practice can and do stem directly from instruction in theoretical principles of teaching. The argument rests on an unwarranted belief in the existence of innate, unimprovable qualities of the teacher. The very concept of teaching fundamentals in any subject area as an aid to the comprehension and improvement of practical activity—the successful foundation of many generations of teaching practice—is not compatible with the idea underlying the 'born, not made' aphorism. To carry the idea to its conclusion would be to negate the very concepts of teaching and learning as activities designed to build on, and complete, our genetic inheritance.

Adaptation, survival and learning

The very survival of an animal depends on its ability to adjust and adapt successfully to changes in its environment. Whether it be the paramecium which can be observed under a microscope moving into obstacles, then backing away and approaching again on a different path, or a flock of feeding starlings which scatters in alarm when the wind raises the tattered arm of a scarecrow, or a mouse which, having been defeated in a fight with another, will attempt to run away at the next approach of the victor, the survival of an animal seems to depend on the existence of a tendency to react in ways which are favourable to its continued existence. This tendency is clearly visible in the reactions of a human being to physiological needs, such as those arising from thirst or hunger, or to the suspected presence of great danger. An inability to react correctly is usually incompatible with continued survival.

Since an animal's environment is subject to the processes of change, animal behaviour must include the capacities to respond to that change. Behaviour has been analysed in formal terms of stimulus and response. A *stimulus* results from a change in the animal's environment. (A 'stimulus' is some physical energy change which activates the sense receptors of an organism, producing a temporary increase of physiological activity.) The animal attempts to adapt to that change— the attempt is a *response,* which may or may not be successful in the circumstances. (A 'response' is the activities of an organism, usually involving muscle or gland, resulting from stimulation.) Where the response is successful and the animal modifies its subsequent behaviour as a result, it may be said to have *learned.*

In more precise terms, an animal, if it is to survive, must make a *correct adjustment or adaptation* to changes in stimuli from its environment. This process necessitates its receiving, interpreting and storing information. In effect, the animal *learns* from its experiences. Learning may be *inferred* from its subsequent reactions to similar stimuli. The octopus which modifies its reactions after being presented repeatedly with a crab attached to an electrified plate, the child which perceives a link between its cries and the swift appearance of its mother and acts accordingly, have learned how to control some aspects of their environment.

The term 'behaviour' is used in this book to indicate the activities of an organism that can be observed by another organism. Skinner defines the term more precisely as 'the movement of an organism or of its parts in a frame of references provided by the organism itself or by various external objects or fields of force'. This definition assumes that all one person can know about another person's awareness and feelings is based on *inferences* from what that other person *does*. Hence, an explanation of 'behaviour' may be provided by a statement of the *functional relationship* between a person's behaviour and those prior events influencing it. By discovering and analysing those prior events that produce relatively enduring changes in people's subsequent behaviour, we are studying the *learning process* that enables them to control themselves and parts of their environment.

The reception, interpretation, storing and retrieval of information are essential operations in the process of control of an environment. In general, the more adequately one is able to carry out these operations, the more precisely one is able to control and, therefore, change the environment according to one's wishes. The formal processes of instruction may be viewed as being linked with man's continuing attempts to control and change his environment so that his survival is the more assured.

Learning in the classroom

Consider four groups of students engaged in the formal activities known as 'the learning process'. The groups are typical of those to be found in a college of further education. The first consists of motor vehicle trade apprentices learning the fundamentals of vehicle servicing; the second comprises BTEC Higher National Certificate students learning the elements of the law of contract; the third is made up of GCE 'A' Level candidates examining a problem of economic theory; the fourth is formed of pre-nursing course cadets working through a topic relating to the structure of the human skeleton.

The motor vehicle apprentices' class is being held in the college's motor workshop, a well-equipped room, with adequate apparatus and visual aids. The lesson has as its objective the learning of the routine servicing of a 'distributor'. Each of the fifteen students is at a work bench, with tools and a distributor kit. The instructor has introduced the topic and is proceeding to an explanation of the practical steps involved. 'Release the clips which, you will observe, are painted red and remove the distributor cap. Watch exactly how I do it . . . Now let me see each one of you in turn do this . . . Good! . . . Next, take hold of the rotor arm. Do you remember it from our last lesson? Here it is on the wall chart . . . The next task is to apply a few drops of thin oil, which you will find in the green can on your work bench, to two points. Here they are, outlined in blue on the wall chart. Do that . . . Let us run through the steps in the process so far. You will see them written on this chart. . . .'

To the casual observer of this lesson, there is visible a group of students listening to a tutor and performing simple tasks according to instructions—a commonplace activity. To the trained teacher, there is evidence of a carefully-structured learning situation made up of a series of planned activities and based on an analysis of the tasks involved in mastery of the skill and of the best methods of performing them. Instructional objectives have been defined, and teaching media and aids needed to make clear the tasks to be performed have been selected. The level of organisation of the abilities of the class has been taken into account in the presentation of the lesson. Stimuli have been presented, and correct responses have been elicited and reinforced. ('Reinforcement' is the process by which the tendency to make a response is strengthened during learning. The concept of reinforcement in learning is an important feature of Skinner's theories, discussed in Chapter 3.) Practice in using patterns of muscular activities from which will result 'psychomotor skills', has been combined with exercise in perceiving relationships. The result has been a modification of the students' behaviour.

The BTEC students are learning how to deal with the principles of commercial law under the direction of a lecturer whose aim is to relate those principles to activities in their environment of which they are aware. Specifically, the lesson turns on the fact that although a contract involves agreement, not every agreement will be upheld by the courts. The lecturer is proceeding by question and answer '. . . Consider, for example, your agreeing with a friend to meet him for dinner, and your failing to appear. Have you broken a contract? Could your friend sue for damages? Think about this for a few minutes, examine the note which you wrote last week, break into your discussion groups, then give me your answer together with reasons for that answer.' Then, after hearing and discussing several answers representative of a variety of points of view: 'Let's consider how the courts have decided similar questions. Here is a note which I shall hand to each one of you, which outlines the facts and the decision in *Balfour* v. *Balfour*. Read it carefully, note the sentences I have underlined and be ready to tell me, in a few minutes' time, whether you agree with the decision and whether you think it 'fair'.'

Here an apparently simple exchange of questions and answers

reveals, on close examination, a prepared scheme based on stimulus and response, a planned progression from the simple to the complex, from the concrete to the abstract, from the general to the special case. The students are encouraged to participate actively and are guided to a path along which they will move to a predetermined destination, recording their observations en route. Cognitive and affective learning (the former concerned with knowledge, comprehension, analysis, etc., the latter with responding, valuing, etc.) will be encouraged by the provision of appropriate stimuli.

The third group is engaged in studying that section of the 'A' Level syllabus in economics which is based on the trade cycle. The teacher's objective is to make the students aware of the quasi-rhythmical pattern and periodicity of movements in production. An overhead projector is being used to display a graph illustrating employment statistics during the first half of this century. Time has been allowed for observation of the graph, questions have been raised and answered and the teacher is developing the lesson from that point. (His precise instructional objective for this part of the lesson is that the students shall recall, after the lesson has ended, the types of period which make up the trade cycle.) '... Look carefully at the movement of the curve between 1900 and 1940.... Note the red arrows which I am marking in so as to show the peaks in 1909, 1921, and 1933. Note, next, the green arrows which I am using to mark troughs.... Which years ought to be marked? ... Good! Mark them on your graphs. Listen now to a short extract from this recording of a recent broadcast on "Unemployment and the trade cycle." Listen, in particular to the speaker's definition of the trade cycle in his second sentence ...'

In this lesson a variety of techniques is employed. Eyes, ears and the associated senses are involved in the process of receiving and interpreting information. Powers of comprehension and deduction are being exercised and the students are moving—as the result of a deliberate plan formulated by the teacher—to a level of understanding higher than that which existed when the lesson commenced. A test, which will be administered towards the end of the lesson, will measure and evaluate that level, so that teacher and students will be aware of progress and attainment.

The nursing cadets are revising for an examination which will be the culmination of their pre-nursing course. The subject of their revision is that part of the anatomy syllabus dealing with the human skeleton. Each is working through a programmed text (see Chapter 20), designed to teach the location and names of the bones and principal parts of the pelvic girdle. Each is working at her own pace and is being guided along a programmed route. In the classroom is a facsimile skeleton. One student has reached that part of the programme which instructs her to look at the skeleton, each part of which is numbered, and to note the numbers which indicate the ilium, the ischium and the pubis. Another student is instructed by the programme to take her completed work book to the course tutor so that he can check her responses to a series of questions on the nomenclature of the bones of the carpus and tarsus.

In this lesson an individual unit of instruction for each student is being used so as to elicit those responses which will aid the process of retention and recall—the very essence of revision. Stimuli have been carefully chosen and each response prepares the ground for the next. A planned sequence of activities is used so as to facilitate comprehension. Continuous assessment of responses, evaluation of achievement and reinforcement of attainment are used as a bridge to the next stage in the instructional sequence. Information is being presented, received, retained and retrieved—the essence of the learning process.

Elements of the learning process

An analysis of the learning situations set out above indicates the component elements of the system to which we refer as the 'formal classroom situation' (with which succeeding chapters will be largely concerned). Those elements include the following:

1. *A learner,* whose nervous systems, senses and muscles are operating in sequences of patterned activity, which we may speak of as *behaviour.*
2. *A teacher,* selecting and organising instructional methods, consciously planning and controlling a situation directed to the achievement of learning.
3. *A series of objectives* related to students' anticipated and desired behavioural changes. We may consider objectives as intended outcomes, the attainment (or lack of it) of which can be observed and measured (see Chapter 8).
4. *A sequence of stimulus-response situations* affecting teacher and learner, resulting in persistent and observable changes in the behaviour of the learner from which we may infer learning. That learning is directed to an enhancement of students' cognitive, affective and psychomotor abilities. (Note, however, that the learner's knowledge acquired in situations such as these interacts with his hereditary, and often unconscious, knowledge.)
5. *Reinforcement* of that behaviour.

6. *The monitoring, assessment and evaluation* of the learner's changes in behaviour in relation to the objectives of the learning process.

Definitions of learning and teaching

How should learning be defined? Dictionary definitions provide a useful guide. 'To get knowledge of (a subject) or skill in (an art etc.) by study, experience, or teaching. Also, to commit to memory...': *Shorter Oxford English Dictionary*. 'To acquire knowledge of or skill in by study, experience, or instruction': *Cassell's New English Dictionary*.

More specific definitions have come from the philosophers and psychologists. 'A change in human disposition or capability, which persists over a period of time, and which is not simply ascribable to the process of growth' (Gagné 1983). 'A relatively permanent change in a behavioural potentiality which occurs as the result of continuous reinforced practice' (Kimble 1963). 'A process of reorganisation of sensory-feedback patterning which shifts the learner's level of control over his own behaviour in relation to the objects and events of the environment': (Smith 1966). 'The process by which an activity originates or is changed through reacting to an encountered situation, provided that the characteristics of the change in activity cannot be explained on the basis of native response tendencies, maturation or temporary states of the organism (e.g. fatigue, drugs, etc.)' (Hilgard and Bower 1981). 'Learning is becoming capable of doing some correct or suitable thing in *any* situations of certain general sorts. It is becoming prepared for *variable* calls within certain ranges' (Ryle 1983). 'Any activities that develop new knowledge and abilities in the individual who carries them out, or else cause old knowledge and abilities to acquire new qualities' (Galperin 1965).

For the purpose of the chapters which follow, *learning* will be considered as *the apparent modification of a person's behaviour through his activities and experiences, so that his knowledge, skills and attitudes, including modes of adjustment, towards his environment are changed, more or less permanently.* By extension, *teaching* will be considered as *a system of activities intended to induce learning, comprising the deliberate and systematic creation and control of those conditions in which learning does occur.*

The significance of an analysis of the learning process for the teacher

The implications of what has been stated above are important for the practising teacher, involved in the day-to-day activities of the classroom, laboratory and workshop. Learning, often thought of as a mysterious event, emerges from the definitions presented above as a complex process, capable of analysis and, as in the case of any other manifestation of human behaviour, generally amenable to the techniques of scientific investigation. The activities which may be inferred as having occurred when changes in a learner's behaviour are observed can be made the subject of close enquiry. In particular, it is necessary that the practising teacher be aware of the research and conclusions of the experimental psychologists in the area of human behaviour.

Because the learning process can be understood, to some extent, it can be guided, therefore, in considerable measure. (But not completely! Dewey reminds us that perhaps the greatest of all pedagogical fallacies is 'the notion that a person learns only the particular thing he is studying at the time' (Dewey 1940).) The task of the teacher is no longer merely to impart information and to hope that it will be received and retained. It is to be seen in terms of *understanding* and *planning* those conditions and activities which will result in effective learning. The guidance of the learning process necessitates activities which are known collectively as 'control'. Control is based on *monitoring* (or *measuring*), *assessing and adjusting*, specific tasks which are central to successful classroom teaching (see Chapter 7).

'The acquisition and proclamation of knowledge' no longer constitute the sum of activities for which the teacher must undertake responsibility. His role is seen in these pages as involving responsibility for all the vital, interpersonal processes of communication. These processes, their techniques and problems, are at the very heart of the teaching–learning situation. The teacher as *communicator*—and the term will be used with an awareness of its precise, scientific meaning and its wider, social significance—figures prominently in some of the chapters which follow. The teacher as *manager* is also discussed.

2

Theories of learning (1): the behaviourists—Pavlov, Watson, Thorndike and Guthrie

If its facts were all at hand, the behaviourist would be able to tell after watching an individual perform an act what the situation is that caused his action (prediction), whereas if organised society decreed that the individual or group should act in a definite, specific way, the behaviourist could arrange the situation or stimulus which would bring about such action (control) (Sahakian 1976).

Responsibility for the provision and control of conditions for effective learning is presented in these pages as a principal duty of the teacher in further education. It is important, therefore, that the teacher shall consider a selection of some of the more important answers given by the experimental psychologists to the fundamental question: 'How does the human being learn?' A study of the learning process in human beings is a central theme of psychology, but no one school of psychologists claims to have offered a complete solution to the many complex problems posed by the phenomenon of learning. Contemporary learning theory is often eclectic and characterised by a very wide range of hypotheses. The teacher who is searching for a single, uncomplicated answer to questions arising from the learning process is likely to be disappointed. He has the opportunity, however, of studying some of the many theories which seek to throw light on those inferred changes in the student, known as 'learning', and of weighing them in the balance against his considered personal experience in the classroom.

Representative theories of learning

It has been suggested that there are as many 'schools' of psychology as there are psychologists, a view which seems not exaggerated when one is confronted with the enormous range of widely-differing opinions in psychology. Four representative groups of theories, each of considerable significance for the practising teacher, are selected for comment.

The behaviourists

Behaviourism is based on a concept of psychology which sees its essence in the examination and analysis of that which is 'publicly observable and measurable'. The method of psychology (according to Hebb) should be

> ... to work behaviouristically, constructing a theory of mind based on the objective facts of behaviour. This means that we know mind, and study it, as the chemist knows and studies the properties of the atom. Atoms are not observed directly ... the chemist has ideas about the atom which he can test by experiment, and modify in accordance with the results (Hebb 1966).

The domain of psychology ought to be the relations between an organism's *responses* (that is, for example, its measurable muscle movements) and *stimuli* (that is, changes in the physical energy of some aspect of the organism's environment). In relation to teaching, behaviourists place emphasis on the teacher's task to provide for and to promote the adhesion of desired responses to appropriate stimuli. Pavlov, Watson, Thorndike and Guthrie are considered in this chapter as representatives of the behaviourist school.

The purposive and neo-behaviourists

Some psychologists have suggested that behaviour is generally directed to some goal: people behave as if they have some 'purpose'. Such behaviour, often directed by anticipations of consequences based on past experience, can be related to the nature of goals to be sought and the means to attain these goals. Behaviour can be described, therefore, as 'purposive'. The neo-behaviourists have investigated in recent years the significance of reinforced, or conditioned, responses in relation to the S–R (stimulus–response) bond. In relation to teaching, the neo-behaviourists stress the importance of the teacher's role in effecting successive and systematic modification of changes in the student's environment so as to increase the probability of desired responses. In Chapter 3, Tolman is discussed as the founder of purposive behaviourism; Skinner and Gagné are considered as representatives of the neo-behaviourists.

The Gestaltists

Gestalt psychology is concerned with the significance of organised forms and patterns in human perception, thinking and learning. Understanding and the perception of relationships within organised entities are of the very essence of learning. For the psychologist, the study of *molar* behaviour (behaviour of the whole organism) is likely to be more productive than concentration on *molecular* behaviour (behaviour analysed in terms of single events). Shifting the emphasis away from what the Gestaltists consider to be the crudities of behaviourism, they would ask not 'What has the student learned to do?', but 'How has the student learned to perceive this new situation?' It is the teacher's task to assist in the promotion of 'insightful learning' and to act so that students may develop and extend the quality of their insights. Koffka, Köhler and Wertheimer are considered in Chapter 4 as representatives of the Gestalt school.

The cognitive school

Cognitive psychologists assume that, in the interactions of an organism and its environment, not only is there a change in the overt behaviour of the organism, there is a change in its knowledge of the environment; this latter change affects present responses and future attitudes to the environment. The student should be viewed as a purposive individual in a continuing interaction with his social and psychological environment. Learning is essentially a process of interaction as a result of which the learner attains fresh insights ('cognitive structures') and sheds or modifies old ones. It is the task of the teacher to assist the student in restructuring his insights. Dewey, Bruner and Ausubel are considered in Chapter 5 as representatives of this school.

Pavlov: the background

Pavlov (1849–1936), a Russian physiologist, was primarily interested in the circulation of the blood and the processes of the gastro-intestinal system. He showed little interest in psychology until his last years. For him, so-called 'mental events' were no more than reflex units of behaviour. As a young man he had been influenced by his fellow-countryman, Sechenov (1829–1905), who had written in his *Reflexes of the Brain,* a work banned by the Tsar's censors: 'All acts of conscious or unconscious life are reflexes . . . Only physiology holds the key to the scientific analysis of psychical phenomena.' The study of the nervous systems of animals led him to methods of investigation from which he discovered the techniques of the *conditioning of behaviour.* On the basis of these techniques was erected a new structure of the investigation of aspects of human behaviour and, in particular, the study of aspects of the learning process. Pavlov's work on the process of conditioning ranks very high in the contributions made by scientists to an understanding of learning.

For Pavlov, so-called 'mental phenomena' could be dealt with objectively and scientifically only if it were possible to reduce them to observable, measurable physiological quantities. The concept of the 'reflex' could be extended so as to embrace not only unlearned responses but also learned reactions. Behaviour in all its varieties was, according to Pavlov, essentially *reflexive;* it was determined by specific events. (His system has been described as 'neurobehavioural'; S–R (i.e. the concept of environmental specifiable stimuli producing responses) is replaced by S–N–R, stimulus–neural process–response.) Unconditioned reflexes were inborn types of nervous activity, transmitted by inheritance. But conditioned reflexes (see below) were acquired by an organism during its life; they were not normally inheritable, according to Pavlov. Human beings learn as the result of conditioning and it was this hypothetical process which formed the basis of Pavlov's research.

The process of conditioning studied by Pavlov was derived from the results of his investigation of salivation in dogs. The parotid gland of a dog was inverted, so that its secretions could be accumulated in a calibrated glass and measured externally, and the animal was placed in a harness. It was then presented with a stimulus such as the sound of a metronome, bell or tuning fork. Initially, the sound did not seem to elicit any observable response. Later, powdered meat was presented to the dog after a short interval of time following the sound, and its salivary fluid was collected and measured. After further trials, in which the sound of the metronome or bell was invariably followed by the presentation of food, *the sound alone produced an anticipatory salivary response.* This may be illustrated as follows:

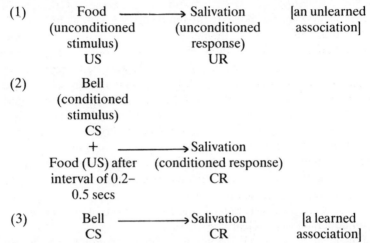

(1)   Food   ——————→ Salivation   [an unlearned
       (unconditioned   (unconditioned   association]
             stimulus)   response)
                US   UR

(2)   Bell
       (conditioned
           stimulus)
               CS
               +   ——————→ Salivation
      Food (US) after   (conditioned response)
      interval of 0.2–   CR
          0.5 secs

(3)   Bell   ——————→ Salivation   [a learned
               CS   CR   association]

Pavlov found that if the paired stimuli (CS+US) were presented repeatedly, the CR gradually increased in strength. This conditioning process was seen by Pavlov and some of his colleagues as a possible explanation of certain aspects of the organisation of behaviour. The techniques of conditioning, it was suggested, could be applied to the training of human beings. *Human behaviour might be amenable to the process of moulding on the basis of the controlled establishment of conditioned responses.* Further, in Pavlov's words, 'Any natural phenomena chosen at will may be converted into a conditioned stimulus . . . any visual stimulus, any desired sound, any odour . . .' (Popper has suggested an interesting reinterpretation of Pavlov's experiment, the point of which will not be lost on teachers. He puts forward the idea that the dogs had 'developed a theory', consciously or unconsciously, that the food would arrive when the bell rang and that this expectation caused the saliva flow, precisely as did the expectation raised by the smell of the food.)

Pavlov believed that the nervous centres involved in the formation of CRs in man were located on the cortex of the cerebral hemispheres. 'Temporary connections' (including CRs) were formed as the result of 'irradiation' of stimuli reaching these hemispheres. Stimulation becomes 'generalised' in the hemispheres so that other areas of the cortical region react similarly to that involved in the original stimulus.

Every learning situation, according to Pavlov, involves an element of generalisation. Further, 'inhibition' (the opposite of 'irradiation') can be induced by training the subject to discriminate among stimuli which seem at first to be similar.

The uniqueness of man

The fact that most of Pavlov's work was carried out on dogs (although in the final stages of his career he used monkeys and gorillas) should not blind teachers to his belief in the unique nature of man. He maintained that man has fewer instincts than animals, so that his behaviour is governed by CRs to a very much higher degree. It is possible to condition man and animals in ways which are similar; but man possesses, uniquely, the rich treasure-house of language. The animal responds to simple 'primary signals'; man responds to the 'secondary signals' conveyed to him in written or spoken form. There is, said Pavlov, no comparison, qualitative or quantitative, between speech and animals' stimuli.

Human behaviour cannot be reduced to the very simple S–R actions of Pavlov's experiments on dogs; nowhere in his writings does Pavlov suggest otherwise. We may learn some important lessons from his study of animals which have application to the human body (described by Pavlov as 'unique in the degree of its self-regulation'), but man himself occupies 'an ontological status superior to that of the animals'. Pavlov, it should not be forgotten, wrote of 'our extra, especially human, higher mentality', and of 'science, the instrument of the higher orientation of man in the surrounding world and in himself'. In a speech delivered in 1909, he referred to his disinclination 'to negate anything which relates to the innermost and deepest strivings of the human spirit. Here and now I only defend and affirm the absolute and unquestionable rights of natural scientific thought . . . who knows where its possibilities will end!'

Pavlov's work and the teacher

The major works of Pavlov, e.g. *Conditioned Reflexes* (1927), have been the basis of much study in recent years on the importance of conditioning in the process of learning. Some of Pavlov's deductions from his experimental data have been reassessed, and conditioning is now seen by some psychologists as more than a mere substitution of one stimulus for another. Conditioned responses (CR) differ from unconditioned responses (UR), and the process of conditioning may result in the subject's acquiring a *new group* of stimulus response patterns—a matter of significance for the class teacher whose work includes the presentation of stimuli in a variety of conditions.

The mere suggestion that Pavlov's work might have lessons for the practice of classroom instruction is rejected firmly by many teachers. Research derived from experiments on harnessed, mutilated animals has, it is argued, no application whatsoever to human learners. The atmosphere of the animal laboratory is, and must remain, a world away from that of the classroom and the purpose of the activities therein. Further, it is stressed, the entire concept of conditioning, with its all-too-familiar connections with 'brain washing', can have no place in the activities of educators. The freedoms which must characterise the classroom are incompatible with the philosophy and processes associated with conditioning.

Others, however, see in some of Pavlov's work the possibility of creating techniques which, when refined, can be used consciously and conscientiously so as to 'shape' human intellectual development—an important objective of teaching activity. The excesses of those who have deliberately misused conditioning techniques ought not to be advanced, it is argued, as reasons for forbidding the use in any circumstances of some of those techniques. For Pavlov, learning was inseparable from 'association'; hence, *what* teachers do, *how* they do it, in what *surrounding circumstances,* to what *ends,* become significant for the study of instruction. Pavlov's insistence on organisms being studied as wholes, 'in all their interactions', and on biological processes being considered as essentially dependent on the environment, has lessons for teachers wishing to understand the significance *of the setting* of instruction. Human personality is determined, according to Pavlov, by environment, biological inheritance and conditions of upbringing, and a person's general behaviour depends largely on his 'acquisitions', i.e. the habits he has formed. The part that can be played by a teacher in the process of habit formation will be obvious. Formal education, strengthened by other experiences, can exert a decisive influence on that process.

Watson: the background

Watson (1878–1958), professor of experimental and comparative psychology at Johns Hopkins University, Maryland, began his career as a researcher into animal behaviour. It was this background which led him to examine psychology in strict behavioural terms. His major works include: *Behaviour: an introduction to Comparative Psychology* (1914); *Psychology from the Standpoint of a Behaviourist* (1919); *Behaviourism* (1925). Psychology, according to Watson, ought to be a purely objective, experimental branch of natural science (the 'science of behaviour') and behaviour could be described adequately in *physiological terms* of stimulus, response, habit formation, etc. Concepts such as sensations, feelings were to be cast aside. The introspectionist's question: 'What is an organism *experiencing*?' had to be replaced by the question: 'What is the organism *doing*?' 'Consciousness' was a term of no value, since it merely reflected the mind–body problem which was of no significance—mind did not exist. Indeed, said Watson, the assumption of consciousness was 'just as unprovable as the ancient concept of man's soul'. Thinking, he suggested might be merely 'subvocal speech movements'.

Behaviour was to be studied in terms of biologically-determined phenomena. (The theoretical goal of psychology should be the prediction and control of behaviour.) Its understanding necessitated a close study of glandular secretions and muscular movements. The principal method of study should be objective observation and experimentation. This required a new vocabulary from which subjective terminology would be eliminated; references to 'introspectively observable phenomena', such as sensation, thought and intention, which were said to intervene between stimulus and reaction, would disappear.

Watson and the learning process

According to Watson, human beings are born with some few reflexes and emotional reactions (such as love, rage, fear), but no instincts (which are merely S–R links); all other behaviour is the result of building new S–R connections. Habit formation may be analysed in terms of its constituent units of conditioned reflexes. Learning, as an aspect of human behaviour, can be studied in terms of the formation of connections in the learner's muscle groups. When S and R occur at the same time, their interconnections are strengthened, and the eventual strength of the connection will depend largely upon the frequency of S and R occurring together. S produces activity in a part of the brain, and R emerges as the result of activity in some other part; S–R neural pathways are strengthened when the two parts of the brain are simultaneously activated. But learning produces no new connections in the brain—they exist already, as part of the learner's genetic constitution. Hence, our behaviour, personalities and emotional dispositions are all learned behaviours. *The human being is no more than the sum of his experiences.*

Given this analysis, *conditioning* was seen as fundamental to learning. The conditioning of the learner, through his environment and experiences, *in which the teacher may actively intervene,* will determine his acquired patterns of behaviour. Heredity and instincts counted for little, in Watson's scheme, as contributions to human behaviour. Learning becomes an all-important factor in the development and modification of an individual's behaviour.

Watson embodied Pavlov's findings into his theory of learning. In a famous experiment involving conditioning, Watson, who had reasoned that young children had no reason to fear animals, showed Albert, an eleven month-old child, some tame white rats, an experience which the child apparently enjoyed. Later, a rat was presented shortly after a loud noise which frightened the child. After several repetitions of the experience, the child showed fear of the rat, even in the absence of the distressing noise. Fear was displayed also in the presence of other furry objects. Watson showed later that, by feeding the child with its favourite dishes and introducing the feared animal very gradually into the background and then into the child's direct view, the fears could be extinguished. (An account by Harris of the experiment throws doubt on the success of the deconditioning of 'little Albert'.)

Watson's work and the teacher

The behaviourist doctrine promulgated by Watson, amongst others, has become an object of unceasing criticism for both psychologists and teachers. It has been condemned as a reductionism which robs man's nature of its dignity, reducing the complexities of human development to mechanistic, deterministic and over-simplified formulae ('the psychology of muscle twitches'). A recent attack, mounted by Talyzina, reflects the views of many opponents of the doctrine:

> It does not overcome an idealistic interpretation of the psyche . . . Behaviourists interpret the subject of their studies in a coarse, mechanistic way: having separated behaviour from the psyche, they reduced it to a system of movements. It is true, of course, that movement is part of behaviour, but behaviour may not be reduced to a sum of movements . . . Behaviourists did not perceive the qualitatively specific properties in

the behaviour of man by comparison with that of animals. They view man not as a social being but as a purely biological one (Talyzina 1981).

To others, however, the behaviourists' emphasis on the significance of environment and experience underlines the role of the teacher. If heredity gives the learner his body only, and if all else is acquired, then the control of the acquisition of knowledge is a vital activity. Control of the learning environment—an essential task of the teacher—becomes a significant factor in the learner's development.

The possibility of the student's being conditioned to respond favourably to the circumstances in which he learns—his class environment, his teacher, the content and overtones of the lesson—reminds the teacher of the importance of planning the learning environment and lesson content with care. Each part of the lesson ought to be examined in the planning stage, and evaluated during class activity, as a contributory factor to the eliciting of those responses which make up desirable criterion behaviour. 'What type of response will be elicited from my students as the result of my teaching activity?' Questions of this nature ought to be posed by the teacher in the preparatory stages of a lesson and his answers ought to affect his lesson content.

The teacher in further education ought not to forget the possibility of students' attitudes to their lessons being formed as a result of the conditioning process of which Watson wrote. A negative attitude to, say, quantitative topics, may be the result of the generalisation of anxieties resulting from difficulties at an earlier period in mathematics classes. It is, unfortunately, a simple matter for that generalised attitude to extend to the wider field of the college curriculum as a whole. Watson's work can act as a reminder to the teacher to take particular care so as to avoid creating the anxieties and hostility which may emerge later as a fixed response to formal instruction of any type.

In the flush of enthusiasm, Watson claimed that, given a dozen 'healthy infants, well-formed', he would guarantee to train any one of them, selected at random, so as to become any type of specialist he might select, 'regardless of his talents, penchants, tendencies, abilities, vocations and race of his ancestors'. Stripped of its zeal and hyperbole, Watson's challenge stands as a reminder of the powerful contribution which can be made by the teacher to the growth and shaping of the learner's personality.

Thorndike: the background

Thorndike (1874–1949) was one of the dominant forces in the study of learning for many years. Almost all his professional life was spent on the staff of a teacher training college. His output was prodigious; a recently-compiled list of his works shows more than five hundred titles, among them his major writings: *Animal Intelligence* (1911), *The Psychology of Learning* (1913) and *The Fundamentals of Learning* (1932). His main interest was animal psychology and, in particular, intelligence and learning. Thorndike's pattern of experiments with animals marked out a route which was followed later by other experimental psychologists, including Skinner (see pp. 35–40).

The basis of Thorndike's approach to problems of behaviour lay in his belief that *human behaviour could be analysed and studied in terms of S–R units.* The essence of behaviour was to be found in the initiation of events and an individual's reactions to them. 'Mind' was no more than a collective term relating to the activities of the body cells which responded to stimuli. Behaviour and, therefore, learning, were explicable through an understanding of *bonds* between sense impressions and impulses to actions; the task of the psychologist was to discover how such bonds are created. (Thorndike's emphasis on S–R bonds led to the categorising of his theories as 'bond psychology' and 'connectionism'.)

Thorndike's theories emerged largely from experiments with cats, chicks, dogs and monkeys, but he believed that some universal laws of behaviour could be derived from that work. Man, in his view, differed from the other animals only in degree. Man's superior intelligence was little more than a reflection of his capacity to form S–R bonds. Degrees of human intelligence signified varying speeds of bond formation; the more intelligent person has more bonds at his disposal to enable him to deal with problems.

Thorndike's laws of learning

Thorndike's contribution to the theory of learning may be summarised by a statement of his major and subsidiary 'laws'. The *law of effect* was formulated thus: an act which results in an animal's experiencing satisfaction in a given situation will generally become associated with that situation, so that when it recurs the act will also be likely to recur. An act which results in discomfort tends to be dissociated from the situation, so that when the situation recurs the act will be less likely to recur. In effect, *the greater the satisfaction or discomfort experienced, the greater the degree to which the S–R bond will be strengthened or loosened.* Pleasurable effects, therefore, tend to stamp in associations; unpleasant effects (such as punishment) tend to stamp them out. (The subsequent modification of this law is mentioned below.) According to the *law of exercise,* a response to a situation will generally be more strongly connected with that situation in proportion to the number of times it has been so connected and to the average strength and duration of the connections. (This, too, was later modified.) The *law of readiness* suggested that a learner's satisfaction is determined by the extent of his 'preparatory set', i.e. his readiness of action.

There were several subsidiary laws. The *law of multiple response* stated that a response which fails to produce satisfaction will trigger off another until success results and learning becomes possible. According to the *law of set,* learning is affected by the individual's total attitude, or disposition. The *law of selectivity of response* suggests that as the animal learns, so it becomes capable of ignoring some aspects of a problem and responding to others. The *law of response by analogy* emphasises that a person's response to a novel situation is determined by innate tendencies to respond and by elements in similar situations to which he has acquired responses in the past. The *law of associative shifting* suggested that a learner responds first to a given stimulus, then transfers the response, by association, to a different stimulus. (This is in line with Pavlov's findings.)

The law of effect was modified thirty years after its publication when Thorndike abandoned his belief that punishment tended to stamp out S–R bonds. His restatement of the law emphasised that punishment merely caused the learner to modify his behaviour until he discovered some act which resulted in reward. Rewarding a connection strengthened it, whereas punishing it had little weakening effect. The law of exercise was also modified: practice *in itself* did not make perfect, but practice in circumstances which allowed the learner to be informed of his results could be valuable in strengthening the S–R links. The *law of spread of effect,* enunciated in 1933, stated that if an act had pleasurable consequences, the pleasure tended to become associated not only with the act and the eliciting stimulus, but also with other actions which occurred at approximately the same point in time.

Thorndike's work and the teacher

Thorndike's theories have been criticised as crude and over-simplified. In particular, his S–R bond explanation of the basis of learning has been condemned as a mechanical interpretation of some few aspects of the complexities of human behaviour. Many psychologists and teachers, however, see his work as that of an important pioneer, mapping a route for others who followed. Thorndike's general view of the relationship of psychology to teaching is significant. He viewed psychology as part of the necessary basis of a scientific approach to the practice of teaching and wrote: 'Just as the science and art of agriculture depend upon chemistry and botany, so the art of education depends upon physiology and psychology.'

There is much in Thorndike's work which is of relevance to the day-to-day tasks of the class teacher. Its emphasis on the significance of the S–R bond reminds the teacher of the importance of viewing *all* his activities (intended and otherwise) as contributions to the learning process. Lesson planning, instructing and evaluation of attainment emerge in the light of Thorndike's analysis as related directly to those responses which make up learning. ('Put together and exercise what should go together, and reward desirable connections.') His modification of the law of effect, which stressed reward as a more effective factor than punishment in the modification of a learner's behaviour, has an obvious lesson for the teacher. The law of exercise suggests the importance of 'doing' and repetition in the learning process, and its modification emphasises the futility of thoughtless 'rote learning'. The law of readiness stresses the importance of preparation for learning and serves to remind the class teacher of the vital part played in the learning process by motivation (see Chapter 6) and of his responsibility for the strengthening of a student's readiness to learn. The necessity of flexibility of approach by the learner and the value of trial and error learning emerge from Thorndike's law of multiple response. His demonstration of the significance of response by analogy reminds the teacher of the responsibility to arrange the conditions of learning so that the identification of common elements in a variety of situations may result in strengthening the ability to generalise.

Thorndike's views on 'understanding' and 'insight' are also of interest to the teacher. Understanding grows out of habits acquired at an early stage in the learner's development. It may be fostered by teaching 'connections' appropriate to general problems of the type being studied. 'Insight', where the learner seems to understand a new situation immediately, is no 'unpredictable spasm'; it arises on the basis of appropriate habits and analogies. 'Both theory and practice', said Thorndike, 'need emphatic and frequent reminders that man's learning is fundamentally the action of the laws of readiness, exercise and effect . . . If we stay lost in wonder at the extraordinary versatility and inventiveness of the higher forms of learning, we shall never understand man's progress or control his education.'

Guthrie: the background

Guthrie (1886–1959) taught psychology at the University of Washington after a period of study based largely on philosophy. He had been influenced in particular by philosophical writings which suggested that a number of the more important problems concerning 'mind' could be translated into concepts of behaviour and comprehended accordingly. His definitive work was *The Psychology of Learning* (1935).

For Guthrie, human behaviour was to be explained precisely in terms of control by eliciting stimuli; a change in a S–R connection could be understood and explained on the basis of simple, mechanistic laws. Some behaviour seemed to Guthrie to be goal-directed, but this was not to be explained in non-physical terms. A person's 'intention' to reach some goal could be explained in terms of 'maintaining stimuli' that keep the organism active and allow muscular readiness to respond and muscular readiness to accept the consequences of that response. Similarly 'attention' can be explained in physical terms as a variety of responses orienting sense receptors towards stimuli. 'What is being noticed becomes a signal for what is being done.'

Guthrie and the learning process

Guthrie's theory of learning is based on one general principle, that of *simultaneous contiguous conditioning*. 'A combination of stimuli which has accompanied a movement will on its recurrence tend to be followed by that movement.' The principle has been paraphrased, by Hill, thus: 'If you do something in a given situation, the next time you are in that situation you will tend to do the same thing again.' Whether the response emerges as the result of an unconditioned stimulus or in any other way is of no matter, according to Guthrie; provided that the conditioned stimulus and reaction occur *together*, learning will take place.

It is important to note that whereas Watson emphasised the principle of frequency (which suggested that S–R bonds vary in strength and are made stronger as the result of 'practice'), Guthrie insisted that conditioning was a 'once-for-all' process and that practice added little to the strength of a bond. (Guthrie had in mind the 'molecular', small movements which go to make up a skilled performance.) 'A stimulus pattern gains its full associative strength on the occasion of its first pairing with a response.' Reinforcement plays no part in Guthrie's theory of learning; a student learns simply by 'doing', not by success or reinforcement. Learning is occurring continuously, although much is replaced immediately it is learned by the learning of successive types of response.

Of particular interest to teachers is Guthrie's remedy for bad habits. He describes three methods for the modification and eradication of undesirable habits; each involves discovering the type of stimulus which evokes the undesirable response and then discovering some method of effecting a dissimilar response in the presence of those stimuli. The 'threshold method' requires the presentation of stimuli in a weak fashion so that the undesirable response is not elicited; the stimuli are increased to full strength in gradual fashion so that the response never occurs. The 'fatigue method' necessitates the eliciting of the undesirable response over and over again until the person responding becomes fatigued and ceases making that response. The 'incompatible stimuli method' involves the presentation of stimuli for the undesirable response at the same time as other stimuli, producing an incompatible response, are presented; the original stimuli become linked with the new, desirable response.

Guthrie's work and the teacher

The mechanistic, deterministic nature of Guthrie's analysis of human behaviour has alienated many educationists. They point to the 'real-life complexity' of behaviour, particularly in the classroom, and argue that such behaviour requires a deeper analysis than that implicit in contiguity theory. Not all teachers are convinced that if a learner does something in a certain situation, he will tend to do the same thing again on the next occasion he is in that situation. But the significance of Guthrie's concept of learning should not be overlooked. His insistence on 'particular responses to particular stimuli' serves to remind the teacher of the significance of the combination of stimuli resulting from classroom environment and teaching activity. It emphasises, too, the overall significance of presenting stimuli in a planned way.

Guthrie emphasises the importance of attempting to elicit desired patterns of behaviour in specific situations. Preparation for formal examinations, for example, involves practising in a situation which has a close resemblance to that of the examination in mind. Situation simulation, which requires a precise analysis of stimuli and responses, can play a very important role in those class activities related to preparation for particular situations. Rewards and punishments, says Guthrie, are of little significance and are, in themselves, neither good nor bad. Whether they are effective or ineffective will be determined by what they cause the learner *to do*. What is really vital in the learning situation is the control of stimuli so that desired responses may be elicited. *'What a person does is what a person will learn.'*

3

Theories of learning (2): the purposive and neo-behaviourists—Tolman, Skinner and Gagné

It is often said that a scientific view of man leads to wounded vanity, a sense of hopelessness, and nostalgia. But no theory changes what it is a theory about; man remains what he has always been. And a new theory may change what can be done with its subject matter. A scientific view of man offers exciting possibilities. We have not yet seen what man can make of man (Skinner 1979).

Early behaviourist doctrines have been extended and modified by psychologists and research workers such as Tolman, Skinner and Gagné, who are discussed in this chapter. Tolman's views, rooted firmly in the principles of behaviourism, flowered in unique fashion and were categorised as 'purposive behaviourism'. Skinner brought scientific precision to the detailed study of the learning process viewed in strict behavioural terms and created a theory based on 'operant reinforcement'. Gagné examined the instructional technology needed for competency-based education and developed a psychology, based upon behaviourism, related to the observable circumstances that obtain when acts of learning occur. Each of these psychologists has made a deep impression on the principles and practice of teaching in our schools and colleges.

Tolman: the background

Tolman (1886–1959) taught psychology at the University of California. Because of his highly-individual approach to the study of behaviour and his findings, he is claimed by both behaviourist and cognitive schools as an advocate of their teachings. He opposed the views of the S–R associationists: for him, the S–R association (see Chapter 2) was not an objective fact, it was no more than an inference. The act of behaviour had to be studied in a *molar* (i.e. large-scale), rather than a *molecular,* way. As a behaviourist he rejected introspection as a mode of inquiry, but the mechanistic views of the early behaviourists seemed too simple for an adequate explanation of behaviour, which he saw as *holistic* (i.e. capable of explanation in terms of the whole system).

His major work, *Purposive Behaviour in Animals and Men* (1932), emphasised his view of 'purpose' in behaviour. We do not merely respond to stimuli, we move towards goals related to our beliefs and our attitudes. 'Organisms pursue goal objects by selecting certain means–object routes.' We can understand behaviour only by examining an entire *sequence* of varied behaviour with some predictable end; we have to examine the whole so as to understand how the sequence is put together and the end achieved. Early behaviourists had viewed anything intervening between stimulus and response as itself in the nature of a response. Tolman rejected this as too simple an explanation, and viewed the determination of behaviour as a result of environmental stimuli and physiological states *plus* the intervention of variables (which he termed 'cognitions'). (Intervening variables include demands and appetites.) Cognitions, demands, appetites, etc., combined so as to produce responses. Behaviour was 'docile', that is, flexible and not invariant.

In thinking about anything a person uses a 'cognitive map', that is, a general appreciation of relationships among different stimuli and a *set of expectancies* about the meaning of those relationships. Such a map was a symbolic representation of the person's environment—physiological, psychological and social—and his possible relations to it. The map would be constructed on the basis of the person's specific goals (or 'purposes'). Goal objects have motivating qualities; the presence of a preferred goal object may result in a performance superior to that elicited by the presence of a less desirable goal object. The *expectations* concerning a goal object are of great importance.

Tolman and the learning process

Learning, according to Tolman, was *the acquisition of expectancies.* By an 'expectancy' he meant that in the presence of a certain 'sign', a particular behaviour will produce a particular consequence. We 'learn' when we establish a series of expectations concerning the contiguity of events based on repeated past experiences of their appearance in sequence. Learning can occur without reward (hence the concept of reinforcement is not essential to an understanding of learning) if the contiguity of stimuli can be repeated often enough. As a person becomes aware of novel behaviour and unsuspected relationships, new behaviour will appear, a learning process very similar to the Gestaltists' concept of 'insight' (see Chapter 4) and called by Tolman 'inventive ideation'.

Tolman distinguished *six different kinds of learning,* as follows:

1. *Cathexis.* This is based on a tendency to seek one goal rather than another when a certain drive is present. When a goal object satisfies a certain drive, a cathexis is formed; the organism has acquired a 'disposition'.

2. *Equivalence beliefs.* These are 'cognitions' that, where reward or punishment is found in a certain situation, the situation itself is *equivalent* to the reward or punishment and is, therefore, in itself, rewarding or punishing.

3. *Field expectancies.* These are built on 'cognitive maps' based on anticipations about the environment in which we function and resulting from repeated experiences. They make possible 'short-cuts' and 'round-about' routes in learning.

4. *Field-cognition modes.* These are biases towards learning one thing rather than another, resulting from the discovery of principles and the changing of one's frames of reference. They make possible new modes of perceiving and inferring.

5. *Drive discrimination.* This involves a learner's ability to distinguish one kind of internal drive stimulus from another.

6. *Motor pattern acquisition.* This involves learning by contiguity, which can be viewed in relatively simple terms of conditioning, based on stimulus–response connections.

Tolman's work and the teacher

Tolman's refinement of early behaviourism has attracted some of the teachers who are repelled by the arid, mechanistic views of Watson and his contemporary advocates. The emphasis on purpose, drive and motivation in Tolman's writings corresponds in many ways to the importance attached by practising teachers to a curriculum and lesson scheme organised around the needs of learners. His insistence on learning as 'sign-expectation', that is, as resulting from an individual's expectation that the environment is organised in certain ways and that 'one thing invariably leads to another', has found an echo in the theory and practice of those teachers who place emphasis on the logical construction of schemes of classroom work. His insistence on the importance of cathexis—the acquired relationship between an object and a learner's drive—and his belief that cathexes are extremely resistant to forgetting, have been embodied in the views and practice of teachers who construct lessons on the basis of a carefully-explored relationship between the perceived needs of students and the objective of those lessons.

Tolman's view of behaviour in molar terms has drawn the attention of teachers to the need for an overall approach to class behaviour, which is not to be viewed in simple terms. The expectancies of students are to be considered along with their apparent reactions to stimuli. Intervening variables have an importance which should be reflected in the teacher's overall awareness of the many factors which go to make up learning. Tolman's listing of age, heredity and endocrine conditions as influencing learning reminds the teacher that classroom learning may not be the only determinant of overall behaviour and that student reactions have to be understood in wider terms than those associated with the simple stimulus–response schemes of some psychologists.

Skinner: the background

One of the most influential of contemporary contributions to the development of learning theory is that of the neo-behaviourist school, led by Skinner (b. 1904), formerly professor of psychology at Harvard University. Skinner is perhaps best known to teachers as one of the founders of programmed instruction (see Chapter 20). The outlines of his work may be found in *The Behaviour of Organisms* (1938), *Science and Human Behaviour* (1953) and *The Analysis of Behaviour: a programme for self-instruction* (1961). A notable collection of essays entitled *The Technology of Teaching* (1968) dealt with topics such as the science of learning and the art of teaching, motivation, teaching machines, etc. In *Beyond Freedom and Dignity* (1971), Skinner moved from the study of behaviour to a searching critique of some of the basic values of our society. *About Behaviourism* (1974) contains a philosophical defence by Skinner of his views. Man is seen, according to this apologia, as capable of controlling his destiny because he knows what has to be done and how to do it.

Skinner's techniques of investigation have been applied to a study of the conditions of behaviour of pigeons, dogs, rats, monkeys and human children. He claims that in spite of considerable phylogenic differences, 'all these organisms show amazingly similar properties of the learning process'. The conditioning experiments associated with his name were based upon the use of the 'Skinner box', an apparatus which allowed him to study the responses of a variety of animals. A hungry (but unconditioned) animal, for example, a rat, is allowed to explore the box. When the rat spontaneously presses a small brass lever, the experimenter drops a pellet of food from a magazine into a tray, thus allowing the animal to eat. This is repeated on several occasions until the rat acquires the habit of going to the tray when it hears the sound made by a movement of the food magazine. Later, the lever is connected directly to the magazine so that the rat's pressure results in the presentation of a food pellet. Conditioning then follows rapidly. Accumulated data on the animal's rate of response were used by Skinner in his formulation of the effect of reinforcement in learning. These techniques were later refined and used as the basis of continued experiments in *the modification of behaviour by operant conditioning* which, for Skinner, is synonymous with the essential characteristic of the learning process. ('Any condition or event which can be shown to have an effect on behaviour must be taken into account. By discovering and analysing these causes, we can predict behaviour; to the extent that we can manipulate them, we can control behaviour.')

The basis of behaviour

A primary objective of Skinner's work has been the 'functional analysis of behaviour'. Behaviour is, for him, 'the movement of an organism or of its parts in a frame of reference provided by the organism itself or by various external objects or fields of force'. The course of behaviour, he claims, can be described in terms of the external stimuli eliciting it and the responses, i.e. the succeeding events. The strength of any response is determined by the intensity of the stimulus; prolongation or repetition has the same effect as an increase in its intensity. A response can become a stimulus for a further response (the phenomenon of 'chaining'). A change in a given response can result in changes in related responses (the phenomenon of 'generalisation').

Behaviour can be considered in relation to two types of response: elicited and emitted. Responses elicited by known stimuli are classified as *respondents:* thus, in a 'respondent situation' a student learns merely by being involved in the situation, i.e. he is 'responding' to his environment. Responses emitted (i.e. not elicited by recognised stimuli) are classified as *operants*. Operant behaviour is typical of the form taken by most human behaviour: it comprises those responses which operate on the environment so as to generate consequences. In an 'operant situation', a student is learning as the result of responses made more probable because of immediate 'reinforcement' (see below).

Human behaviour is to be understood, according to Skinner, entirely on the basis of a study of physiological responses; the analysis of stimuli is unnecessary, as is the analysis of other 'intervening variables'. States, such as 'need' and 'desire', have to be specified in precise, operational terms, so that an animal's drive, for example, is to be seen as no more than those operations which affect its behaviour in particular ways. ('An adequate science of behaviour must consider events taking place within the skin of the organism, not as physiological mediators of behaviour, but as part of behaviour itself.') In the case of an animal's need for food, its drive is a function of the number of hours during which it has been deprived of it. Drive is neither a stimulus nor a physiological state; it refers solely to certain types of operation.

The learning process

An organism learns, according to Skinner, by producing changes in its environment. At the basis of his view of the nature of the learning process is the concept of *reinforcement* as a stimulus which increases the probability of a response. Skinner differentiates positive and negative reinforcement. *Positive reinforcement* is the presentation of a stimulus which, when added to a situation, increases the probability of occurrence of a response. *Negative reinforcement* is the termination of some unpleasant ('aversive') stimulus, which, when removed from a situation, increases the probability of occurrence of a response.

It is the *conditioning of operant behaviour* which is of great importance in Skinner's analysis of the learning process. *Learning is, in essence, the creation of conditioned connections between the learner's operant behaviour and its reinforcement; it is a change in the form or the probability of responses.* The strength of a *learned response* is generally determined by the amount of reinforcement it receives.

Behaviour can be shaped by reinforcement—this, perhaps, is one of the most striking of Skinner's conclusions. When each step in a complex act is reinforced by the reward of the selected responses which comprise it, chains of reflexes are established. In this process the technique of *reinforcement scheduling,* i.e. the systematic application of reinforcement, is of great importance. Skinner lists four types of scheduling.

(a) *Fixed interval:* the first correct response made after a fixed interval of time is reinforced;
(b) *Variable interval:* the first correct response made after a variable period of time is reinforced;
(c) *Fixed ratio:* the first correct response made after a fixed number of responses is reinforced;
(d) *Variable ratio:* the first correct response made after a variable number of responses is reinforced.

Schedules (b), (c) and (d) tend to produce high rates of response; schedule (a) is characterised by bursts of response preceding the usual time of reinforcement, with low rates of response following on it.

In *operant conditioning,* the important stimulus is that which immediately *follows* the response, it is *not* that which precedes the response. The result is the strengthening of any emitted response that leads to reinforcement. The strengthening of *general tendencies* to make responses is the result of operant conditioning—a vital matter in the learning process, according to Skinner. The essence of operant conditioning is related to the *probability* that classes of responses will occur in the future.

'The discriminative stimulus does not elicit a response, it simply alters a probability of occurrence.' Hence, it is *not* correct to say that a man behaves because of the consequences which *are* to follow his behaviour; it is more appropriate to say that he behaves because of the consequences which *have* followed similar behaviour in the past. It is the changing of contingencies of reinforcement in the direction of desired behaviour that leads to such behaviour—the very essence of 'learning'.

Skinner's direct application of operant conditioning findings to the problems of classroom learning culminated in his advocacy of programmed instruction (see Chapter 20) and the teaching machine. ('We have every reason to expect . . . that the most effective control of human learning will require instrumental aid.') The concepts of immediate reinforcement of emitted behaviour and the gradual withdrawal of stimulus support from the learner ('fading' of learning cues), which characterise programmed instruction, were derived directly from his success in the shaping and conditioning of animal learning through reinforcement.

Skinner's work and the teacher

Skinner's view of the learning process has attracted trenchant and persistent criticism: see, for example, the onslaughts from Chomsky and Koestler. He has been accused of 'extrapolating well beyond his data', and his generalisations concerning human behaviour have been attacked as reflecting the study of animals which are totally unlike human beings. The shaped behaviour of a pigeon taught to dance has been held to be irrelevant to an explanation of the complex activities which form human behaviour. Nor, it has been argued, should the conditions of the operant conditioning chamber be used as the basis of suggestions for the conditions which ought to exist in the classroom. Additionally, the basic objections to behaviourism's rejection of the mentalistic explanations of human activity have been hurled with special vigour at Skinner and his associates. It is objected, further, that he seems to consider learning to be of one type only, whereas there may be many types.

Skinner has replied to many of these criticisms and has reasserted his views. (A typical reply, in *Beyond Freedom and Dignity*, is '"Animal" is a pejorative term, but only because "man" has been spuriously honorific . . . Man is much more than a dog, but like a dog he is within range of scientific analysis.') Teaching remains, for him, 'the arrangement of contingencies of reinforcement under which behaviour changes'. This is a view which has important implications for the class teacher. Teaching, he reminds us, should not be a random, hit-or-miss affair, nor is it an unfathomable mystery; it is a process which is amenable to investigation, and which requires the methodological application of techniques based in part on the results of the experimental analysis of behaviour. A student is 'taught' in the sense that '. . . he is induced to engage in new forms of behaviour and in specific forms on specific occasions'. *The teacher's task is to shape behaviour and this requires an awareness of objectives and the techniques of attainment.* It requires, additionally, a knowledge of the basis of reinforcement and of results of types of reinforcement scheduling. Indeed, the infrequency of reinforcement is regarded by Skinner as 'the most serious criticism of the current classroom'. In essence, the teacher's role should be that of practitioner of a technology designed 'to maximise the genetic endowment of each student . . . [leading him] to make the greatest possible contribution to the survival and development of his culture'.

Dembo derives the following practical advice for teachers from

Skinner's work. First, in teaching a new task, act so as to reinforce immediately rather than allowing a delay between student response and reinforcement. Secondly, reinforce each correct response in the early stages of a task. When learning is seen to occur, insist upon more correct responses before reinforcement and move gradually, but methodically, to intermittent reinforcement. Thirdly, do not expect a perfect performance of a task by the student on the first occasion; attempt, rather, to reinforce students' steps in the direction of mastery. Finally, do not reinforce in any way undesirable behaviour. (Dembo's comments have particular relevance for the teaching of skills: see Chapter 16.)

Skinner has emphasised that a really effective educational system cannot be constructed until the processes of learning and teaching are properly understood. Human behaviour, he insists, is far too complex to be left to casual experience, or even to organised experience in a classroom environment which is, by its very nature, restricted. 'Teachers need help. In particular, they need the kind of help offered by a scientific analysis of behaviour.' Skinner's words affirm the importance for the class teacher of practice based firmly on theory. Education is, for Skinner, 'the establishing of behaviour which will be of advantage to the individual and to others at some future time.' The role of the teacher is the engineering of that advantageous behaviour.

Gagné: the background

Gagné (b. 1916) is an educational psychologist who has occupied the chairs of psychology at the Universities of Princeton and Florida. His work has been concerned largely with a consideration of the general processes of learning so that the design of education might be improved. His most important books are *The Conditions of Learning* (1965), *Essentials of Learning for Instruction* (1974) and *Principles of Instruction Design* (with L. J. Briggs) (1974).

'Human beings acquire most of their human qualities through learning.' Learning must be linked, according to Gagné, with the design of instruction 'through consideration of the different kinds of capabilities that are being learned.' Those external events we call 'instruction' must have different characteristics 'depending on the particular class of performance change that is the focus of interest.' Instruction is, for him, an arrangement of external events designed to activate and give support to the internal processes of learning. Instructing means 'arranging the conditions of learning that are external to the learner.' We must not forget that the most important aspects of a learner are 'his senses, his central nervous system and his muscles.'

Gagné and the learning process

Learning is described by Gagné as '. . . a change in human disposition or capability, which persists over a period of time, and which is not simply ascribable to the process of growth.' It is a *process* taking place in the learner's brain; it is called a 'process' because 'it is formally comparable to other organic processes such as digestion and respiration.' People do not learn in any general sense, rather in the sense of changed behaviour that can be described 'in terms of an observable type of human performance.' The change in a student's performance is what leads to the conclusion that learning has occurred.

Gagné enumerates *five major categories of human capability that can be considered as outcomes of learning.* They are 'learned capabilities . . . supported by particular sources of internal and external events'.

1. *Verbal information* ('man's primary method of transmitting accumulated knowledge . . .').
2. *Intellectual skills* ('learned capabilities which enable the learner to *do* various things by means of symbolic representations of his environment').
3. *Cognitive strategies* ('internally organised capabilities which the learner makes use of in guiding his own attending, learning, remembering, and thinking').
4. *Attitudes* ('acquired internal states that influence the choice of personal action').
5. *Motor skills* ('making possible the precise, smooth, and accurately timed execution of performances involving the use of muscles').

Learning is viewed by Gagné as a 'total process', beginning with a phase of *apprehending* the stimulus situation, proceeding to a stage of *acquisition,* then to *storage* and, finally, to *retrieval.* The teacher must ensure that a student has the prerequisite capabilities for the learning task he is to undertake. There is a 'learning hierarchy' which depends on prerequisite intellectual skills. Gagné enumerates *eight types of learning,* each requiring its own teaching strategy.

1. *Signal learning.* Here the learner associates an available response with a new 'signal' (i.e. stimulus).

2. *Stimulus–response learning*. Here the learner acquires exact responses to discriminated stimuli.
3. *Chaining*. The learner acquires a number of S–R bonds, e.g. the sets of motor responses needed to change a typewriter ribbon, set up a drilling machine, finger A-flat on the oboe.
4. *Verbal association learning*. Here the learner acquires verbal chains, selecting the links from his previously-learned repertoire. 'The chain cannot be learned unless the individual is capable of performing the individual links.'
5. *Multiple discrimination*. The learner acquires the capacity to discriminate between apparently similar stimuli and to make the correct response.
6. *Concept learning*. The learner is able to make common responses to classes of stimuli and to recognise relationships, known as 'classes'.
7. *Rule learning*. The learner is able to form chains of two or more concepts. A rule is 'an inferred capability that enables the individual to respond to a class of stimulus situations with a class of performances'.
8. *Problem solving*. This is 'a natural extension of rule learning, in which the most important part of the process takes place within the learner'. It is characterised by 'discovery' of relationships.

Gagné suggests the use of 'instructional sequences' consisting of: informing the learner as to what form of performance is expected after completion of learning; questioning the learner so as to elicit recall of previously-learned concepts: using cues eliciting the formation of chains of concepts or 'rules'; questioning the learner so as to obtain a demonstration of rules; requiring the learner to make a verbal statement of the rule.

The phases of learning

The 'information-processing model' is considered by Gagné to represent 'a major advance in the scientific study of human learning'. According to Gagné's interpretation of the model, an act of learning, no matter what its duration in time, comprises several phases. It begins with an intake of stimulation from the learner's receptors and concludes with feedback, following his performance. A number of 'internal processing events' also take place. The teacher's task comprises several different types of external stimulation which affect the processes of learning.

The following *phases of learning* are noted by Gagné.

1. *The motivation phase.* This involves striving to attain some end. The identification of students' motives, and channelling them into 'activities that accomplish educational goals' form a task for the designer of instruction. The generation of student expectancies is essential in this phase; the teacher can assist by informing the learner of the objectives—'expectancies of the learning outcome'.

2. *The apprehending phase.* Attention and selective perception constitute this phase. The teacher's specific task here is the direction of attention, so that the learner is ready to receive appropriate, prepared stimuli. Selective perception involves the teacher in arranging stimuli which will emphasise those features of his presentation which it is intended shall be stored in the learner's short-term memory (see p. 127). The highlighting of aspects of presentation (by repetition, audio-visual aids, and verbal and pictorial emphasis) is an essential feature of 'foundation learning' in any subject area.

3. *The acquisition phase.* Coding and storage entry characterise this phase of learning. The process of coding involves transforming information into a pattern appropriate for storage in the memory. The provision of learning guidance, the 'stimulation of recall of necessary prerequisites and other supportive material from the learner's long-term memory' comprise the teacher's principal task in this phase. Verbal directions eliciting the utilisation of previously-learned material are important. Questions, cues, have a part to play here.

4. *The retention phase.* Memory storage, following storage entry, is the essence of this phase. Instruction designed to ensure retention—practice, tests, feedback—is necessary here.

5. *The recall phase.* Retrieval is the appropriate internal process for this phase. The provision of a variety of external cues within the learner's frame of knowledge is the teacher's task at this point. Thus, the learner may be required to apply what he has learned to novel types of problem in a variety of circumstances.

6. *The generalisation phase.* Transfer of learning (see p. 135) is the objective of this phase; the teacher's task is its promotion. Gagné views transfer of learning as taking the form of lateral and vertical movement. *Lateral transfer* is a process of generalising that 'spreads over' situations at approximately the same level of complexity, e.g. as where the acquired ability to recognise parts of speech is carried over from English to, say, French. *Vertical transfer* involves the use of learned capabilities at one level in learning at a higher level, as where the knowledge of handling clay is utilised in the design of pots.

7. *The performance phase.* The eliciting of an appropriate performance, reflecting newly-acquired capability, is essential if the
   teacher is to have evidence of the learner having attained his
   objective.
8. *The feedback phase.* This final phase, in which the learner is made
   aware of the degree to which his performance approaches
   required standards, acts as a reinforcement, strengthening newly-
   learned associations and their recall.

Gagné's work and the teacher

The practical significance of Gagné's work has been recognised by the
many teachers who build their lesson schemes and plan their instruction on the basis of the concepts adumbrated in *The Conditions of
Learning.* Gagné sees the teacher as a designer and manager of the
process of instruction and an evaluator of learning outcomes. He
emphasises, above all, the importance of the *systematic design of
instruction* based on intended outcomes and linked with awareness of
the internal conditions of learning. Gagné's view of the 'hierarchical
nature' of the learning process serves as a reminder to the teacher that
the learner must be adequately prepared to enter a particular phase of
instruction. The teacher must ensure that 'relevant lower-order skills
are mastered before the learning of the related higher-order skill is
undertaken . . . First, find out what the student already knows; second,
begin instruction at that point.'

The *importance of feedback* in the classroom is stressed by Gagné.
'Every act of learning requires feedback if it is to be completed.' This
necessitates communication to the student, as swiftly and accurately
as possible, of the outcome of his performance (see Chapter 7) and
calls for careful and regular evaluation in the classroom. The planning
of feedback is one example of the design of instruction—with the
learner in mind—which characterises the neo-behaviourism of which
Gagné is a powerful advocate.

4

Theories of learning (3): the Gestalt school—Koffka, Köhler and Wertheimer

> The harmony that results from the simultaneous sounding of all the strings [of a lyre] is obviously different from the sounds produced by the individual strings . . . The totality that emerges from the harmony of all the strings plucked together differs from the totality produced when the strings are plucked individually (Philoponos c. AD 500).

Gestalt psychology (*Gestalt,* configuration, structure, pattern) arose out of the work of Koffka (1886–1941), Köhler (1887–1967) and Wertheimer (1880–1943) and stands in opposition to the methods and conclusions of the structuralist and behaviourist schools of psychology. The basic theories of the Gestalt psychologists are set out and elaborated in Koffka's *Principles of Gestalt Psychology* (1935), Köhler's *Gestalt Psychology* (1929) and Wertheimer's *Productive Thinking* (1945). The influence of the Gestaltists on theories of the nature of learning and classroom techniques has been profound.

Objections to structuralism and behaviourism

Structuralists (e.g. Titchener (1867–1927)) attempted to understand mental states and processes by examining and analysing their composition and arrangement. The Gestaltists condemned this approach, insisting that any analysis of the mind which merely attempted to reduce it to elements was misleading. Mental patterns could not be reduced, they claimed, to combinations of smaller elements, to 'bundles of sensations'. The components of an individual's mental life,

45

such as learning and thinking, could be analysed successfully only in organised, complete structures.

Behaviourism as represented by Watson, for example (see Chapter 2), was also rejected by the Gestaltists. The reduction of human behaviour to S–R patterns was criticised as over-simplified. In its place the Gestaltists offered a concept based on a pattern symbolised by S–O–R (stimuli pattern–perceptual organisation by the organism–response based on perception). They maintained that 'organisms do not merely respond to their environment, they have *transactions* with the environment' (Robinson 1981).

To 'cut to pieces living and thinking processes' in an attempt to get at the elements of thinking, was to blind oneself to the importance of structure as a whole. It was to the pattern and meaningfulness of the mental process as a whole that the Gestaltists turned their attention.

The essence of the Gestaltist approach

'The whole is greater than the sum of its parts; we are dealing with wholes and whole-processes possessed of inner intrinsic laws'—this is the essence of the Gestaltist approach to a study of the phenomena with which psychology is concerned. It is the total, structured forms of an individual's mental experience with which the psychologist ought to be concerned and the attributes of the whole are not entirely deducible from an analysis of constituent elements. The whole itself possesses properties, as well as its individual components. The structural form of a Bach fugue is 'greater than' the notes of which it is made; the structure of a screw-cutting lathe is 'greater than' the mere sum of the carriage, spindle, cutting tool, etc., of which it consists. The complex perceptions which are involved in thinking and learning, are much more than the mere 'bundles of sensations' of which they are said to be constituted. A learner's experience has a pattern, a 'wholeness', which is more than the sum of its 'parts'. It is a *structure* of psychological phenomena with properties which cannot be understood by a mere summation of those phenomena.

An individual's experiences, his behaviour, are not explicable, argued the Gestaltists, by atomistic theories. Phenomena such as learning have to be studied as complex, highly-organised structures *(Gestalts)*. The aspect of behaviour which we call 'learning' is, in this view, *a pattern of activities*. Fundamental to an understanding of those activities is the concept of the Gestaltists, known as *insight*.

Insight

'Insight' is used by Gestalt psychologists in a very specific sense. It is said to emerge when the learner suddenly becomes aware of the relevance of his behaviour to some objective and is the result of a sudden *reorganisation by the learner of his field of experience*. The learner suddenly experiences a 'flash of inspiration', a 'new idea'. Archimedes' legendary cry of 'Eureka!' ('I have found it!') when he suddenly discovered the key to the principle of floating bodies—according to the account of Vitruvius—might be taken to symbolise insight in this sense. But insight should not be confused with the random, 'lucky guess'. There can be no insight in the absence of appropriate knowledge. ('Fortune favours the prepared mind' (Pasteur).)

The sudden 'flash of illumination' which throws new light on a hitherto intractable problem is well known in the history of scientific discovery. Poincaré tells of how his discovery of the essence of Fuchsian functions came to him suddenly during a seaside walk. The physicist de Broglie recounts how 'quite suddenly and usually with a jolt there occurs some kind of crystallisation, and the research worker perceives instantly . . . the main outlines of the new concepts that had been latent in him.' Nicolle has told of how he solved in a moment of 'creative illumination' the problem of the transmission of typhus by fleas. Kekulé is said to have discovered the concept of benzene rings while 'in reverie' on the top deck of a London bus. Sir William Hamilton, the Irish mathematician, wrote of how, while walking, he experienced a flash of inspiration involving his 'new algebra' (relating to discarding the communicative postulate for multiplication). (Note, however, that some scientists are critical of this concept as it applies to a person attempting to construct a new point of view. Gruber, for example, says: 'The sudden insight in which a problem is solved, when it is solved suddenly, may represent only a minor nodal point,like the crest of a wave, in a long and very slow process—the development of a point of view.')

Insight, according to the Gestaltists, does not result from separate responses to a series of separate stimuli; it is a complex reaction to a situation *in its entirety,* a perception of a whole group of relationships, a discovery of 'a previously unrecognised but fundamental unity' in a variety of phenomena, in effect, a 'suddenly occurring reorganisation of the field of experience'. Insight and thought are, in this sense, virtually synonymous.

Köhler's well-known study of insight learning in chimpanzees involved tests of the animals' abilities in the solution of problems, some necessitating the use of implements. In one of these experiments, the animal under observation appeared, at one stage, to act very suddenly (giving the impression of carrying out some plan of operations) in order to reach bananas suspended out of its reach. It placed boxes on top of one another, climbed them and seized the fruit. In another experiment it put together, after many attempts, some jointed sticks which it then used to reach fruit placed outside its cage. Köhler interpreted these actions as being discontinuous with the animal's previous trials and errors; he saw them as exhibiting a pattern of learning which he recognised as insight.

On a much higher level the phenomenon is observed in the learner who is struggling to find the correct solution to an algebraic problem. He may seize on an apparently important feature of the problem and reformulate it in terms of that feature. Eventually his perception becomes sufficiently 'structured' to allow him to 'see into' the problem and to solve it. The sudden 'I have it! I need to multiply the square root by 3, and there's the answer . . .' is the result of no magic, no fortituous assembling of the elements of the problem in their correct order; it is, say the Gestaltists, the result of the learner's perceiving *the structural essence of the total situation posed by the problem.* The learner has made an imaginative leap 'from present facts to future possibilities'. ('Making things explicit leads to the construction of a structure which is partially new, even though contained virtually in those structures which preceded it' (Piaget).) The learner 'sees where he saw not before'. Gestaltists hold that, in general, learning resulting from insight is characterised by the following features:

(a)   the solution to a problem comes suddenly;
(b)   the solution can be repeated subsequently and without any error, on the presentation of further problems of the same type;
(c)   the solution can be retained for long periods of time and be transposed to problems which possess the same basic features as the original problem, but which are in very different contexts.

The laws of Gestalt psychology

The basic laws of the Gestaltists arise from the belief that the fundamentally biological process of perception is governed by principles of organisation, so that the human being imposes on his physical environment a certain *Gestalt.* They may be formulated as follows:

1.   *Law of figure-ground relationship.* An individual's perceptions are

organised into 'figures' which tend to stand out from their background. Consider, for example, the letters which are printed on this page. They stand out from the spaces which separate them. Yet, although figures *and* space form the field of perception, the spaces are not 'perceived' by the reader. Similarly, the pattern in which acts take on their meaning from their context in time and place is based on relationships of this nature.

2. *Law of contiguity.* Things tend to be perceived as a unity according to their proximity in time or space. The closer they are, the more likely are they to be perceived as 'grouped'.

3. *Law of similarity.* Items which are similar to one another in some way, e.g. form, tend to be perceived in a group or pattern, other things being equal.

4. *Law of Prägnanz.* Percepts tend to make the best patterns possible under the circumstances, i.e. figures will be perceived in their best possible form, in the shapes most characteristic of form or structure. (The brain tends generally to interpret a form as an integrated whole.)

5. *Law of closure.* Figures and actions which are incomplete may be perceived as though symmetrical or complete, e.g. gaps in a learner's visual field tend to close in order that he may recognise complete units.

6. *Law of transposition.* Patterns may be changed or distorted without their recognisable identity disappearing, e.g. the tune of the national anthem will be recognised whether played by a solo piccolo in G-major or a full orchestra in C-major.

The laws have been summarised thus: '. . . that immediate experiences come organised in wholes; that certain items "belong" to one constellation rather than another; and that experienced features are modified by being together' (Allport 1955).

Learning and productive thinking

Learning, in Gestalt psychology, is no mere linking of associations or the workings of formal logic in the mind of the learner. It results from the learner's restructuring and reformulating his perceptions of situations involving problems. These perceptions lead to a sudden solution based on insight and reflect the learner's cognitive understanding of the relevant relationships. Learning is a *dynamic process,* not constituted by mere bundles of discrete S–R events which are transformed, somehow, into new concepts acquired by the learner.

The acquisition and retention of insight form, according to the Gestaltists, the core of the learning process. Persistent changes in knowledge, skills and attitudes constitute learning and this is not always reflected in a learner's overt behaviour. 'Learning by doing' is not recognised by Gestaltists except where a learner's 'doing' assists in changing his cognitive structures; learning results where the doer is aware of the *consequences* of his acts. Koffka defined learning in precise terms which are of much interest for the teacher: '. . . the modification of an accomplishment in a certain direction . . . in creating trace systems of a particular kind, in consolidating them, and in making them more and more available both in repeated and in new situations'.

An aspect of learning which was of much importance in the theories of the Gestaltists, particularly Wertheimer, was so-called 'productive (or creative) thinking'. Blind attempts to solve a problem, which are typical of the learner's uncritical application of rote-learned formulae, were contrasted with the dynamic creative process in which the learner applies himself with understanding to the discovery of a solution, based on his growing awareness of the structure of the problem. (Bell, describing the process of creating new knowledge, speaks of 'taking fragments of intellectual mosaics whose larger shapes cannot be predicted in advance and fitting them together in different ways or by regarding large conceptual structures from a new angle, which opens up wholly new prisms of selection and focus'.)

Wertheimer's experiments led him to conclude that although a potential capacity for creative thinking may be present in many learners, it is often unrealised and goes to waste because of the blind, drill-like procedures of instruction to which they have been subjected. Productive solutions are usually related, said Wertheimer, to the 'whole characteristics', and not the isolated aspects, of problems. Productive thinking, he asserted, necessitated the learner's grasping the essential relationships within a problem, grouping them into 'wholes' and restructuring the problem. (Duncker, who experimented with university students in problem solving, concluded that the solving of a problem often demanded its formulation in 'productive terms', i.e. the students had to see the problem afresh in terms of related stages (Duncker 1945).)

'Productive thinking' was analysed by Wallas, who suggested that thinking of this type usually involves four stages: (1) *preparation,* in which the learner explores the problem and defines it; (2) *incubation,* in which the learner rests and, in effect, dismisses the problem from his conscious thoughts; (3) *illumination,* in which solutions may occur to the learner in an unexpected manner; (4) *verification,* in which the solutions are investigated and checked by the learner (Wallas 1926).

Gestalt psychology and the teacher

The concept of insight which is at the heart of Gestalt psychology as it applies to learning, has brought criticism from some psychologists and teachers. It has been suggested that the solutions to some of the Gestaltists' experimental problems arose out of the subjects' transfer of previous learning. Harlow's experiments with monkeys taught to solve problems based on the presence of an odd object in a group, convinced him that a trained animal might acquire a 'learning set' which allowed it to solve problems without *apparent* trial and error. What seems to be insight might be the result not of a sudden understanding of the essence of the problem, but of the recall of past learning. Teachers have pointed out also that no insight appears necessary for the learning of many things, such as simple facts. (The history student does not learn the names of the wives of Henry VIII by insight.) Psychologists, such as Gagné, have reminded the Gestaltists that insight is not a prototype for a great deal of learning which people generally undertake.

In spite of these and other criticisms of the fundamentals of Gestalt psychology, the concept of learning outlined by the Gestaltists has found a sympathetic response in the practice of many class teachers. That learners often mentally organise the components of a task and perceive with 'sudden vision' the solution to a problem (or, as teachers and students might put it, 'the penny suddenly drops') is a common experience in classroom teaching. Learners commonly select from new material that which seems important, so that new terms emerge leading to insight. That insight becomes more highly-structured until it produces a solution to the problem. To plan a lesson, to arrange a problem situation so that it leads to the learner's discovery of patterns, relationships and solutions, is often a difficult, but necessary and worthwhile task. To prepare students for the unexpected emergence of novel concepts during contemplation of a problem is to assist in the development of insight. 'He who does not expect the unexpected will not detect it: for him it will remain undetectable and unapproachable' (Heraclitus).

The Gestaltists' approach to learning emphasises for the teacher the importance of so arranging lesson structure that the learner finds the route to the solution of a problem *and* sees his efforts as directed to that end. Considerable progress may be made in lessons in which learners are brought to a particular point and then asked to examine and explain how they have arrived at that point and how they see their work as linked to the next steps in the solution of the problem. In these cases learning will be facilitated where an 'overview' is presented and the interrelationships of course topics have been explained.

Wertheimer's warnings against mechanical and blind drill are echoed in those lesson structures based on comprehension and understanding as opposed to mere memorisation. Katona's work, involving experiments inspired by Wertheimer's theories, led him to conclude that the individual who has learned solely by rote memorisation has little advantage over an unpractised learner when both are faced with new problems, and that where a skill has been acquired with insight, repeated tests in novel situations often result in a continuously improved standard of performance (Katona 1940). (Teachers who have arrived intuitively at similar conclusions, or as the result of careful and direct observations in classroom, laboratory and workshop, will be encouraged to learn that their conclusions are supported by much formal research.)

Retention and transfer of knowledge—important objectives of the teaching process—appear in the light of Gestalt theory not as the product of repetitive drills, but as the result of the learner's discovery of patterns and relationships and their effective transposition to a new, wider range of situations. In short, Gestalt theory suggests that the teacher should aim to elicit productive thinking based on the perception of phenomena as integrated wholes. The teacher's task is, in the light of this theory, the arranging of the conditions of learning so that perception of this nature is facilitated.

The importance of practice is stressed by the Gestaltists: they suggest that teachers should consider the advisability of providing for students continued opportunities for the observation of novel patterns and relationships. Awareness and understanding of those relationships can be utilised by the teacher through a series of planned, systematic exercises, so that problem-solving can be carried out (in Hilgard's words) 'sensibly, structurally, organically, rather than mechanically, stupidly, or by the running off of prior habits' (Hilgard and Bower 1981).

5

Theories of learning (4): the cognitive school—Dewey, Bruner and Ausubel

Discovery is in its essence a matter of rearranging or transforming evidence in such a way that one is enabled to go beyond the evidence so reassembled to additional new insights (Bruner 1974).

Cognitive theories stand in total contrast to those of the behaviourists. The cognitive psychologist is concerned with the learner's 'internal processes' in knowing and perceiving. He assumes that a learner's behaviour is based on 'cognition', i.e. acts of knowing or thinking about the very situation in which that behaviour occurs. The formation and use of concepts, knowledge of the environment as the result of interactions by the learner and his surroundings, the organisation of knowledge, are of basic interest to the cognitive school. The S–R explanation of learning is generally rejected. The task of the teacher is related directly to the development of 'cognitive strategies' in the learner, i.e. his capabilities to select and modulate his individual internal processes of thinking, perceiving and learning. Dewey, Bruner and Ausubel are considered below as illustrating some of the views known collectively as 'cognitive learning theory'.

Dewey: the background

Dewey (1859–1952), one of America's leading educationists, made outstanding contributions to several areas of knowledge. As a philosopher, he occupied the chairs of philosophy at the Universities of Chicago and Columbia and was one of the founders of pragmatism—

the philosophy based on the doctrine that the only real test of the truth of philosophical principles or human cognitions is their practical result. As a psychologist, he was a founder of the school of functionalism, which viewed mind in terms of its adaptive significance for the organism. As an educationist he helped to mould American thought and practice in the classroom by a prodigious output of articles and books. His systematic philosophy was expounded in *Experience and Nature* (1925). Some of his writings on education include: *Democracy and Education* (1916); *The Way Out of Educational Confusion* (1931); *How We Think* (1933); *The Need for a Philosophy of Education* (1934).

Dewey viewed education as 'intelligent action', characterised by the learner's continuous evaluation of his experiences, the eventual product of which is a 'redefinition of purposes'. Education proceeds 'by the participation of the individual in the social consciousness of the race', so that a student becomes an inheritor of 'the funded capital of civilisation'. The only 'true education' comes through the stimulation of one's powers by the demands of social situations. An educational process has two sides, one psychological and one sociological; the former is probably the more significant. Indeed, without the educator's insight into the psychological structure and activities of the student, the educative process can be only haphazard and arbitrary.

Education should train one's powers of 'reflective thinking'. Genuine freedom, says Dewey, is intellectual; it rests in the trained power of thought, in the ability to 'turn things over', to examine a problem in depth. Reflective thinking is based on *five steps* between the recognition of a problem and its solution: suggestions for a solution; clarification of the essence of the problem; the use of hypotheses; reasoning about the results of utilising one of the hypotheses; testing the selected hypothesis by imaginative or overt action.

A sound educational theory is essential for sound educational practice, according to Dewey, if one accepts his concept of education as a 'conscious, purposive and informed activity'. There are *four central notions* involved in education, each requiring deep theoretical analysis. First, the 'aim of the activity'—educational ends and immediate aims had to be postulated with care, but the exact aims of instruction could not be 'legislated' because they depended on groups of variables unique to particular times and places. The second notion concerned 'the teacher', whose task was to prompt ideas of development in the student by providing a setting which would be conducive to learning. The third notion concerned 'the learner', whose desires, interests and purposes 'fired and sustained' the educational process. The final notion concerned 'the curriculum', the means by which educational aims were achieved, and this was to be based, not on the dictates of tradition, but on the principle of relevance of live issues.

Dewey and the learning process

In an early seminal article on the reflex-arc concept, Dewey attacked psychological 'molecular' thinking. He argued that the behavioural act in a reflex movement does not remain a 'meaningful' act if reduced to its sensory-motor elements. Rigid distinctions between sensations, thoughts and acts were to be avoided; they were no more than artificial abstractions from the 'organic unity' of the arc. Reflexes and all other types of behaviour had to be interpreted in the light of their significance for adaptation. The study of the human organism *as a whole,* functioning in its environment, was the proper subject matter for psychologists.

According to Dewey, every event, external or internal, calls for some kind of response. All human behaviour is the result of events and is guided by anticipation of consequences and other intervening variables. That behaviour also determines events which follow it. Learning has to be viewed as part of a 'whole', as part of an interaction of the learner and his environment.

Learning is *'learning to think'.* It arises as the result of the 'formation of wide-awake, careful, thorough habits of thinking'. The process of learning involves the exercise of the intelligence ('every intelligent act involves selection of certain things as means to other things as their consequences') and the comprehending of information so that it can be used in new situations. Mere activity does not constitute experience; 'learning by doing' is impossible, unless the 'doing' effects a change in the learner's cognitive structures.

Dewey warns against the notion that learning suddenly blossoms in adolescence after a period of unreflective thought. 'Adolescence is not a synonym for magic.' The adolescent has to be guided towards utilisation of his powers of reflective thinking and this is part of the teacher's overall responsibility. Appropriate guidance necessitates viewing the adolescent within the context of his environment and developing his cognitive abilities (in particular, his inductive and deductive powers of reasoning) so that learning may result from the 'active, persistent and careful consideration of any belief or supposed form of knowledge in the light of the grounds that support it and the further conclusions to which it tends.' Dewey warns also against the tendency of skill studies to become 'purely mechanical'. Mere imitation, dictation of steps to be taken and mechanical drill may give quick results, but they may strengthen 'traits likely to be fatal to reflective power'. True learning of skills necessitates their acquisition as the result of the use of the intelligent powers of the mind.

Dewey's work and the teacher

Dewey places great emphasis on the role of the teacher 'as a stimulus to response to intellectual matters'. Everything a teacher does in the classroom, as well as the manner in which he does it, 'incites' the student to respond in some way or other and each response tends to set his attitude in some way or other. *The teacher's influence is paramount,* even in those situations which Dewey describes as 'pupil-centred' (i.e. in which the student's personal desires, level of attainment and motivations are taken carefully into account). The teacher's responsibility for the development of 'reflective thinking' in his students is also emphasised. If the complete act of thought generally follows the pattern suggested by Dewey and other cognitive theorists (arousal of interest, leading to exploration, selection and verification of hypothetical solution to problems), then teaching must recognise the organisational steps necessary for the training and development of thinking. Instruction should be organised so as to pace development (but not to outstrip it). The motivation of cognitive learning is related directly to the learner's standards of intellectual achievement and to the guidance of his teacher.

Dewey's stress on the importance of curriculum content—to be related to the student's environment and his intellectual needs rather than the demands of tradition—calls for an awareness of the real nature of that environment. This, in turn, demands from the teacher an ability to differentiate the purely ephemeral from the fundamental. Dewey reiterates in his writings his belief that the true centre of correlation of subjects is the student's own social activities.

The classroom cannot be separated from the environment of which it is an important part. Teaching is a process, not simply of the training of students, but of 'the formation of the proper social life'. The real end to be sought by teachers and learners is 'growth' which will emerge from a 'reconstruction of accumulated experience' directed to social efficiency. Classroom activity is not set apart from society's progress; it is a prerequisite of that progress. The teacher is, therefore, a 'social servant' concerned with 'the securing of the right social growth'.

Translated into practical terms, this necessitates a curriculum and modes of instruction designed consciously with the learner's purposes and the aims of society in mind.

Bruner: the background

Bruner (b. 1915) has occupied the chairs of psychology at the University of Harvard (where he established a research centre for cognitive studies) and Cambridge. His work has been influenced in great measure by the thinking of Piaget, particularly in relation to the development of thought processes. Among Bruner's many writings on education are: *A Study of Thinking* (1956); *The Process of Education* (1960); *Toward a Theory of Instruction* (1966); *Learning about Learning* (1966); *The Relevance of Education* (1973).

Learning is viewed by Bruner in terms beyond the mere acquisition of knowledge; he sees its end as the creation of 'a better or happier or more courageous or more sensitive or more honest man'. The institutions in which formal learning takes place—the schools and colleges—are responsible for the important task of 'amplification of intellectual skills'. That 'amplification' involves instruction concerning the place of the student in the culture of his society; indeed, intelligence is seen by Bruner as, 'to a great extent, the internalisation of tools' provided by that culture. Cultural variations produce variations in modes of thinking so that a student's cognitive growth will be influenced directly by social patterns.

Students should be trained to develop their capacities to the full. 'Understanding of principles' should be developed if students are to be given confidence in their capabilities. They must be taught *how* to analyse problems, how to search for relevance and structure and how to 'economise in the use of mind' in seeking for solutions to questions. What students should be learning is not 'particular performances', but *competence,* and central to the attainment of that end is the acquisition of *correct modes of thinking.* (Bruner's emphasis on 'understanding of principles' mirrors an earlier important statement by Whitehead:

Whatever be the detail with which you cram your students, the chance of their meeting in after-life exactly that detail is almost infinitesimal; and if they do meet it, they will probably have forgotten what you taught them about it. The really useful training yields a comprehension of a few general principles with a thorough grounding in the way they apply to a variety of concrete details. In subsequent practice the student will have forgotten your particular details; but he will remember to apply principles to immediate circumstances (Whitehead 1929).

Bruner and the learning process

The cognitive school of psychology has been concerned with the 'building of a mental bridge' between the stimulus and response in the S–R process. Bruner emphasises the role of 'perception' in that process. 'Perception' is the operation by which the learner interprets or gives some meaning to sensory material and that 'meaning' will result from the context of the stimulus (in the learner and his environment) and the learner's past experiences with similar types of sensory stimulation. The brain, according to Bruner, 'selects' some stimuli in accordance with the learner's needs, values, attitudes, etc. Stimuli which are of a 'threatening' type are ignored. The process is called 'perceptual defence'. Sensory experience is organised by the learner's brain in relation to past experiences so as to interpret the current situation. As the result of 'fixation' the recurrence of a stimulus is accompanied by the recurrence of the same type of perceptual experience produced on its previous appearances.

Learning is a cognitive process involving the learner's *acquiring* new information, *transforming* his state of existing knowledge and *checking* the adequacy of that state of knowledge against the demands of new situations. (In Popper's words: 'Knowledge is always a modification of earlier knowledge . . . [it] goes back, ultimately, to inborn knowledge' (Popper 1979).) We learn best, not by committing a body of knowledge to mind, but by 'participating in the process that makes possible the establishment of knowledge'. *Knowledge is a process, not a product.* The acquisition of knowledge is an active process and depends for its effectiveness on the learner's relating incoming information to previously-acquired frames of reference. The learner gradually acquires 'internal models', giving him a pattern of meaning in his experiences so that he is able to extrapolate on the basis of that pattern. He constructs hypotheses to explain incoming information and tests them so as to produce meaningful interpretations of reality.

Learners construct 'models' of the external world and those models will be determined largely by the culture of society. An adequate model will not only explain objective reality, but will predict 'how the world might be'. The models become 'expectancies' allowing the learner to make short-cuts and leaps from partial evidence, reflecting the human tendency to 'categorise'. The construction of categories involves the learner's ability to create 'strategies', i.e. sequences of mental events related to goals. Inherent in any strategy are three factors. The first is the *informational situation* which will determine whether more information needs to be gathered by the learner before he arrives at a conclusion. The second factor is the *certainty of cognition*, that is, the intensity of the thinking needed to arrive at a conclusion. The third factor is the *general consequence of failure*, that is, the 'risk' involved in the result of cognition. These factors interact to produce a learner's strategy of movement towards a learning-goal. (Gagné criticises the concept of strategies. To know a strategy is not even a substantial part of what is needed. The learner cannot solve problems effectively until he has acquired 'masses of organised intellectual skills'.)

Growth in learning capacity is *not,* according to Bruner, a gradual accretion of associations or S–R connections; it is 'a matter of spurts and rests . . . the spurts ahead in growth seem to be touched off when certain capacities begin to develop'. These spurts do not necessarily depend on the learner's age, but rather on his ability to organise incoming information within frames of reference and models of reality. The development of that ability is one of the teacher's principal tasks. But the difficulties of this task should not be underestimated. Butterfield, the historian of science, reminds us: 'Of all forms of mental activity, the most difficult to induce even in the minds of the young, who may be presumed not to have lost their flexibility, is the art of handling the same bundle of data as before, but placing them in a new system of relations with one another by giving them a different framework.'

One of Bruner's most controversial statements is that 'any subject can be taught effectively in some intellectually honest form to any child at any stage of development'. It is merely a matter of 'representing the structure of that subject in terms of the child's way of viewing things'. Ausubel has attacked this statement as ignoring the fact that some abstractions are so inherently complex and difficult that they cannot be made understandable to persons below a certain level of cognitive maturity. In a pointed criticism of Bruner's statement, Tyler asks: 'Do common experience and observation not convince us of the impossibility of teaching such a class of responses as "solving linear equations" to a neonate?' (Tyler 1964). (Bruner's response is that he had phrased his statement so as to suggest the possibility of teaching 'meaningful aspects of any subject' at certain age levels.)

Bruner's work and the teacher

Interpreting the cultural patterns of society for the learner and assisting him to achieve mastery of the processes inherent in 'creative thinking'—these are the tasks of the teacher, according to Bruner. Students must be taught in a manner which allows them to comprehend single instances in terms of broad generalisations and principles. Bruner stresses that the student learning physics 'is a physicist, and it is easier for him to learn physics behaving like a physicist than doing something else'. The class teacher has the responsibility of ensuring that methods of teaching are 'realistic' in that they allow *discovery activity;* purely expository teaching on its own is of little value, according to Bruner, in helping a student to acquire the capacity to think creatively and critically.

Bruner's call for 'discovery learning' reflects his belief that 'the curriculum of a subject should be determined by the most fundamental understanding that can be achieved of the underlying principles that give *structure* to that subject'. Teaching will be most productive where the subject matter is 'gutted' so that its bare bones—its structural elements—are revealed and made a foundation for the acquisition of principles. A student who knows the principles of a discipline has the power to investigate and solve problems within its terms.

In discovering the 'meaning' of principles, a student is learning concepts and relationships. Bruner suggests that the activity of discovering has four advantages. (These should be of interest to the further education lecturer involved, in particular, with first-level and foundation courses.) First, there is a growth in 'intellectual potency'—the student acquires the ability to develop 'strategies' in approaching and analysing patterns in his environment in an organised manner. Secondly, intrinsic motivation becomes a preferred alternative to extrinsic rewards—the student achieves satisfaction from discovering solutions on his own. Thirdly, the student who has mastered the techniques of discovery learning is able to apply them to the solution of real problems outside the classroom. Fourthly, improvements in memory seem to be associated with the organisation of one's knowledge—retrieval of information stored in the memory (see p. 126) becomes easier where the student has organised his knowledge in terms of his own system.

Building on Bruner's views, Taba (1963) outlines some general steps in discovery learning. First, the learner should be confronted with a problem that initiates a 'feeling of bafflement'. No important generalisations should be offered by the teacher at this stage; the learner must be encouraged to explore the problem for himself. Next, he should be prompted to utilise previously-acquired knowledge so as to understand new patterns and structures from which will emerge solutions to the problem facing him. He should then be given an opportunity to demonstrate in relation to other problems the principles he has now acquired. In this way the teacher has provided the conditions facilitating the learner's discovery of 'organising principles'.

Mastery of specifics is essential if the student is to make progress and it is the teacher's task to ensure such mastery. 'Lower-order regularities' must be mastered if there is to be movement towards higher-order learning. Students must be given an opportunity to master specifics by developing skills related to immediate problems in which their knowledge may be put to use. The 'exploration of alternatives' must be part of the instructional process and it should be linked with a 'general understanding of the structure of subject matter'. The acquisition of a generalised set of basic ideas is an important aim of classroom instruction; indeed, according to Bruner, one of the true tests of learning is whether the student has grasped, and can use, 'the generic code' he has been taught. Speed of learning, resistance to forgetting, transfer of learning, creation of ability to generalise and to create new hypotheses are some of the criteria of instruction. A *spiral curriculum*, built on rudiments acquired at an early age, moving upwards and circling back to previous understanding is essential for the successful structuring of subject matter. Such a curriculum ought to be built 'around the great issues, principles and values that a society deems worthy of the continual concern of its members'. Development and redevelopment of the learner's capacities, so that he is able to deal with problems at advancing levels of complexity, are the prerequisites of successful learning and this necessitates appropriate planning of instruction in the classroom.

From the variety of teaching techniques suggested by Bruner, Dembo selects four which, taken together, could constitute an effective teaching model for many college courses. First, teach the *basic structure* of the subject, emphasising concepts, fundamental principles and relationships. Next, experiment with discovery learning techniques so that students are motivated and assisted in the acquisition and retention of principles. Thirdly, consider the advisability of commencing instructional periods with a problem that calls for the utilisation of previously-acquired knowledge in order to assist students in the search for solutions at a new level of knowledge.

Finally, pitch the instruction at a level appropriate to a student's over-all cognitive functioning so that concept formation is encouraged (Dembo 1981).

Ausubel: the background

Ausubel (b. 1918) has carried out much of his work in the City University of New York in which he directed the Office of Research and Evaluation. The principles of his thought are set out in *Educational Psychology—A Cognitive View* (1968); his other important writings include *Theory and Problems of Adolescent Development* (1964) and *The Psychology of Meaningful Verbal Learning* (1963).

Educational psychology is, according to Ausubel, concerned primarily with 'the nature, conditions, outcomes, and evaluation of classroom learning'; it should not involve itself with topics such as the nature and development of needs, animal learning and conditioning. Further, it should take into account only those kinds of learning that take place in the classroom—reception and discovery learning (i.e. meaningful 'symbolic' learning). Rote learning and motor learning are considered by Ausubel to be so inconsequential a part of classroom learning as not to warrant consideration in a treatment of educational psychology. Ausubel's condemnation of much rote learning derives from his observation that the learner is unable to relate the results of such learning to his existing cognitive structures. (O'Neil emphasises this view: 'Rote memorisation usually involves multiple readings of the material with little or no effort devoted to assimilation. Therefore, the material learned through this method usually is not meaningfully related to other stored information, which limits the facility with which such information can be retrieved at a later date' (O'Neill 1978).)

Ausubel and the learning process

The principal factors influencing 'meaningful learning and retention' are, according to Ausubel, the *substantive content* of a learner's structure of knowledge and the *organisation* of that structure at any given time. If cognitive structure is unstable and disorganised, it will inhibit meaningful learning; if it is stable and well-organised it will assist in such learning. To have appropriate 'background knowledge' of concepts and principles is essential for problem solving. Prior experience with related problems is necessary for a learner to deal successfully with novel situations.

Ausubel differentiates carefully 'reception' and 'discovery' learning. In 'reception' learning a learner is presented with the *entire content* of what is to be learned in its *final form;* the presentation is 'meaningful' if it allows him to reproduce it, with understanding, at some future date. The presentation of a geometrical theorem in terms which give the learner an opportunity to comprehend its structure, is an example. 'Discovery' learning involves the learner's discovering the principal content of what has to be learned *before* it can be incorporated meaningfully into already-existing cognitive structures. Following such learning, the student's capacity to transform facts and integrate them into previously-acquired experience will be increased.

'Meaningful learning'—to which classroom activity should be directed—involves the acquisition of 'new meanings'. 'New meanings' allow a learner to relate and 'anchor' new material to his cognitive structure, to integrate the essence of new experiences with existing patterns. In contrast, 'rote learning' does not result in the acquisition of new meanings; it involves no logical perception, no comprehension of relationships, but only arbitrary constructs. The basic type of meaningful learning is 'representational', that is, learning the meaning of symbols. 'Propositional learning' allows the learning of the meaning of verbal propositions expressing ideas 'other than those of representational equivalence'. 'Concept learning' involves the acquisition of 'generic' ideas. Each of these three types is important for true learning.

Sequential organisation of learning is of considerable importance. The arrangement of topics in a subject-matter field should be the result of an understanding by the teacher of the importance of the fundamental 'anchoring concepts'. A learning unit ought to be a link in a chain; its acquisition by the learner should be an achievement in its own right and should provide the appropriate scaffolding for the next unit in the sequence. Antecedent steps should be consolidated if the learning of subsequent steps is not to be vitiated. Consolidation requires, according to Ausubel, 'confirmation, correction, clarification, differential practice and review'.

Ausubel criticises the Gestaltist concept of 'insight' (see Chapter 4). He stresses the emergence of insight as dependent on the learner's prior experience. It rarely appears in the 'Eureka' form; it tends rather to follow 'a period of fumbling and search, of gradual emergence of a correct hypothesis'. It is important for the teacher to understand, however, the circumstances in which an apparently unproductive period of thought is followed by a sudden 'seeing the light'.

Ausubel's work and the teacher

Ausubel's emphasis on 'meaningful learning' will remind teachers that learning, designed to ensure mastery of a situation by an extension of the student's powers of reasoning, involves the careful *design of instruction* with that end in mind. His stress on linking units of instruction to form a continuous process necessitates a 'programmed' approach to classwork so that sequential learning might be achieved and the learner assisted in the discrimination of old and new ideas.

Ausubel has advocated the use of 'organisers', that is material introduced in advance of the learning material itself, presented 'at a higher level of abstraction, generality and inclusiveness'. They may take the form of a short statement in continuous prose or a diagram, or networks indicating relationships. The principal function of an organiser, according to Ausubel, is 'to bridge the gap between what the learner knows and what he needs to know before he can successfully learn the task at hand'. An 'expository organiser' is used when the new material to be learned is totally unfamiliar; it will emphasise context and link the essence of the new material with some previously-acquired concepts. It 'reminds the learner of meaningful context already available in memory and relevant to the new learning'. A 'comparative organiser' is used when the material to be learned is not entirely novel; it will point out ways in which that material resembles and differs from that which is already known.

Note, however, that 'organisers' may take other forms. Joyce and Weil point out that the 'organiser' might be an entire lesson which precedes the other lessons constituting a unit of work. The form of the organiser, they claim, is less important than the fact of its being continuously related to the material it is organising (Joyce and Weil 1972). (Davies suggests that 'advance organisers' can help to ensure that meaningful learning, rather than rote learning, results from instruction, and that they can provide an alternative to instructional objectives (see Chapter 8). He sees their functions as: the provision of a linking structure; the differentiation of ideas, leading to their acquisition with clarity; and the preservation of the identity of new ideas, ensuring that they are not absorbed totally into an existing structure, with the loss of their distinctive features (Davies 1976).)

Examples of 'organisers', used successfully in a management

course, are: a chart showing the main institutions of the capital market in Britain and illustrating their interrelationships, used as an 'expository organiser' for a unit of instruction on one of those institutions (the London Stock Exchange); a short film sequence, based on the eruption and subsequent handling of a shop-floor work dispute, used as a 'comparative organiser' for a unit of instruction dealing with the management of conflict.

Ausubel suggests that class learning can be improved through use of the technique of 'progressive differentiation'. The most general, inclusive concepts of a subject discipline should be taught first, followed by the less inclusive concepts, thus setting the stage for the teaching of specific information. Ease of assimilation and retention of information should result, since the learner's cognitive structure will then contain stable 'hooks' on which new material can be placed. Ausubel advocates, additionally, the adoption of 'integrative reconciliation' in the classroom. This technique concerns the overall organisation of content within a subject area. New ideas must be integrated with those previously learned during a course: it is unhelpful to students to devote one lesson, early in the course, to a discussion of 'ideas and concepts' and to fail to refer to those concepts at later stages of the course. This is to introduce barriers between subject elements and relationships. There should be reference throughout the course to previously-learned ideas, definitions and principles, so that they are integrated into course content as a whole.

On the matter of teacher responsibility for the content of the curriculum, Ausubel takes an uncompromising stand against the advocates of a system in which student decisions entirely determine that content. 'Teachers cannot in good conscience abdicate this responsibility [of structuring subject-matter content] by turning over to students, in the name of democracy and progressivism, the direction of education.' The content of the curriculum takes into account the student's needs; its formulation remains, however, the teacher's, not the student's, responsibility.

PART TWO

COMMUNICATION, CONTROL AND TEACHING OBJECTIVES

6

Communication and control —the essence of the teaching process (1)

You cannot speak of ocean to a well-frog—the creature of a narrower sphere; you cannot speak of ice to a summer insect (Chuang-Tze).

Consider the teaching activities outlined in Chapter 1. Each involves complex sets of relationships between teachers and learners, the most important being those resulting from *communication*. The relationships reflect, in part, the teachers' conscious manipulation of conditions, so that the students might achieve desired objectives. Manipulation of the teaching environment in relation to goals is, in effect, a type of *control,* a process which will be examined later. In this chapter we consider *communication,* i.e. the 'exchange of meanings' between teacher and students, without which there can be no effective teaching or learning, and *motivation,* i.e. the general desire of a student to enter into the learning process.

What is communication?

Communicate [L. communicare (communis, common)], *v.t.* To impart, to give a share of, to transmit; to reveal; to give Holy Communion to. *v.i.* To share, to hold intercourse, to confer by speech or writing . . . communication, *n.* The art of communicating; that which is communicated . . . *(Cassell's New English Dictionary)*

The essence of communication is the transmitting and receiving of information through a common system of symbols, whether in the form of writing or other signs, expressive movements, or the spoken

69

word. It takes place when the behaviour of one person acts as a stimulus for the behaviour of another; in the words of I. A. Richards, 'Communication takes place when one mind so acts upon its environment that another mind is influenced, and in that other mind an experience occurs which is like the experience in the first mind, and is caused in part by that experience.'

The following definitions of communication are of interest:

(a) 'the process by which people attempt to share meaning via the transmission of symbolic messages' (Stoner 1982);

(b) 'an interactional process in which meaning is stimulated through the sending and receiving of verbal and non-verbal messages' (Tortoriello 1978);

(c) 'the achievement of meaning and understanding between people through verbal and non-verbal means in order to affect behaviour and achieve desired end results' (Mondy 1983).

An important characteristic of man, which divides him from other creatures, is his capacity for the expressive vocalisation which we call *speech*. It may be that the early growth of civilisation depended in large part on man's ability to communicate with his neighbour by speaking, and the later stages of civilisation have reflected, in some measure, the invention of more complicated media of communication, such as the printing press and the radio. The development of formal teaching, in particular, is linked to the expansion of communication methods. From the spoken discourse to the printed textbook, the TV lesson and the computer, the teaching process has depended on the ability and technique of the teacher to convey to the learner in an appropriate form the fruits of human thought—that is, to communicate.

In the teaching situation, communication by the teacher is generally intended to influence the learner's behaviour. Its mode will be determined, therefore, by that situation which will reflect the lesson's objectives. To that end, communication in the classroom may be verbal or non-verbal, formal or informal, one-way or two-way, designed to elicit a verbal or non-verbal response, intended to state a fact or pose a problem. Its primary function in the teaching process is *the creation and maintenance of a community of thought and feeling which will lead to learning.*

Communication in relation to teaching

Class teaching requires the presentation of stimuli and the eliciting of learners' responses. Effective presentation of stimuli is, in itself, a form of communication. Whether pointing to a chart, tapping a ruler on a desk so as to attract attention or asking a subtle question which demands interpretation and insight for its solution, the teacher is engaged in the process of communicating. Consider, for example, the following situations in typical further education classes:

1. Day-release students are being taught the elements of vehicle maintenance. They and their tutor are examining a mechanism at which he is pointing. He states: 'Our next job is to lubricate the accelerator control linkage and cable and the pedal fulcrum. Here they are.' He then ensures that his statement has been understood.
2. Secretarial students are studying business documents. An overhead projector displays an illustration of a bill of exchange. The teacher says: 'This obviously isn't a cheque, which we looked at a few minutes ago! Why not?' Answers are elicited and considered by teacher and class.
3. BTEC students have been listening to one of their group reading his essay on 'Cures for Inflation'. He has reached his final sentence: 'Inflation can be cured, I submit, only by the abolition of the market price system.' The students turn their attention to the tutor, awaiting his reaction. He raises his eyebrows in mock, exaggerated surprise. The students observe, and understand, his reaction.

In these examples we can discern a variety of modes and media of communication. They include statements of fact, expressions of opinion, comment on opinion, questions, replies to questions, the posing of problems. The media and channels of communication include the voice, gestures (pointing, facial expressions—the so-called proto-linguistic signs, which are of great importance in the classroom), visual aids. In each of these varied examples of classroom communication will be found the following elements:

(a) an objective (e.g. to achieve an understanding of the functions of a bill of exchange);
(b) an awareness by the class teacher of the path to that objective;
(c) the creation of a link, or 'channel', between teacher and class, the effectiveness of which will be determined in large measure by the teacher's skill and the learner's initial motivation and continuing interest;
(d) the adoption by the teacher of appropriate modes of communicating his 'message', calculated to elicit responses and modify behaviour;
(e) the reception and comprehension of the message, of which the teacher becomes aware ('feedback').

Communication in the classroom is, therefore, not merely a matter of an instructor's addressing a class; it is the outcome of a number of interrelated activities. Where any one of these activities is omitted, the effectiveness of the communication may be vitiated or destroyed, so that the probability of successful learning is reduced accordingly.

Communication theory: a useful analogy

Attempts have been made in recent years to analyse the basis of information transmission so as to formulate a general theory of communication. The mathematical theory of communication, put forward by Shannon and Weaver, draws on information theory to present an explanation of communication systems which has important analogies with the teaching process. (The aim of information theory is the discovery of laws which can be couched in mathematical terms concerning systems designed to communicate or manipulate information. The term 'information' is used in a highly-technical sense as 'that which resolves uncertainty'; it can be measured in terms of changes in probability (Shannon and Weaver 1949). In less formal terms, Paisley describes 'information' as denoting 'any stimulus that alters cognitive structure in the receiver . . . Something that the receiver already knows is not information' (Paisley 1980).)

Consider a very simple system of communication, say, that existing where one person speaks to another. The system includes the following three elements:

(a)   a *source* (or transmitter)—the speaker;
(b)   a *channel*—the air which carries the speaker's voice;
(c)   a *receiver*—the listener.

Such a system may be represented by the simple diagram in Figure 6.1. Figure 6.1.

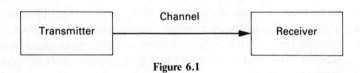

Figure 6.1

Shannon and Weaver utilised a relatively simple model of the communication process: a message flowed along a selected channel from source to receiver. Emitted signals were decoded by the receiver. In modelling information flow, the problems to be answered were: '*Who* says *what*, in *which channel*, to *whom*, and with *what result?*' The model was seen later to require modification since, in particular, it seemed to ignore the important role of feedback in the process of communication.

A later model emerged from the work of Berlo. He drew attention to the significance of feedback and stressed the significance of cultural influences and communication skills on the sender's message. Common experiences and shared meanings among participants were seen by Berlo as essential to effective communication (Berlo 1960).

More recently, Barnlund has revealed the dynamic, transactional nature of communication. His model shows communication as a dynamic process ('continually responsive, continually changing') in which the interaction of all elements within the process must be studied. Each participant shares the processes of encoding and decoding; participants 'exchange roles' continuously during some types of communication. According to Barnlund, the process of communication should not be viewed as a unidirectional, linear activity, but more in the nature of a mutual, reciprocal, transactional phenomenon (Barnlund 1980).

Certain general features have emerged from the above models. First communication is viewed best as a process, that is, a series of sequential activities directed to some end. Secondly, communication involves an interpersonal relationship. Thirdly, communication involves 'traffic in symbols' which, by their very nature, are mere approximations to the concepts intended to be transmitted. Finally, communication, if it is to be effective, necessitates a community of meaning attached to its symbols.

Figure 6.2 is a diagram delineating the fundamental features in the communication process. (Note that 'noise' occurs throughout the

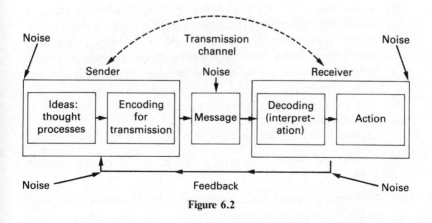

Figure 6.2

system, and that the dotted line joining sender and receiver should be interpreted as suggesting an interchange of roles at many stages in the process.)

The system is made up of the following elements:

(a)   an *information source* from which the message material originates;
(b)   a *transmitter* which transforms (or 'encodes') the message into a form suitable for the channel;
(c)   a *'noise source'* which interferes (not only in the auditory modality) with the flow of information between transmitter and receiver and reduces the probability of the message being received correctly to less than 1. (Indeed, as Shannon pointed out, the efficiency of a communication system as a whole is defined in part by the probability that noise will change the information content of the message. 'Noise' is used here in its communication engineering sense of unpredictable, random and unwanted signals that mask the information content of a communication channel.)
(d)   a *receiver* which decodes the message encoded by the transmitter;
(e)   a *destination* for the message;
(f)   *feedback* (see p. 83).

The analogy with the classroom situation in which a teacher is engaged in the processes of communication should be apparent. The importance when designing a lesson of allowing for the interference of 'noise' is clear.

The communication system of a typical lesson may be considered as consisting of the following elements:

(a)   an *information source*—the brain of the teacher;
(b)   a *transmitter*—the teacher's voice mechanism which produces a signal (words) which is transmitted through a channel (air);
(c)   *'noise'* which distorts the signal and which may result from distractions in the classroom environment, for example, or an irrelevant meaning 'read into' the message on the basis of a previous experience;
(d)   a *receiver*—the students' sensory organs;
(e)   a *destination*—the students' brains;
(f)   *feedback*—e.g. by question and answer.

Shannon and Weaver identify three levels of communication problems:

1.   With what accuracy can the very symbols of a message be transmitted?—the problem of *technique.*

2. With what precision do the symbols convey the meaning of the message?—the problem of *semantics*.
3. With what effectiveness does the received and perceived meaning affect behaviour?—the problem of *effectiveness*.

These problems may emerge when a teacher analyses the lesson he has given, in the form of the following questions:

1. 'How accurately have I conveyed the meaning of the lesson, i.e. did I employ the appropriate mode of communication?'
2. 'How precisely, in practice, did the lesson content resemble that which I had in mind?'
3. 'How did perception of the lesson content modify the behaviour of the students as judged by their responses, and, in general, how effective was I?'

The analogy presented by the theoreticians' model emphasises for the teacher the complexities of communication and draws attention to some of the factors which are necessary for the attainment of teaching goals.

'Noise' as a barrier to effective communication

The best-planned lesson can fall on 'deaf ears' and there must be few tutors in further education who have not suffered the chagrin which arises from the confrontation of a teacher, anxious to present a carefully-prepared lesson, and a class, apparently indifferent and unwilling to participate. 'They didn't respond in any way!' 'I put everything I had into it—diagrams, models, notes—and it fell flat!' 'As soon as the lesson started, I could tell we weren't on the same wavelength!'

The effectiveness of communication in the classroom may be weakened by the deficiencies of the 'source' and 'transmitter', by 'noise' and competition from a variety of sources, and by inadequacies of the 'receiver'. Often, the very environment in which the class works acts as a 'noise source' which interferes with and distorts reception of the teacher's message. Physical conditions, e.g. lighting, temperature, seating, may be such as to distract from and therefore weaken reception of the message. A badly set-out room in which the teacher can be neither seen nor heard properly is a common source of interference with information flow. Where a classroom in a college is set out in formal 'school style', the recall of unhappy experiences or of failure associated with school may interfere with the reception of communication by adult students. Controlling the teaching environment, in the sense of ensuring that it does not function as a 'noise source', is an important task for the class tutor. This is not to be taken as implying that effective communication and teaching cannot take place save in a carefully-illuminated, thermostatically-controlled room! On the contrary, it is well known that extremely efficient instruction does take place in ill-ventilated Nissen huts or in badly-illuminated, noisy laboratories overlooking railway shunting yards. In analysing the reasons for poor communication, however, it is necessary to consider the effect on the class of *all* types of distracting stimuli including the physical environment.

The 'source' and 'transmitter'—the teacher himself—may be responsible for the erection of barriers to effective communication. His personality and mannerisms will obtrude on the communication process. An aggressive manner, a nervous disposition (which may reflect inadequate knowledge or poor lesson preparation), the proto-linguistic signs which are swiftly interpreted by students as evidence of hostility or lack of interest in the subject matter, may block the pathway to learning. Adolescents are often adept in the swift detection of insincerity, so that there is unlikely to be effective learning where the tutor reveals, by an inflexion of voice or a display of indifference in response to a question (so-called 'proto-linguistic symbols') that he is out of sympathy with the purpose of the lesson. An incorrect choice of the medium of communication—a long verbal explanation of the contents of a document, for example, rather than a discussion using its image projected on a screen—may weaken the effectiveness of message transmission. A lesson pitched at too high a level or out of sequence with previous lessons will usually ensure that the class is 'on a different wavelength', so that communication is impossible. A rate of delivery which is too swift for comprehension and assimilation of the message, or too slow to maintain interest, can prevent effective transmission. A badly-structured, disjointed lesson plan may produce signals so erratic that no part of the intended message reaches the class; the signals may also produce 'overtones' resulting in a distortion of meaning. (William James' reminder that 'the mind is, at every stage, a theatre of simultaneous possibilities', is of relevance here.)

The learner—the 'receiver' and 'destination of the message'—may function in a manner which weakens or renders meaningless the communication. He may be incapable of receiving or 'decoding' (i.e. comprehending) the content of a lesson because he is inadequately prepared. A strong desire to learn how to use a computer will not recompense for a total lack of knowledge of programming processes. A well-planned lesson designed to improve speeds of typing, utilising taped dictation, will have little value for those members of the class whose spelling is poor. Where effective interpretation of messages received by the senses is impossible because of lack of acquaintance with the technical vocabulary employed, comprehension of the message is impossible. Where there are variations in the learner's level of intensity of interest, his reception of information is influenced directly; there is no communication where the learner's mind is 'elsewhere'.

Effective barriers to communication may be set up where a teacher is unaware that the language he is using is, by reason of its structure, style and syntax, so far removed from that to which his class is accustomed that the disjunction of transmitter and receiver is almost total. The work of Bernstein in uncovering the different 'class codes' of communication is of great significance for the class teacher. Bernstein draws attention to the existence of two types of language-codes—'working class language', a highly-predictable, 'public' language in which individual selection and permutation are severely restricted, and 'formal language' in which the speaker is able to make a highly-individual selection and permutation (Bernstein 1971). (For a critique of Bernstein's views see the writings of Labov.)

Parry has enumerated the following factors as barriers to effective communication (teachers will recognise swiftly some of the causes of breakdown in lessons): limitation of the receiver's capacity (e.g. cognitive limitations, preventing recognition of exceptions to generalities—the 'reductive listening' which causes students to think that what is presented as new material is no more than old knowledge 'rehashed'); distractions (often from competing stimuli and environmental stress); the use of unstated assumptions (so that cognitive barriers arise between teacher and students, who are, effectively, at cross-purposes); incompatibility of 'schemes' of understanding (whereby differing reaction patterns and expectancies lead to misinterpretations); intrusion of unconscious or partly-conscious mechanisms (such as fear, leading to the rejection of disturbing and unwelcome information); confused presentation of information (which ignores the fact that as information becomes more complex, so, for many learners, comprehension difficulty is intensified) (Parry 1966).

Probably the most effective barrier to communication in college classes is the learner's lack of motivation. In the absence of those conditions which arouse and sustain his interest in the learning process and its outcome, the chances of the teacher's eliciting the desired responses to a stimulus message are very slender. It is to the problem of motivation in the process of classroom communication that we now turn.

Motivation: its general nature

Motivation (*motus, movere* = to move) has been defined variously by psychologists as: 'the phenomena involved in a person's drives and goal-seeking behaviour'; 'the tendencies to activity which commence with a persistent stimulus (drive) and end with an appropriate adjustive response'; 'the arousal, regulation and sustaining of a pattern of behaviour'; 'the internal state or condition that results in behaviour directed towards a specific goal'. The term will be used here in a general sense to refer to a person's aroused desire for participation in a learning process. Dewey speaks of the teacher in his role of guide and director as steering a boat, '... but the energy that propels it must come from those who are learning'. The arousal, regulation and sustaining of the student's enthusiasm for learning, that is, the harnessing of his power of motivation in the service of the lesson, constitute an important task for the teacher.

The presence of motivation is considered by most teachers to be essential to effective communication and learning. Davies enumerates four effects of motivation that are of importance in instruction: motivation arouses, sustains and energises students; it assists in the direction of tasks; it is selective, in that it helps to determine students' priorities; it assists organising students' activities (Davies 1971). Tutors in further education are aware of the relative ease of teaching highly-motivated students and of the frustrations and difficulties arising from lessons with students who, for example, see no link between their aspirations and the content of a curriculum. The former usually exhibit behaviour which is calculated to assist the process of communication; the latter may display a resistance which makes effective communication difficult or impossible.

Motivation: its psychological basis

Psychologists tend to speak of the concept of 'motive' in terms of that which accounts for a learner's energy, direction and persistence of behaviour; hence it becomes possible to *infer* a learner's motives from observation of his use of learned behaviour, from the direction of that behaviour and from its persistence in pursuing and attaining a goal. A learner's motives include those related to his physiological needs (hunger, sleep, etc.) and those related to self-esteem, ability to deal with his environment, etc. An individual's 'stored motives' depend on their strength and on the 'cues' in a situation which give him information as to the desirability of the goal and probabilities of attainment. Where motives are in conflict, the stronger motive generally prevails; where the motives are of equal strength, compromise or uncertainty will result.

Some psychologists speak of a 'motivational cycle' which is based on the following components: *need* (which arises when conditions felt to be necessary for optimal chances of survival veer from their optima); *drive* (some purposeful activity initiated by a need state of the organism); *goal* (the terminal point of the drive); *satiation* (resulting in the cessation of the drive activity).

Maslow (1908–70) saw motivation in terms of an individual's striving for growth; he sought to explain it by reference to a 'hierarchy of human needs'. He believed that at any given moment a person's behaviour is dominated by those of his needs which have the greatest potency. As his 'lower', physiological needs are adequately satisfied, motives at a 'higher' level in the hierarchy come into play. The hierarchy is made up as follows:

1. *Physiological needs,* e.g. hunger, thirst, leading to a desire for food and water.
2. *Safety needs,* e.g. security. (A highly-anxious student may be experiencing these needs.)
3. *Belonging needs,* e.g. friendship.
4. *Esteem needs,* e.g. success.
5. *Self-actualisation needs,* e.g. desire for self-fulfilment.

Motivation at levels 4 and 5 (often referred to as *intrinsic motivation*) is very important and should be taken into account in the planning of work which is related to the ultimate goal of the realisation of students' potential abilities.

Alderfer (b. 1926) has reformulated Maslow's hierarchy into three levels.

1. *Existence needs,* e.g. physiological and safety needs.
2. *Relatedness needs,* i.e. needs involving social and interpersonal relationships.
3. *Growth needs,* i.e. all those needs relating to the development of human potential.

In addition to Alderfer's hierarchy being based on a 'need satisfaction process', it incorporates a 'need frustration regression process'. Thus, where a student experiences repeated frustration in his efforts to satisfy some higher-order need, he will place greater importance on the preceding lower-level needs (Alderfer 1972).

Herzberg (b. 1923) believes that persons are affected by 'motivators' and 'hygiene factors'. 'Motivators' are the factors directly associated with the *content* of an activity. He enumerates as examples, recognition, responsibility and the feeling of accomplishment. To the degree that they are present, motivation will occur, having a positive effect on learning. 'Hygiene factors' are those primarily associated with the *context* of an activity. As applied to the classroom setting, examples of such factors are the style of instruction adopted by the teacher, security of the learner, interpersonal relationships in the classroom. When present, hygiene factors prevent dissatisfaction, but do not necessarily lead to satisfaction (Herzberg 1959).

Motivation in the classroom

The teacher has the task of creating a learning environment which relates the learner's activity to his needs and aspirations, so that his competence is developed and strengthened and his sense of self-improvement heightened. This may necessitate a combination of teaching techniques which will deliberately keep alive, utilise and strengthen the learner's initial motivation. These techniques should take into account the following matters:

1. The individual learner's motivations and goals should be understood and the aims of the course should be clearly defined and explained to him.
2. 'Goals that are too hard or too easy to attain are neither motivating nor reinforcing when attained' (Hilgard and Bower 1981).
3. Short-term goals should be seen to be related to long-term achievement.
4. Lessons should be planned by the teacher *and seen by the student* as part of a sequence eventually leading to the attainment of desirable ends.
5. Tasks set should be appropriate to the student's level of abilities. 'Nothing dampens motivation as much as an unrelieved diet of failure and frustration' (Ausubel 1978).
6. Attainment of a required level of competence ought to be explained and accepted not as an end in itself, but as a key which opens the door to higher levels of understanding and achievement.
7. Lesson material and communication ought to be meaningful, ought to arouse intellectual curiosity and ought to involve

students actively and personally. 'The intensity of our interest in an activity, as well as the amount of effort that we expend on it, depend on our feeling of personal involvement in that activity' (Kolesnik 1978).

8. The level of communication during a lesson ought to be pitched carefully so that there is no 'comprehension gap' between teacher and student.

9. The fatigue which accompanies boredom and which destroys motivation ought to be avoided by a planned variety of teaching and learning activities. Cognitive drive should be maximised by arousing intellectual curiosity.

10. Assimilation of lesson material ought to be tested regularly.

11. Evaluation of test results ought to be conveyed to students as swiftly as possible and ought to be interpreted in the context of immediate and long-term aims.

12. Competence and mastery ought to be recognised and reinforced by praise.

13. Temporary failure ought to be considered by student and teacher as an occasion for a fresh attempt to overcome difficulties.

Does the absence of appropriate motivation preclude the success of a lesson? Ausubel suggests that the teacher should consider ignoring lack of motivation and concentrate on teaching the student as effectively as the situation allows. This, he claims will produce some degree of learning, and the motivation for further learning may result. Davies suggests that it is not always necessary to postpone learning until the appropriate motivation exists. The teacher should ignore initial motivational states and rely on lesson presentation which will capture and develop interest.

Effective *control* which, together with successful *communication*, helps to ensure the attainment of teaching objectives, is considered next.

7

Communication and control —the essence of the teaching process (2)

One has control by controlling a few developments which can have significant impact on performance and results. One loses control by trying to control the infinity of events which are marginal to performance and results (Drucker 1974).

Without communication, teaching is impossible. But communication will not suffice in itself to create an effective teaching situation. The teaching process, of which communication is a part, has to be directed to some desired end and movement towards the objective necessitates a planned progression. The use of a strategy of instruction designed to attain a teaching objective requires *control*—the alternative could be a meander which may, or may not, bring the learner to that objective. Control, its elements, its application to classroom teaching and, in particular, its relation to the concept of *information feedback,* ('knowledge of results') will be examined below.

Terms such as 'control' and 'manipulation of the environment' are not welcomed by many teachers, for whom they are associated with undesirable circumstances such as loss of freedom, denial of human rights, etc. But the argument presented below turns on the belief that in *any* system, such as that constituted by a class and tutor, some control is essential, and some manipulation of environmental factors is needed, if organisational objectives are to be accomplished efficiently. 'To control does not mean to suppress or impose on the process a course that contradicts its nature. On the contrary, it implies that the nature of the process in question is taken into consideration to the maximum possible extent, and that each influence on the process is applied in accordance with the process's own logic' (Talyzina). The classroom processes suggested below involve an understanding of, and respect for, the student for whom the provision of effective learning conditions is the essence of teaching activities.

The basis of feedback: a control analogy

Information feedback may be considered as *the return of a signal which indicates the result of an action and which can be used to determine future actions.* (In physiological terms, as applied to the learner, feedback is the sensory input resulting from his own effector activity.) Consider, for example, seemingly simple feedback actions such as those of a vehicle driver noting a change in the contact between his car tyres and the road surface, thereby sensing the presence of ice and reducing speed, or the automatic excretion of moisture through the pores of the skin in response to signals indicating excessive body heat, i.e. the process of sweating. Investigation of any system, natural or artificial, the behaviour of which is *purposive* and *adaptive,* reveals some circularity of action between its parts, so that the system's output can be assessed and the input modified.

The basic principles of feedback—which will be considered later in relation to classroom practice—can be illustrated by considering two processes which, outwardly, seem totally different from each other: the steering of a vessel and the lifting of a pencil.

1. Consider, first, a helmsman steering his craft through a turbulent sea, his eyes fixed now on the stars, now on the faint outline of land ahead, sensitive to each movement of his vessel which he is guiding to a selected harbour. Helmsman and craft form a *system* which has a *goal* (the harbour). The process of *control* (steering the craft) is determined by the *response* of the helmsman to the information which reaches him (i.e. his *assessment*) concerning his environment (stars, sea, craft, land).

2. Consider, next, a student intending to lift a pencil from his desk. Hand and eye, brain, nerves and muscles which regulate movement form a *system* which at that moment has a specific *goal* (i.e. lifting the pencil). The hand is *controlled* and guided to the pencil by muscles which act on *signals* coming from the body's central nervous system. Signals from nerve endings in the retina of the student's eye result from *responses to information* presented by the position of the pencil (e.g. how far it is from the desired position) and are fed back to the brain, which *assesses* them and *regulates* the action of muscles in the arm and hand. Here is an example of *informational feedback* by which the student learns the effect of his responses on the environment. (The term 'affec-

tive feedback' is used to refer to an organism learning whether a changed situation will be pleasant or unpleasant.)

From these and other similar activities we may generalise concerning feedback, that:

(a)   it is a characteristic of a goal-seeking system (e.g. a class and its teacher);
(b)   it arises where a system is furnished with continuous signals as to its environment and its functioning within that environment;
(c)   it allows the system to respond to information provided by signals;
(d)   it enables a response to be made which results from an assessment of signals and an adjustment of activity in relation to the system's goals.

(The examples above are of *negative feedback,* i.e. that which leads to corrections restoring a system to equilibrium. *Positive feedback* results in attempts to improve a system before variations occur; but if uncontrolled, it can result in an unstable 'runaway' and a breakdown of the system.)

Feedback in the classroom

The general classroom situation may be considered in terms of a system, i.e. a *set of interrelated elements,* characterised by a particular structure and behaviour. In terms of *structure* it consists, basically, of teacher and students each reacting to the other. Its *behaviour* is that of a goal-seeking body, the goal being, at any given moment, pre-determined learning objectives. The teacher's activities are directed to the control and *transformation* of the system of which he is a part, i.e. the changing of the level of class attainment.

Any teaching activity may be viewed in system terms. A lesson designed to increase typing speeds, a class discussion on the theories of town planning—each may be interpreted as a *directed process* intended to alter some element of the system's components, in these cases the speed of response of students, or their understanding of their environment. A 'directed process', however, demands that the director be *aware of the state of the system,* its approach to and deviation from its goal, as often as possible. Consider the situation of the motorist rendered temporarily 'blind' because of a shattered windscreen, or the army commander who is out of touch with his forward troops. In each of these cases the 'knowledge' which is necessary for the successful control (perhaps survival) of the system is unavailable. Control and, ultimately, viability, of the system come to an end. ('When a system's negative feedback discontinues, its steady state vanishes and at the same time its boundary disappears and the system terminates' (Miller 1955).) Analogously, *control of the teaching system (i.e. the class) demands that the teacher shall know its state and its rate of progress towards its goal.*

The nature of the typical lecture or lesson may make a flow of information feedback difficult or impossible. The lecturer engaged in a one-way communication process can have very little knowledge of audience reactions save in a superficial way (see Chapter 17). The teacher confronted with twenty students cannot easily monitor twenty different sets of reactions throughout his lesson. Circumstances such as these, which in theory and practice reduce the general possibility of feedback and control to a very low level, necessitate extraordinary steps by the teacher if some assessment is to be made practicable. The lesson plan which does not allow for the testing of progress, which omits the use of any corrective device allowing the teacher to 'keep on course', has small chance of success—if that success is to be measured by attainment of a desired goal. Explanations interspersed with tests, recapitulations followed by question and answer sessions—these are some of the methods of obtaining the signals of progress without which the class teacher's activities may be compared with those of a blind helmsman.

The elements of control

The role of the teacher which is presented in this book is based on his tasks as manager, planner, executive and controller. In his capacity as controller he undertakes the direction of the lesson, his goal is some defined teaching objective, his strategy is aimed at attainment of that objective. To that end he requires feedback which enables him to 'adjust future conduct by reference to past performance'. His control function is not an end in itself; rather is it the means whereby he and his students are able to perform a specified function, i.e. achievement of the lesson objective.

The components of a control system may be enumerated in very general terms as:

(a) a *control characteristic,* i.e. an indicator of the performance for which standards need to be set;

(b)   a *sensory device* which measures that characteristic;

(c)   a *control unit* (or comparator) which will compare and assess deviations from the desired goal and bring into play a *corrective device;* and

(d)   an *activating unit* which will change the basic operating system.

From a consideration of the processes mentioned in this and the previous chapter there emerge the *essential constituents of a control activity,* whether in the classroom or elsewhere:

(a)   measurement;

(b)   assessment;

(c)   adjustment.

Control cannot be effective in the absence of any one of these activities. Thus, the successful driving of a car (an exercise in precise control) involves continuous cycles of *measuring* distances, *assessing* speeds, *adjusting* the position of levers, so that the car's direction and speed are controlled. Effective staff promotion policy in a business organisation necessitates a process of *measuring* staff performance, *assessing* that performance in relation to potential, *adjusting* responsibilities, so that total performance is more effectively controlled.

Control in the teaching situation

All the activities constituting control ought to be utilised during the teaching process. The 'output of the system', i.e. its accomplishment in terms of learner achievement, ought to correspond to the teacher's desired objective. Achievement is, therefore, the 'controlled characteristic' which must be assessed. 'Sensory devices' take the form of tests and similar procedures. The 'control and activating units', which respond to an assessment of the learner's deviation from his expected performance, are represented by the teacher's application of corrective action.

Where possible the teacher must *measure* attainment. This does not necessarily involve absolute precision, although the more precisely he is able to measure a learner's level of attainment at any moment, the more effective will be the quality of his control. If his measurement can be expressed in numbers (e.g. as a percentage, a deviation from an average, a rank order) then the ensuing assessment may be easier. (Lord Kelvin reminded us: 'When you can measure what you are speaking of and express it in numbers, you know that on which you are discoursing. But if you cannot measure it and express it in numbers, your knowledge is of a very meagre and unsatisfactory kind.' But remember, too, Whitehead's warning against 'false concreteness'!)

The teacher must then *assess* the significance of his measurement—not always an easy task. Consider the case of a student who has scored over seventy-five per cent in three successive tests and who suddenly plummets to twenty per cent in the fourth test. Consider a situation in which only half of the members of a class respond adequately to a series of 'snap questions' put in mid-lesson. The assessment of this kind of signal requires a knowledge of one's objectives, of the students abilities and of those 'boundaries of toleration' which mark out, at their lower level, a 'danger zone'. Upon the teacher's assessment will depend his next actions.

The final stage in a cycle of control procedure is reached when the teacher decides to *adjust* the situation and takes steps to do so. This may require remedial work for an individual student or a swift adjustment of the teaching plan as it relates to an entire class. Control demands that the teacher shall act to reinforce success and correct shortcomings. *It is the ability to react swiftly and appropriately to a changing classroom situation which marks out the teacher who has mastered the technique of lesson control.*

In the next chapter we consider the definition of 'teaching objectives', a concept which is linked closely with effective control and communication in the classroom.

8

The definition and construction of teaching objectives—a behavioural approach

> If you don't know where you are going, it is difficult to select a suitable means for getting there. After all, machinists and surgeons don't select tools until they know what operation they are going to perform . . . Instructors simply function in a fog of their own making unless they know what they want their students to accomplish as a result of their instruction (Mager 1955).

The theory of communication and control in the classroom which was outlined in previous chapters involved a reference to goals, or objectives, and their attainment. The problem of the precise definition and statement of those objectives in behavioural terms is now considered in some detail.

Aims, goals and objectives

A perusal of many of the texts relating to teaching objectives indicates that there is now a standardised nomenclature which differentiates sharply the three concepts of aims, goals and objectives.

(a) *Aims* are general statements representing ideals or aspirations. Thus, the Schools Council defined the aim of humanities teaching as 'to forward understanding, discrimination and judgement in the human field'. The Business and Technician Education Council (BTEC) describes its fundamental aim as ensuring 'that students on BTEC courses develop the necessary competence in their careers in their own, employers' and the national interest'.

(b)   *Goals* describe the actual 'destination' of learning, in general terms. Thus the goal of BTEC (in relation to its aim outlined above) is the provision of a series of appropriate courses leading to BTEC awards.

(c)   *Objectives* are statements, often of a quantifiable, operational nature, indicating events from which mastery of desired activities may be correctly inferred. An objective is defined by Mager as 'an intent communicated by a statement describing a proposed change in a learner—a statement of what the learner is to be like when he has successfully completed a learning experience. It is a description of a pattern of behaviour we want the learner to be able to demonstrate'.

The essence of teaching objectives

How ought a teaching objective to be defined? Given the definition of learning which was adopted in Chapter 1, a learning event may be said to culminate in a change in the learner's behaviour. The result of that change may be observed (and learning may be inferred) by noting what the learner can *do,* as compared with what he was unable to do before the learning event. *A statement which describes what a learner will be able to do on the completion of an instructional process is known as a behavioural objective.* In Bloom's words: 'An objective states an attempt by the teacher to clarify within his own mind or communicate to others the sought-for changes in the learner' (Bloom 1981). Thus we could state that: following an introductory lesson on the carburettor, the learner 'will *name* correctly the different components of the carburettor'; or, that, following a unit of instruction relating to the industrial trade cycle, the learner 'will *describe* in their correct sequence the events which make up a trade cycle'. The *naming* and *describing* refer to types, or to forms of *behaviour* from which one can observe whether the objectives of the lessons have been attained, or not.

Lesson notes prepared by student teachers usually contain statements of the 'object of the lesson'. Often, however, the 'object' is couched in very wide terms ('. . . to teach the use of the micrometer'), or in a style which makes its attainment incapable of assessment ('. . . to instil an appreciation of management techniques'), or in a manner so terse as to render impossible any interpretation of the teacher's real aims ('Ohm's Law'). The method of defining and stating objectives which is outlined below is rigorous, precise and based on considering those objectives *in terms of student performance* ('the *learner* will describe ...'), rather than in terms of teacher performance ('... to *teach* the use of ...').

Two types of teaching objectives will be considered:

1. *The general objective:* this is usually stated in terms of that part of the syllabus which forms the unit of instruction.
2. *The specific objective:* this states the observable behaviour of the student which is expected at the end of the period of instruction.

An example, based on a course in elementary economics, might read as follows:

General objective: At the end of this period of instruction the student shall apply correctly the basic principles of the theory of rent to a consideration of a variety of economic phenomena.

Specific objectives: The student shall:

(a)   state the theory of rent in his own words;
(b)   distinguish correct and incorrect applications of the theory;
(c)   outline the concepts of profit and wages in terms of economic rent.

A further example, based on an elementary science course, might read as follows:

General objective: Following this lesson the student shall demonstrate correctly an understanding of the properties of carbon dioxide and of its production from chalk by the action of an acid.

Specific objectives: The student shall:

(a)   recall and make a sketch of the apparatus used;
(b)   specify the process of preparation;
(c)   identify three properties of carbon dioxide.

The teaching functions of behavioural objectives

There are three principal teaching functions of behavioural objectives in the context of classroom teaching. First, they impose on the teacher the discipline of selecting and formulating the *steps* which he considers necessary in the process of instruction. Second, they provide him with an overall view of the *structure* of his instructional task. Third, they present him with the basis of a suitable *assessment procedure*.

A statement of objectives presupposes a planned series of instructional *steps*. Each step has to be seen as a link in a process; each should be considered as starting from an ascertained level of student performance; each should be planned so as to contribute to a movement of that performance to a higher level. This is not an easy task since it involves the teacher in posing and answering many questions, including: 'What is the student able to *do* before the instruction commences?' 'What do I want him to be able to *do* after the period of instruction?' 'What resources will be available to the class?' 'What are the constraints (e.g. time available for instruction)?' Without answers to questions of this kind the defining of lesson objectives will be less than precise.

From the pattern of steps formulated in terms of objectives should emerge the *structure* of the lesson designed to achieve the defined instructional ends. The 'total view' of the lesson, or series of lessons, in terms of ends, of the means to achieve those ends and of the modes of recognition of their attainment, is important because it gives the teacher a 'general line of advance'—a prerequisite for the control of instruction.

A further prerequisite for that control is *assessment* of the student's progress. Such an assessment is built into the very process of formulating behavioural objectives. Attainment of the learning objective can be recognised and, therefore, assessed and evaluated, in terms of student behaviour.

The defining and stating of objectives in terms of student attainment

Consider a teacher's statement of his lesson objective in the following terms: 'to show students that no loss of matter accompanies chemical change'. Couched in these terms, the objective presents some difficulties of interpretation. It views the outcome of the lesson solely in terms of the *teacher's activities* ('to *show* students . . .'). It does not provide a statement of the desirable outcome of those activities in terms of what the *students* will have learned. A teacher could, in fact, 'show students' an experiment designed to illustrate the indestructibility of matter without their learning anything! As a 'declaration of intent' the statement is of some interest; as a formulation of direction and outcome it is of little value.

Consider next a teacher's statement formulated in terms of *lesson outcome* and viewed from the point of *student attainment*. Assume that the section of the general science syllabus on which the lesson or series of lessons will be based reads, simply: 'indestructibility of matter: simple experiments'. The teacher must interpret this phrase and decide on the appropriate teaching method. He should then state his objectives *in terms of the outcome he would wish to see as the result of his teaching.* Next, he should specify how that outcome can be satisfactorily demonstrated and evaluated. *He states his objectives, therefore, in terms of an instructional product which can be assessed,* thus:

General objective: Following the series of lessons, the student will:
- (a)   understand the meaning of the term 'indestructibility of matter'; and
- (b)   evaluate correctly the three experiments to be undertaken together with their results.

Specific objectives: The student will, within a period of one hour, and without the use of books or notes:
- (a)   recall and define the term 'indestructibility of matter';
- (b)   illustrate in essay form the concept, 'all chemical changes take place without loss of matter';
- (c)   analyse in essay form the results of the experiment involving the burning of phosphorus in a closed flask;
- (d)   analyse in note form the results of the experiment involving . . .;
- (e)   analyse in note form the results of the experiment involving . . .

It will be noted that the teacher's *general objective* as stated above is 'understanding' and 'correct evaluation'. The *product of instruction* is stated in the form of a group of *specific objectives,* i.e. certain types of *behaviour* which will demonstrate to the teacher that the students understand and are able to evaluate correctly. That demonstration allows him to assess their progress in relation to his overall objective. In sum, objectives ought to be defined and stated in terms of *learning outcomes,* i.e. *student attainment.* In that way their use may contribute to the control of the learning event; that is their real significance.

The stating of specific objectives as learning outcomes

Assume that the general instructional objectives have been selected and formulated. The teacher has now defined the general purpose of his lesson, i.e. the goal to which he and his class should move. Specific objectives must be designated next as precisely as possible on the basis of the teacher's personal experience of instructing in the subject area and in relation to the level of attainment of the class.

More precisely, the statement of specific objectives should take into account the *terminal behaviour* which will demonstrate attainment of the objective, the *conditions* under which attainment is to be demonstrated and the *criteria of success* upon which evaluation will be based.

1. *Terminal behaviour.* This should be couched in terms of the *outcomes* which the teacher expects. The terms should be more precise than those used in the general objective—'lists', 'defines', 'enumerates' as contrasted with 'comprehends', 'evaluates', 'recognises'. The action verb with which the statement of the specific objective begins ought to refer to *observable behaviour*, e.g.:
   (a) '*defines* correctly the terms "profit" and "interest"';
   (b) '*lists* three of the main points of difference between an inland and a foreign bill';
   (c) '*draws* a diagram illustrating the working of a thermostat'.

   The verbs with which these specific objectives begin introduce *behavioural tasks* which can be observed and assessed by the teacher. Each refers to a *specific learning outcome* which will be related to a wider, general objective.

2. *Conditions under which the behaviour is to be demonstrated.* The specific objectives may be formulated so as to include stimulus conditions and desired constraints. The teacher may wish to specify the information, the equipment, the materials which are to be made available to the student, restrictions of time, etc. This is illustrated in the following extracts from specific objectives:
   (a) 'without the use of calculators . . .';
   (b) 'with the typewriter keys masked . . .';
   (c) 'within an examination period of thirty minutes . . .'.

3. *Criteria of success.* These will be stated in accordance with the teacher's experience. Performance will be evaluated in relation to the criteria. An acceptable 'minimal mastery level' should be stated, as in the following examples:
   (a) '. . . must state correctly at least three of the four principal points . . .';
   (b) '. . . must make not more than five errors in the transcription . . .';
   (c) '. . . must list all six procedures . . .'.

The selection of objectives

Selection will reflect closely the content and requirements of the syllabus to which the class teacher is working. The selection of wide, general objectives becomes relatively easy when the published syllabus elaborates subject headings, rather than when they are stated tersely in a few words. Compare, for example, the following extracts from two syllabuses relating to commercial studies:

Syllabus A   *'The modern office'.*
Syllabus B   *'The modern office: functions; personnel; organisation; mechanisation'.*

Extract A (typical of those syllabus statements which cause some difficulty for teachers seeking to interpret the precise requirements of examination boards) provides little help in the formulation of precise objectives. In such circumstances objectives ought to be selected after an examination of current commercial practice, previous test papers, appropriate chapters in textbooks and manuals, etc. Extract B suggests immediately a number of relevant objectives.

Curriculum guides may provide a further source of general objectives. They may be obtained from teaching institutes, professional and trade educational bodies and, in some cases, examination boards.

A fruitful source of examples of objectives and, in particular, their formulation in terms of classroom practice, may be found in the analytical studies of Bloom and Ebel. The *taxonomies of teaching objectives* which they and others have produced are outlined in the next chapter. (See Bloom *et al.* 1981.).

Tyler's 'general objectives'

Tyler advocates, in contrast to those who support the writing and use of specific objectives, a concentration on the design and use of *general objectives*. 'More general objectives are desirable rather than less general objectives.' The most useful way of defining an objective is, according to Tyler, to consider two 'dimensions'—behaviour and content. 'Behaviour' is described by Tyler as 'the kind of behaviour to be developed in the student'. 'Content' means 'the content or area of life in which the behaviour is to operate'. An objective requires, additionally, *context*. What, asks Tyler, is the precise significance of a behavioural objective requiring a student to 'think rationally'? About *what* ought he to be thinking? What is the point of content devoid of context? What is the learner supposed to *do* with the law of diminishing returns or the calculus? Tyler insists on objectives based on behaviour *and* content.

Mere lists of objectives provide, according to Tyler, no real indication of the very *structure* of knowledge, with which their compiler ought to be concerned. A useful statement of objectives involves the utilisation of a graphic two-dimensional chart so as to discover 'concise sets of specifications'. Along one axis is 'behaviour'; along the other is 'content'. Intersections of vertical and horizontal columns are marked where they suggest a direct relationship between content area and behavioural aspect; absence of a mark suggests absence of such a relationship or the presence of a trivial, immaterial relationship. The marked relationships can be used as the basis for a formulation of course objectives. Tyler suggests that, in general, one year's work in a subject area necessitates seven to fifteen behavioural categories and ten to thirty content categories (Tyler 1949 and 1964).

The controversy on instructional objectives

The principle and use of instructional objectives in the classroom have attracted the severe criticism which is levelled against other manifestations of behaviourism, such as programmed instruction (see Chapter 20) and objective tests (see Chapter 23). Education, the non-behaviourists emphasise, is a process, the outcome of which can be neither defined nor measured in strict behavioural terms. (Objection has been taken, also, to the 'input-output' formulations of some advocates of instructional objectives; it has been stated, for example, that 'the language of the production line is inappropriate to describe the processes of instruction'.) To suggest that overt behaviour is the sole criterion of a learner's cognitive attainment is to miss—it is argued—the 'real point' of education. Further, the learning outcome, by its very nature, defies the precise, quantitative analysis upon which the theory and use of instructional objectives rest. To attempt to formulate this outcome in exact terms is, it is claimed, to trivialise the really important ends of instruction.

Eisner, a trenchant critic of the use of educational objectives, makes four points. He claims that the outcomes of instruction are too complex and numerous for educational objectives to encompass. The quality of learning which stems from student interaction is very difficult to predict, so that the teacher cannot specify behavioural goals in advance. Next, there are some subject areas in which the specification of instructional objectives is impossible—even if it were desirable. In the arts, for example, how can one state criteria and objectives? And ought not instruction in these areas to yield behaviour which may be unpredictable and which, therefore, comes as a surprise to teacher and learner alike? Further, he argues, most of the outcomes of instruction need not be specified in advance. The teacher ought not to ask: 'What am I trying to accomplish?' Rather ought he to ask: 'What am I going to *do*?' From his doing will stem the accomplishment. ('We can only know what we wanted to accomplish after the fact.')

Hogben has drawn attention to the practical problems of drawing up objectives. He refers to the sheer number of statements which would be involved in translating a curriculum into behavioural terms and emphasises that the type and quality of much classroom learning is largely unpredictable, so that objectives cannot always be stated realistically in advance of the lesson. There is more to education, he urges, than objectives that can be stated unambiguously in terms of student behaviour. In particular, 'responsive diversity' must be encouraged. He makes five suggestions: first, that although some course objectives can be stated they need not be framed in specific, behavioural terms; second, that long-term objectives (which may not become apparent to students until long after the end of a course) ought to be stated; third, that unexpected and unintended outcomes ought not to be ignored; fourth, that the objectives in their totality ought to mirror the goals which generated them; finally, that objectives which cannot be easily assessed ought not to be ignored in the building of a curriculum (Hogben 1972).

Popham advances the following arguments against the validity of objective tests. First, because trivial learner behaviour is the easiest to cast in objective form, the really important outcomes of education may not receive appropriate emphasis. The stating of explicit goals prevents advantage being taken of those opportunities unexpectedly occurring during a lesson. Behavioural changes are not the only type of important educational outcome. Further, in some subject areas (the fine arts, for example) it is very difficult to identify measurable student behaviour. Measurability generally implies accountability and teachers might be judged on ability to change behaviour alone (Popham 1970).

Macdonald-Ross emphasises the following objections to behavioural objectives. First, there are no well-defined prescriptions for their derivation. Defining objectives before the event often conflicts with the exploration which should characterise the learning process. Unpredicted classroom events (often important) cannot be utilised fully in the context of pre-specified goals. In some disciplines appropriate criteria can be applied only after the event. Finally, lists of behaviours are not an adequate reflection of the real structure of knowledge (Macdonald-Ross 1973).

The case against the use of instructional objectives may be summed up in metaphoric terms thus: 'Education is an exciting journey, the precise destination of which cannot be known in advance. It recognises no bounds, it cannot be constrained by paths and marked roads. It needs no compass, no guide other than the sun, moon and stars. Maps and milestones rob the journey of its real meaning. Those who make the journey must be allowed to wander as they will, to use roads only when they wish, to walk into unknown territory if they so desire. It is better to journey hopefully than to arrive and the exciting prospects of discovery must be allowed to every traveller.'

In answer, it has been emphasised that the basic rationale of instructional objectives is the effective utilisation of human and other resources so as to achieve desired ends; this is impossible to attain save by reference to standards and criteria of achievement. It is—arguably—more interesting to travel hopefully than to arrive, but it is vital to know one's destination and necessary to be able to recognise it! It is also of importance that travellers should not be exposed unnecessarily to the hazards of falling by the wayside and never completing the journey. Nor may we ignore the fact that most educational travellers have a very limited time in which to complete a very arduous journey. The lesson viewed as a planned, exciting journey, with instructional objectives used as milestones along the route, in no way removes the wonder of learning and the satisfaction which comes with achievement. Further, the use of instructional objectives does not necessarily destroy the spontaneity of class response which can enrich a lesson. Nor does it prevent a teacher effectively utilising the side winds, the unexpected issues, which often arise during a lesson.

Macdonald-Ross stresses the following advantages claimed for behavioural objectives. First, they encourage teachers to think and plan in a detailed fashion and to make explicit previously unstated values. They provide a rational foundation for evaluation and provide a basis of a self-improving system which can achieve internal consistency and realise in practice aims set in theory.

If a lesson is viewed as an unprepared activity, with no discernible objective, if its content is to be determined by whim and its course by improvisation on the spur of the moment, instructional goals may be irrelevant. If, however, the efficiency of the instructional process is to be tested by its success in leading students to desirable goals, then those goals ought to be stated as accurately as possible and the paths to their attainment ought to be charted with precision. The use of instructional objectives may contribute to that end.

Instructional objectives in the classroom: some practical matters

The following points relating to the use of objectives in the classroom are among those reiterated frequently by teachers in further education who have experimented with the design of curricula.

1. The use of instructional objectives in the classroom may involve a complete break with some traditional views of teaching; it necessitates a highly-structured and carefully-planned situation in which the teacher plays a predominant role.
2. Planning a scheme of objectives is all-important. The objectives—which must never be of a trivial nature—must be planned and listed in schematic, sequential form on the basis of 2–5 objectives per lesson. (Have as few objectives as possible.)
3. The use of time must be planned carefully. Periods of at least one-hour seem to be needed.
4. Continuous assessment during periods of instruction may be essential and can present problems in relation to time available. But without assessment, movement to objectives cannot be monitored and, therefore, cannot be evaluated. Assessment in the form of multiple-choice objective tests is often useful.
5. Records of student achievement must be kept carefully.
6. Failure to attain an objective is not to be viewed by teacher or students as a catastrophe! The aphorism suggesting that an unattained objective is an incorrectly-drawn objective does not take into account the phenomenon of 'noise' in communication channels (see Chapter 6).
7. Instruction by the use of detailed objectives makes unusually heavy demands on a class. Concentrated effort is required for extended periods; control of the class throws a heavy burden on the teacher. It is often advisable that a lesson be 'broken up' by short 'buzz group' sessions, for example.
8. Students should be informed carefully of the purpose of this' mode of instruction. Where it is possible to issue lists of instructional objectives at the beginning of a session, motivation can be heightened; the objectives can act as a useful reference point and check list for the students.
9. Consider carefully the concept of objectives as providing 'roads to travel, rather than terminal points'.

9

Taxonomies of teaching objectives

The era of contentment with large, undefined processes is rapidly passing. An age of science is demanding exactness and particularity (Bobbitt 1924).

A useful setting in which to consider the problems of definition and statement of instructional objectives, which were raised in the previous chapter, is provided by the types of classification known as *taxonomies.* 'Taxonomy' refers to a formal classification (*taxis*=arrangement, *nomia*=distribution) based on relationships. Classifications of this type are used extensively in sciences such as zoology, entomology and biology. In biology, for example, organisms may be grouped and classified on the basis of class, order, genus, species, etc. Lower classes are subordinated to higher, until, finally, the *summum genus,* or most inclusive category with which the science is concerned, is reached.

The most widely-known taxonomy of educationa! objectives is that associated with the name of the American psychologist, B.S. Bloom, of the University of Chicago. It was first set out in 1951 at a symposium of the American Psychological Association at Chicago entitled 'The Development of a Taxonomy of Educational Objectives'. Bloom's taxonomy (as it has come to be known) continues to be of much interest for the teacher in further education since its influence may be perceived in areas such as syllabus and examination-paper construction, objective tests, schemes of marking and evaluation, and the identification of training needs in industry and commerce.

The background to Bloom's taxonomy

'Curriculum theory' in the USA has for long been concerned with the search for 'reliable' educational objectives. Thus, Franklin Bobbitt, a pioneer in curriculum theory, argued in *The Curriculum*, published in 1918, that the teacher's task is to study life so as to discover the 'abilities, habits, appreciations and forms of knowledge that men need'. These would form the objectives of a curriculum which would be based on the skills needed for their attainment. In *How to Make a Curriculum*, published in 1924, he enumerated 160 educational objectives classified in nine areas. For Bobbitt, an effective curriculum necessitated the clear formulation of specific *instructional objectives*.

Following a meeting of American college examiners at Boston in 1948 it was decided to mount a series of discussions on the formulation of a theoretical framework to be used to facilitate communication among examiners. Out of these discussions emerged the goal of a *systematised classification of educational objectives*. The classification was to be derived from three sets of principles, educational, logical and psychological. Value judgements concerning objectives and behaviour were to be avoided. The use of a *taxonomy* might assist teachers in labelling their objectives in terms of 'properties' and might help teachers in obtaining ideas as to the most appropriate sequences in which objectives should be placed.

Three important questions were raised early in the discussions. First, was it really possible to classify educational objectives? Second, would the availability of an educational taxonomy result in stultifying the thinking and planning of class teachers in matters concerning the content of the curriculum? Third, might not the use of a taxonomy lead to an undesirable fragmentation of educational purposes which ought to be considered as integrated wholes?

The first problem was met by the assertion that educational objectives *could* be expressed adequately in behavioural terms. The second was answered by an expression of hope that the very consideration of a taxonomy would help teachers in their work in the wide field of relating curriculum objectives and teaching procedures. The third question was recognised as embodying a real and very deep fear and was countered by the assertion that if the taxonomy were to be stated in *general terms*, educational purpose should not be affected too seriously.

The essence of Bloom's taxonomy

Bloom's taxonomy comprises general and specific categories which embrace the likely outcomes of instruction. What was being classified, Bloom insisted, was the 'intended behaviour' of students—the ways in which they are to act, think or feel 'as the result of participating in some unit of instruction'. The taxonomy would assist in explicit formulations of 'the ways in which students are expected to be changed by the educative process'.

Three major divisions, or domains, are delineated:

1. *the cognitive*
2. *the affective*
3. *the psychomotor.*

The cognitive domain is concerned largely with information and knowledge. The affective domain relates to attitudes, emotions and values. The psychomotor domain involves muscular and motor skills.

The cognitive domain

This domain is based on a continuum ranging from mere knowledge of facts to the intellectual process of evaluation. Each category within the domain is assumed to include behaviour at the lower levels. There are six major categories within this domain.

1. *Knowledge.* This is based on recall and methods of dealing with recalled information. It comprises:
   (a) knowledge of specifics (terminology and specific facts);
   (b) knowledge of ways and means of dealing with specifics (conventions, trends and sequences, classifications and categories, criteria and methodology);
   (c) knowledge of the universals and abstractions in a field (principles and generalisations, theories and structures).
2. *Comprehension.* This is the ability to grasp the meaning of material. It embraces 'translation' from one form to another (e.g. words to numbers), interpretation (e.g. explaining, summarising), and extrapolation (predicting effects, consequences).
3. *Application.* This involves the ability to utilise learned material in new situations. It necessitates the application of principles, theories, rules, etc.

4. *Analysis.* This involves the ability to break down learned material into component parts so that organisational structure is made clear. The analysis of relationships, and the identification of the parts of a whole is vital.
5. *Synthesis.* This refers to the ability to combine separate elements so as to form a new whole. Deduction and other aspects of logical thought are involved.
6. *Evaluation.* This concerns the ability to judge the value of material, such judgements to be based on definite criteria.

The affective domain

This domain is 'attitudinal' in concept and ranges very widely from heeding the simple reception of stimuli to the complex ability to characterise by the use of value concepts. There are five major categories within the domain.

1. *Receiving.* This involves 'attending', that is, heeding messages or other stimuli. Awareness, willingness to attend and controlled attention are subsumed under this heading.
2. *Responding.* This involves the arousal of curiosity and the acceptance of responsibility in relation to response.
3. *Valuing.* This involves recognition of the intrinsic worth of a situation so that motivation is heightened and beliefs emerge.
4. *Organising and conceptualising.* This involves the patterning of responses on the basis of investigation of attitudes and values.
5. *Characterising by value or value concept.* This involves the ability to see as a coherent whole matters involving ideas, attitudes and beliefs.

The psychomotor domain

This domain involves the motor skills. No report has yet appeared from the committee set up to study this field, but some suggestions have been made, based on Bloom's general approach. Harrow's taxonomy is as follows.

1. *Reflex movements.* These are the involuntary motor responses to stimuli. They are the basis for all types of behaviour involving bodily movement.

2. *Basic fundamental movements.* These are inherent movement patterns built upon simple reflex movements.
3. *Perceptual abilities.* These assist learners to interpret stimuli so that they can adjust to the environment. Visual and auditory discrimination is an example.
4. *Physical abilities.* These are the essential foundation for skilled movement. Speed, exertion and flexibility are examples.
5. *Skilled movements.* These are the components of any efficiently-performed complex movement. They cannot be acquired without learning, and necessitate practice.
6. *Non-discursive communication.* This comprises the advanced behaviours involved in the type of communication relating to movement, such as ballet. Movement becomes aesthetic and creative at this level of the domain (Harrow 1972).

Bloom's taxonomy and instructional objectives: an application

Examples of general and specific instructional objectives (in an economics course) based on the *cognitive domain* are given below.

1. *Category: knowledge*
   (General objective.) At the end of the period of instruction the student will know the functions of cheques. *(Specific objective.)* He will:
   (a) define a cheque;
   (b) state to which class of document it belongs;
   (c) list the parties to a cheque ...
2. *Category: comprehension*
   At the end of the period of instruction the student will understand the principle of diminishing utility. He will:
   (a) explain the principle in his own words;
   (b) illustrate the principle by means of a graph ...
3. *Category: application*
   At the end of the period of instruction the student will predict the effects of some specified changes in the variables constituting the quantity equation of exchange. He will:
   (a) demonstrate the result on the level of prices of increased supplies of money;
   (b) relate changes in the volume of trade to changes in the general level of prices ...

4. *Category: analysis*
    At the end of the period of instruction the student will analyse the assumptions in an article on prices in *The Economist*. He will:
    (a)   identify the assumptions of the writer in terms of economic principles;
    (b)   criticise those assumptions ...
5. *Category: synthesis*
    At the end of the period of instruction the student will formulate one hypothesis relating data on wage rates and unemployment. He will:
    (a)   design a model illustrating the relationship;
    (b)   discuss the relationship in quantitative terms ...
6. *Category: evaluation*
    At the end of the period of instruction the student will evaluate the weight of a given argument on population and agricultural development. He will:
    (a)   identify the positive and normative statements in the argument;
    (b)   appraise the basis of the argument in terms of economic principle ...

Given the behavioural basis of Bloom's taxonomy, the verbs which may be used for the specification of objectives are of particular importance. Since the objective states what the student will be *doing* as the result of the learning event, a *precise 'action' verb* must be selected. Commonly-used verbs are as follows:

(a)   *knowledge:* lists, names, describes, states, measures, labels, recalls;
(b)   *comprehension:* identifies, illustrates, explains, classifies, indicates;
(c)   *application:* performs, uses, manipulates, assesses, changes, demonstrates;
(d)   *analysis:* analyses, discriminates, criticises, infers, concludes;
(e)   *synthesis:* combines, discusses, argues, derives, reconstructs, designs;
(f)   *evaluation:* supports, attacks, defends, appraises, judges, justifies, clarifies.

Other taxonomies

R. L. Ebel is one of several educationists who have put forward taxonomies which appear to be simpler than Bloom's classification. His taxonomy is based on the following:

(a) understanding terms;
(b) understanding facts, generalisations;
(c) ability to explain or illustrate;
(d) ability to calculate;
(e) ability to predict;
(f) ability to recommend an appropriate course of action;
(g) ability to evaluate (Ebel 1979).

A. E. Matten, of the Associated Examining Board for the GCE, has formulated the following taxonomy which, although produced specifically in relation to economics, has a very much wider application:

(a) recall of information other than principles or terminology;
(b) recall of terminology;
(c) recall of principles;
(d) comprehension (direct interpretation) of statistics or diagrams;
(e) comprehension of principles;
(f) application of a principle (numerical) to a theoretical situation;
(g) application of a principle (diagrammatic) to a theoretical situation;
(h) application of a principle (linguistic) to a theoretical situation;
(i) application of more than one principle to a theoretical situation;
(j) synthesis of principles and background information to 'real' situations;
(k) evaluation of theoretical situations;
(l) evaluation of 'real' situations.

H. Sullivan, in an argument directed against Bloom's taxonomy, presents an alternative system, based on six categories of 'performance terms' which will allow the classification of those behaviours relative to the cognitive tasks involved in learning:

(a) identifying;
(b) naming;
(c) describing;
(d) constructing;
(e) ordering;
(f) demonstrating (Sullivan 1969).

The value of Bloom's taxonomy to the teacher

Criticisms of Bloom's taxonomy have tended to be based on three grounds; first, that since it is formulated in behavioural terms, it is derived from the 'fallacious view' of learning inherent in behavourism; second, that it is derived from a naive and therefore inadequate theory of human knowledge; third, that its cognitive/affective dichotomy is inaccurate.

The taxonomy clearly accepts learning as a response to stimuli, the desired response being the behavioural outcome, or objective. The armoury of anti-behaviourist arguments has been drawn on heavily for an attack on the implicit assertions of the taxonomy. In general, Bloom has been reminded that educational objectives should not be merely behavioural, and that outcome ought not to be equated necessarily with learning. Conceivably, one may learn without being able to convey to another evidence of having learned. Assessed behaviour, it is argued, ought not to be accepted as the only reliable indicator of the attainment of those goals set by a teacher. The taxonomy is condemned, therefore, as simplistic and inadequate as a guide for the class teacher.

A more fundamental criticism of the taxonomy is its view of human knowledge. Bloom, it has been argued, has ignored much of the contemporary analysis of the cognitive processes associated with epistemology. (Epistemology is the study of the nature, methods and validity of human knowledge. It seeks to answer fundamental questions, such as: 'What does it mean to say that "one knows"?' *or* 'By what means can knowledge be acquired?') Consider his first category in the cognitive domain—*knowledge*. Has 'knowledge' any real significance in isolation from 'comprehension' and 'application'? Can a student be said to have 'knowledge' of Pythagoras' theorem if he is able to recall the precise wording of the theorem, but is unable to use it so as to solve a simple problem requiring the calculation of the length of the hypotenuse? Does a student 'know' the functions of money if he is able to recall faultlessly the textbook explanation, but is unable to explain why trading stamps are not 'money'? 'Knowledge' of the name of the discoverer of 'dephlogisticated air' stands on a different level from that occupied by 'knowledge' of the motives of the Birmingham mob which burned his laboratory and house. (Consider the precise significance of the word 'know' in the following statements: 'I know his name.' 'I always know when it's time for lunch.' 'I think I know what he means.' 'I know that my Redeemer liveth.' The famous translator, Ronald Knox, has written of the difficulty in translating 'know'.)

Bloom's separation of the cognitive and affective domains has been criticised as unreal. Consider, for example, the third category of the affective domain—*valuing*. Can this category have any meaning if it is dissociated from cognitive objectives, such as comprehension and evaluation? Has each level in Bloom's hierarchy an immediate relationship with the other levels?

Advocates of Bloom's taxonomy retort that, in spite of its alleged theoretical inadequacies, it has, nevertheless, provided an organised framework within which objectives can be stated and classified. It has given, they claim, an intensive stimulus to the search for a means of stating syllabus content in a balanced way. It has obliged some examiners to keep in mind that most searching question: 'What are we testing?' It has warned against ambiguity in the definition of teaching objectives and has assisted in the construction of statements of goals which enable teachers to evaluate attainment by reference to a yard-stick—albeit not perfect. Its detailed analysis of the outcomes of instruction has provided a new vantage point from which the content of the syllabus and the examiner's scheme might be surveyed and scrutinised in detail.

Bloom's taxonomy may assist the teacher in answering the funda-mental questions: 'In what ways should my students have *changed* as the result of my teaching and what evidence for the change will I accept?' The very posing and consideration of these questions consti-tute a step towards the provision of some of the conditions for effective learning.

PART THREE

THE MANAGEMENT AND TECHNIQUES OF THE TEACHING PROCESS

10

The management of the teaching situation (1)—the teaching environment, syllabus and course design

> Unless we understand that the manager's job is very complex, we will fall into the trap of assuming that management is nothing more than 'common sense'. But common sense is common sense only when we know the important factors that affect a situation, when we are able to divine what must be done (Tosi and Carroll 1982).

In Part Two, the teacher was seen as 'communicator' and 'controller'. These roles—at the very heart of teaching—form part of a wider responsibility which may be termed *the management of teaching and learning*. In this and the following chapters the teacher is considered as the *manager* of a situation in which effective learning is the objective and in which he is required to exercise certain functions broadly associated with management, in its wider sense.

The essence of management

In its wider sense, management may be considered as comprising *those processes by which persons direct and operate organisations based on human effort*. In general, it involves the planning, direction and co-ordination of human activities through the medium of organisational structures. Specifically, the manager is concerned with the setting of objectives, the formulation of plans, the organisation of activities and the direction and control of operations. In more formal terms, the manager may be considered as engaged in directing the transformation of inputs into outputs.

The essence of management, whether in the context of a factory, bank or classroom, is to be discovered in its nature, purpose and chosen modes of operation. Its *nature* is that of a 'process'—a continuous and systematic series of activities. Its *purpose* is related, invariably, to the achievement of organisational aims and objectives. Its *modes of operation* are based on the techniques of co-ordination—the assembling of resources and the planning and synchronisation of procedures necessary for the attainment of desired ends.

The functions of management are universal, in that they may be discerned in one form or another in any type of management process. Outwardly, the planning of a factory production-line schedule may have little in common with the class tutor's formulation of lesson objectives and appropriate modes of tuition; fundamentally, however, both types of activity reflect the essence of planning—the process of 'thinking before doing, the devising of a line of action to be followed, the stages to go through and methods to be used'. Management functions, whether in a classroom or elsewhere, are not always exercised in a fixed sequence, and, in some circumstances, may coalesce: a class teacher or personnel director of a commercial enterprise may find it necessary to engage almost simultaneously in direction and control of an activity, for example.

The teacher's overall function in the classroom may be viewed, in the words of Haimann and Scott, as 'a facilitating activity that allocates and utilises resources, influences human action, and plans change in order to accomplish rationally-conceived goals'. (Haimann and Scott 1978).

The management of instruction

The teacher as manager is responsible, in effect, for the *deployment* of resources and the *planning* and *administration* of instruction so that the student will learn most efficiently. Specifically he has responsibility for the following activities, some of which have been discussed in previous chapters:

1. The creation and maintenance of a classroom environment in which learning can take place.
2. Construction and/or interpretation of a syllabus.

3. Selection and statement of teaching objectives.
4. Selection of appropriate modes of instruction.
5. Class motivation and control.
6. Instruction.
7. Assessment of student performance.
8. Provision of informative feedback to students.
9. Ensuring retention and transfer of knowledge.

In management terms, these and related activities may be classified under four headings: *planning; organising; directing; controlling.*

As *planner,* the teacher has to define the necessary instructional objectives (see Chapter 8) based upon his appreciation of what ought to be achieved, and what can be achieved, given a variety of constraints. As *organiser,* he has to determine a teaching strategy based on his objectives and resources. As *director,* he has to carry out his strategical task and this involves the highly-important functions of motivating and encouraging students. As *controller* (see Chapter 7), he has to monitor and assess his students' progress and adjust his teaching so that his objectives are attained.

In more precise terms, *the purpose of management of the teaching/ learning situation is the modification of the learner's behaviour in accordance with predetermined objectives, the attainment of which should enrich and advance his personal growth.* The teacher/ manager's functions have significance only as a contribution to that end.

The teaching environment: setting the stage for learning

There can be very few occasions on which the teacher is able to exercise control over the wider environment in which he works. The shape of the classroom, its situation in relation to other rooms, its general facilities, cannot often be altered. But the important details which have a direct effect on the process of instruction—the lay-out of the room, the relative positions of teacher and students, the position of teaching aids, temperature, illumination, ventilation, i.e. the accommodation arrangements, require *organisation.* Inadequate accommodation can often play a disproportionate role in the outcome of a lesson. Classroom temperature or illumination which is outside the desirable range is likely to divert students from the immediate learning task. Where such conditions can be controlled, the teacher ought to experiment so as to achieve the most satisfactory environment for his class.

The lay-out of the classroom is often under the control of the teacher and it is desirable that it be arranged in accordance with the specific requirements of the mode of instruction which is being employed. A discussion group demands a lay-out of furniture which is quite different from that needed in a formal lecture. The use of an overhead projector or a TV receiver necessitates a class arrangement which will differ from that needed in a case study discussion (see Chapters 18 and 21). The teacher in further education ought not to accept as immutable the traditional arrangement whereby a class is seated in neat rows and columns, facing a blackboard which is placed exactly in the centre of the front of the room. Some alternative arrangements have proved successful and experimentation by individual class teachers is essential.

Prints and photographs of late-nineteenth and early-twentieth century schools reveal an obsession with symmetry, presumably derived from the belief that order and symmetry were equivalent. School buildings laid out with the geometrical regularity of Fourier's phalansteries, or Bentham's Panopticon (the better to observe the prisoners therein!), were paralleled by precise rows of fixed desks in each classroom. The teacher's place was usually slightly below the middle of the front row, or on a raised platform in that position. This arrangement, now hallowed by time, is followed slavishly by some teachers, under the impression that 'you can be seen and heard from there by all the class'. This is often not the case; the best position from which to speak, from which to control the class, has to be discovered by individual experiment.

The syllabus: interpretation and compilation

The teacher in further education will usually be involved in the preparation of a class for a public or internal examination and will be expected, therefore, to 'work to' a syllabus. This often determines his general aim and teaching objectives. His tasks as teacher/manager necessitate his *interpreting* the syllabus so as to *plan* a programme of work based on objectives and to *organise* the appropriate resources.

A syllabus generally lists a series of *topics* which should be covered during a course and which may form the basis of examination questions. It may be drawn up in wide terms, which makes the teacher's interpretative task very important; it may, on the other hand, be presented with a wealth of detail which allows little in the way of individual interpretation. Thus, a recent syllabus for 'O' level economics published by an examinations board consisted of sixteen lines. This should be compared with a similar examination syllabus published by another board in the same year, which covered several pages. Where there is an absence of detail, the teacher may be at a disadvantage. He should then make an appreciation of the situation in the following terms: 'How important is the segment of knowledge mentioned very generally in the syllabus in the wider areas of the subject?' 'What details are important to the student at this stage of his development?' 'Will past examination papers, examiners' reports, give any indication of the detail required?' The teacher should then plan and organise on the basis of the detail he considers necessary. (It should be noted that there are now signs of a growing tendency towards the 'outline syllabus' which states guidelines only, leaving the teacher free to interpret them as he wishes.)

A syllabus will not generally indicate the relative importance of its topics or the order in which they are to be studied. In some cases, those who compile a syllabus tend to follow the traditional textbook 'order of contents', or a pattern prescribed by a 'logical approach' to the subject, or—consciously or unconsciously—the shape of a university course in which they may have participated. Often, however, the teacher will feel that the subject demands a different approach. Thus, the fact that many textbooks on economics, and syllabus schemes apparently based on them, begin with a definition of the subject and a discussion on the nature of economic laws, does not invalidate a lesson scheme which begins with that section of the syllabus dealing with an examination of industry. Where the teaching of the syllabus can be planned so that it coincides with teaching of related areas in other subjects, the chances of 'meaningful learning' occurring are increased. 'Localisation of industry', taught as part of an economics syllabus, is enriched when linked with 'the distribution of resources', taught as part of the economic geography syllabus.

The interpretation of the syllabus presents the teacher with the necessity of making management-type decisions based on answers to the following questions:

1. 'What ought to be the *content* of my teaching scheme?'
2. 'What ought to be the *shape* of that scheme?'
3. 'What should be my precise *objectives*, the attainment of which will ensure that the syllabus, as I have chosen to interpret it, is largely covered?'
4. 'What *modes of instruction* are necessitated by my choice of objectives?'
5. 'What *modes of assessment* are necessitated by the type of instruction I have selected?'
6. 'What *allocation of course time* is to be made for each part of the syllabus?'

In some circumstances a teacher may be asked to prepare his own course syllabus. A request for a *general syllabus* usually necessitates a comprehensive summary of the course content headings. An *extended syllabus* requires further detail, of the kind usually found in the syllabuses of some major examining bodies, i.e. main headings, sub-headings, specific content. A *working syllabus* generally contains the order of topic development which will be followed by the teacher, and which will form the basis of his lesson plan and notes (see Chapter 8). The compiling of a syllabus by the teacher may draw on standard texts, existing syllabuses and schemes of work, past examination papers and—above all—the teacher's own interpretation of the learner's needs *at his current stage of development.* 'What *must* he know of the subject matter at this stage?' 'What *should* he know?' 'What *could* he know?' What *must* be known will form the *core* of the syllabus. Its *outer layers* may include what *should* be known and, where time allows, what *could* be known. The syllabus content and the suggested allocation of time, as finally decided by the teacher, will reflect clearly his personal interpretation and assessment of the needs of his class in relation to their *initial behaviour* (i.e. their level of attainment at the beginning of the course) and their *desirable terminal behaviour* (i.e. their required level at the end of the course).

is wrong to assume that students attending their first lesson are aware of the published syllabus—many may not know of its existence! The preliminaries of the course ought to include a *discussion of the syllabus* with the class: its overall purpose, its general contents, its relation to the students' development, order of topics to be followed and allocation of time. Where the teacher knows that he will be unable to cover all sections of the syllabus, he ought to inform the class of this at the beginning of the course. Plans may then be announced so that the uncovered sections can be learned as part of a private study scheme, which will be organised and directed by the teacher. This may necessitate advice on private study and the teacher must be prepared to suggest schemes of systematic study. The uncovered part of the syllabus must not be forgotten by the teacher, and references to it should be made from time to time. Where the teacher makes a planning decision which deliberately *omits* a section of the syllabus in its entirety—perhaps because he considers it irrelevant or out of date—his reasons ought to be made known to the class.

Course design

The task of designing a course in its entirety usually falls to a senior member of staff. It may be delegated, however, on some occasions to other members of staff, so that the fundamentals of the task, requiring the exercise of management functions, ought to be known by all teachers in further education. Thus, a firm with which the college is associated may ask for a 'six-week block release course for our young supervisory staff, aimed at introducing them to the principles of management' or for 'an intensive week's revision course on motor vehicle maintenance schedule operations'. The course designer must then plan and organise a scheme, taking into account the time available, the number of students and staff, accommodation and other resources.

The task of design may be based, initially, on consideration of the process illustrated by Figure 10.1.

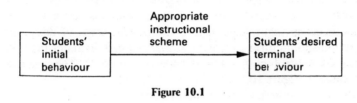

Figure 10.1

What *can* the students *do* when they enter the course? What *must* they be able to *do* when they leave the course? The subtraction of one level of behaviour from the other will produce a 'remainder', the content of which should determine the content of the course. Where a course is to be based on the teaching of an industrial or commercial *skill* a detailed task analysis may be necessary. (The Cambridge Industrial Training Research Unit uses a method of training design based on a classification of the task to be taught according to the specific nature of the learning which is required and the essential nature of the task. Five categories of learning are involved (their initials form the word *CRAMP*, by which name the method is known). The designer of the training course categorises the objectives of the learning situation by posing five questions: is the objective the development of general understanding? (*c*omprehension); is it the production of swift and reliable patterns of response? (*r*eflex development); is it the development of new attitudes? (*a*ttitude formation); is it the remembering of specific facts? (*m*emorising); is it to acquaint the trainee with a group of procedures? (*p*rocedural learning).) Psychomotor skills—invariably based on organised patterns of muscular activities reflecting responses to signals from the environment—

require much practice in co-ordinated activities (see Chapter 16), and the course design must allow for this.

Whether the course involves skills or wider types of behaviour, its design necessitates that account be taken of the students' levels of attainment at the point of entry to the course. What may be expected as a level of attainment, for example, from 'young supervisory staff'? Will they understand the simple organisational techniques upon which general management principles rest? Will the motor vehicle students be acquainted with the general requirements of a maintenance schedule? Discussions with the firm's training officers and, where possible, the administering of pre-course tests, can assist the early planning stages of the course. The desired "terminal learning behaviour" of the students must be based on a realistic assessment of what *is* possible, given the limitations of the situation, and this may result in some modification of the original aims of the course.

Course design is, however, much more complicated than the previous diagram might suggest. The component steps of design and execution should form a *coherent sequence* which includes those elements of control outlined in Chapters 6 and 7. The steps are illustrated in Figure 10.2.

It should be noted, with reference to this chart, that:

(a) the 'suggested course aims' will not often emerge unaltered as the 'agreed course aims';

(b) a terminal test should be constructed as soon as the terminal objectives are drawn up;

(c) the actual programme of work may necessitate the agreement of the departmental head;

(d) the results of the terminal test ought to be compared with the terminal objectives and an assessment made;

(e) the feedback loop between 'process of instruction' and 'tests' is a reminder that without relevant informative feedback, i.e. monitoring and assessment of performance, the level of attainment represented by the terminal objectives is unlikely to be reached.

Selecting the mode of instruction

'I understand the content and overall requirements of the syllabus and I am able to identify my appropriate objectives. What must my students *do* to learn? How may I best facilitate their learning? Ought I to use the lecture form of instruction? Would the formal lesson be

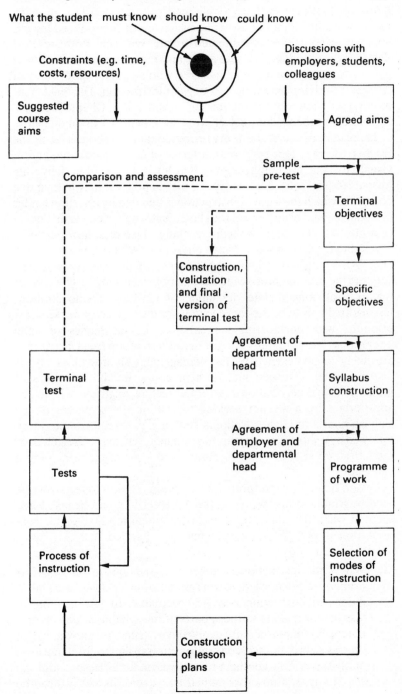

Figure 10.2 *Design and execution of courses.*

more appropriate? Is there a validated programmed lesson which might be useful? Should I use a film which has been produced for this very type of course? Would directed private study achieve the results I desire for my students?' These and similar questions must be posed and answered by the teacher/manager, who has the responsibility of designing and implementing a strategy of instruction. The most commonly used modes of instruction are considered in Chapters 15–20. A general approach to the selection of these modes is outlined below.

There may, of course, be a very restricted range of choices facing the teacher. He may lack resources in terms of accommodation, audio-visual aids, etc. He may recognise that his lack of skill in delivering formal lectures rules out this type of instruction. He may belong to a college in which the form of instruction is decided by a section leader or departmental head. Where the choice is his, however, his first question must be: 'Given my specific teaching objectives, how best do I attain them?' (Gagné suggests two questions: 'What is to be learned?' and 'What kinds of stimulation external to the learner will best support the internal processing necessary for learning?') The subject matter itself may dictate the mode of teaching. Demonstration-lessons are likely to be the chosen mode for the instructor working, for example, with engineering students on the techniques of lathe operations. The case study and the discussion group (see Chapter 18) are likely to be selected by the management studies tutor who is instructing an advanced management course in the principles of industrial wage negotiations. A formal lecture might be selected as appropriate by a teacher seeking to outline the structure of the English courts to Higher National students. A brief lesson and test, followed by a short film as recapitulation material, may be selected for the introduction of pre-nursing students to some of the principles of child care.

Lesson objectives interpreted, perhaps, in relation to the structure used by Bloom in his taxonomy (see Chapter 9) could be taken into account when the selection of an instructional mode is under consideration. In very general terms it may be suggested that:

(a) Where the instruction is linked to objectives in the *cognitive domain,* e.g. knowledge, comprehension, analysis, etc., most modes of instruction may be acceptable. In the planning of instruction relating to those parts of the syllabus which involve relatively simple cognitive objectives (such as knowledge of specifics, terminology, conventions or translation from one level of abstraction to another) formally-structured lessons and the use of appropriate programmed texts (see Chapter 20) can be considered.

(b) Where the instruction is related to objectives in the *affective domain,* e.g. valuing, organising, conceptualising, etc., most modes of instruction may be utilised successfully. Where the objectives are relatively advanced, such as those necessitating the organisation of value complexes, the tutor may find that case studies, group discussions, directed private study periods and tutorials are most productive.

(c) Where the instruction has objectives in the *psychomotor domain,* the 'practical lesson', the demonstration, the employment of visual aids, models, machines, will be valuable. In particular, instruction based on demonstrations of skills, followed by periods of concentrated practice, is essential if mastery is to be achieved. This applies to diverse and precise objectives such as attaining 40 w.p.m. in typing, decreasing the period of time in which a fractured gas pipe can be repaired, or the fluent playing of scale passages on the clarinet.

The students' general abilities and attitudes will be an important factor in the selection of the mode of instruction. It has been suggested (Davies 1981) that the more able students tend to prefer the so-called 'permissive styles' of tuition (e.g. discussions, directed private study and projects, tutorials), while the less able tend to prefer the so-called 'autocratic styles' (e.g. the formal lesson). In spite of the many exceptions to this generalisation—and the teacher in further education should refer here to his own experiences with students of varying abilities—it remains a useful rule-of-thumb for the selection of a mode of instruction by the teacher/manager.

BTEC schemes of instruction

Many colleges of further education have introduced BTEC courses, and their management has now become a major responsibility of departmental staff at all levels. The Business and Technician Education Council (BTEC) was formed as the result of a merger of the Business Education Council and the Technician Education Council, and became operative in October 1983. Members of the Council represent a partnership of industry, commerce and education. The general policy of BTEC in relation to courses is derived from the purpose for which it exists, i.e. the advancement of the quality and availability of work-related education both for those in, and those preparing for, employment in business, technician, professional and related occupations. The Council seeks to ensure: that the availability, accessibility and design of BTEC courses, the quality of student learning and standards of achievement are relevant to occupational requirements; that BTEC courses provide a challenging educational experience and effective preparation for success at work; and that BTEC courses help students to progress to the highest educational and professional achievement within their potential.

Four broad types of education and training come within the Council's scope: pre-vocational, vocational, higher vocational, continuing/post-experience for adults. In the case of *Business and Related Studies* (business and finance, computing and information systems, public administration and distribution), courses are as follows.

(a) *BTEC General Certificate/Diploma in Business Studies.* No special examination passes are needed for entry. The course for the Certificate is two years (part-time); for the Diploma, one year full-time, or two years part-time.

(b) *BTEC National Certificate Diploma in areas such as business, finance.* For entry, either four GCE 'O' levels/CSE grade one passes, or a BTEC General Award in Business Studies with Credit, are required. The course for the Certificate is two years part-time; for the Diploma, two years full-time, or three years part-time.

(c) *BTEC National Certificate/Diploma in Computing.* Entry requirements are either four GCE 'O' levels/CSE grade one passes, a BTEC General Award in Business Studies with Credit, or four BTEC level one units.

(d) *BTEC Higher National Certificate in areas such as business and finance.* Entry qualifications are either at least one GCE 'A' level and three GCE 'O' level passes, plus a BTEC conversion course or an appropriate BTEC National award. The Certificate course is two years part-time; the Diploma course is two years full-time or three years part-time.

(e) *BTEC Higher National Certificate/Diploma in Computing.* For entry, four GCE passes, including one at 'A' level and one in mathematics, or an appropriate BTEC National award, are needed.

(f) *BTEC Post-Experience Certificate in Business and Related Studies.* Students must be at least 21 and have appropriate business experience. (For General and National awards, students must be at least 16; for the Higher National awards, at least 18.)

In the case of *Technician and Design Studies* (agricultural subjects, construction, design, art, engineering, science and hotel and catering), courses are as follows.

(a) *BTEC Technician Studies Course.* This is a pre-vocational course built around a core of basic skills (e.g. numeracy) and additional skills.
(b) *BTEC National Certificate.* Entry qualifications are three CSE passes (minimum grade III) in mathematics, English (or a subject requiring English as a means of communication) and a science subject. The length of the course is three years by day-release but less by block-release. The course is reduced to two years for students with relevant GCE 'O' level/CSE grade one passes in at least four subjects.
(c) *BTEC National Diploma.* Entry requirements are three GCE 'O' levels/CSE grade I passes in relevant subjects. The course lasts two years (full-time), or two–three years (by 'sandwich' study). Students with CSE grade II or III passes in at least three relevant subjects may be able to enter a three-year course.
(d) *BTEC Higher National Certificate.* Entry is by possession of an appropriate BTEC National award, or suitable GCE 'A' level passes. The length of course is two years by day-release, but less by block-release.
(e) *BTEC Higher National Diploma.* Entry requires an appropriate BTEC National award, or equivalent qualification, or a pass in at least one appropriate GCE 'A' level subject. Length of course: 2 years (full-time); three years ('sandwich' study).
(f) *BTEC Post-Experience Awards in Technician/Design Studies.* Entry is according to qualifications and experience.

Centres offering BTEC courses require the approval of the Council. This is forthcoming only where the Council is satisfied with the qualifications and experience of staff, with the availability of specialist equipment (including computer systems), with learning resource support, and with the extent and method of the centres' co-operation and consultation with industry and commerce. Course content, and the operation of classes, require approval from assessors and moderators acting on behalf of the Council.

11

The management of the teaching situation (2)— retention of knowledge and transfer of learning

There are often simple processes underlying the complexities of nature but evolution has usually overlaid them with baroque modifications and additions. To see through to the underlying simplicity, which in most instances evolved rather early, is often extremely difficult (Crick 1979).

Two further aspects of the teacher/manager's role are discussed in this chapter: first, his responsibility for so organising learning that it is retained by the learner for as long as possible; second, his responsibility for the provision of instruction which results in the acquisition by the learner of principles which can be transferred from one type of problem to another, and from the classroom to the world outside. The subject-matter of this chapter is *memory* (remembering and forgetting) and the *transfer of learning*.

Retention of knowledge: the problem

'I revised the work with them only last week and today they can't answer a single question about it!' Statements of this nature must have been made in most college staffrooms at one time or another. They express the bewilderment of the teacher confronted by a class unable to recall the content of a recent lesson. For the student, too, there is dismay in discovering that, although he can recall effortlessly the words and tune of a song heard (and never consciously 'learned') five years ago, he cannot recall lesson material 'committed to memory' five days ago. It is a responsibility of the teacher/manager to arrange instruction so that knowledge is retained by the learner for as long as possible.

Three important questions arise:

1. What is the basis of 'memory'?
2. Why do we forget?
3. How can the process of instruction be structured so as to aid retention and recall?

The memory

By 'memory' we refer to those processes essential for most intelligent behaviour, including learning, by which a person is able to recall past experiences to his present consciousness. Smith speaks of it as 'an organised and integrative process combining both perceptual and motor activities.' Gerard states: 'Memory involves the making of an impression by an experience, the retention of some record of this impression and the re-entry of this record into consciousness (or behaviour) as recall and recognition' (Gerard 1953).

There can be no learning without remembering; but learning and remembering are not equivalents, they are different aspects of the same phenomenon. To 'remember' is to retain the effects of experience over a time; to 'learn' is to retain information over a period of time. Hence, memory is implicit in all types of learning. 'There could be no learning if there were no memory, for the effects of experience could not carry over from one time to the next' (Donahoe and Wessells 1980). In order to demonstrate that a student has *learned,* it is necessary to show that he has *remembered,* i.e. that, given the passage of time and the effects of interference (see p. 131), he is able, nevertheless, to retain and retrieve information learned on a previous occasion.

The comments above concerning the phenomenon we speak of as 'remembering' should serve to remind teachers that memory is not a 'central storehouse' located at some fixed points in the brain. Rather is it to be thought of as a series of functions of the central nervous system, involving the registration and storing of an individual's experiences and the later recall of what has been stored. The views of early physiologists, such as Gall (1758–1828) and Flourens (1794–1867), suggesting that mental powers, such as memory, were localised in separate, identifiable regions of the brain, have been discredited by the recent work of Lashley and Penfield. Luria, the Russian neuropsychologist, argues that no psychological ability exists in isolation and that man's mental processes in general and his conscious activity in particular require the participation of *all* the appropriate functional units of the brain. A commonly-held view of many contemporary brain research workers is summarised by Stein and Rosen: 'In contrast to the view of functional localisation, we are proposing that the brain be viewed as a dynamic organisation of differentiated, but highly interrelated, structures . . . Input into any one area of the central nervous system can affect activity in all areas of the brain' (Stein and Rosen 1974).

In recent years a number of 'models of memory', i.e. representations of systems believed to account for the phenomena involved in remembering, have been constructed. A number of these models reflect the 'information processing' approach, which views memory as involving three processes—registration, retention, and retrieval of information.

(a) *Registration* comprises the perception, encoding, and neural representation of stimuli at the time of a learning experience. Perception involves the set of events following stimulation that occur in the brain's input part. Encoding involves the selectivity of registration: perceived stimuli are transformed into an organised, conceptual 'meaningful' mode. Encoding processes may emerge as diagrams, images, etc. The teacher should note that a student's motivation, attention, previously-acquired knowledge, will affect the selection of stimuli for registration.

(b) *Retention* allows the neurological representation of the student's experiences to be 'stored' over a period of time for later use. (Hence, to 'forget' may be considered as failure to retain that which has been registered.)

(c) *Retrieval* allows the student to have access to information previously registered and retained.

The Waugh–Norman model suggests that items first enter one's primary memory (PM), which has a very limited capacity. Rehearsal (i.e. 'going over' something in one's memory repeatedly) maintains the items in the PM and assists in transferring them to the more permanent secondary memory (SM). When new material is introduced to the PM, old material is displaced. An item in the PM is in the student's consciousness; an item recalled from the SM has been absent from his consciousness (Waugh and Norman 1965).

The Atkinson–Shiffrin model involves three components: a sensory memory (SM), a short-term store (STS), and a long-term store (LTS).

The information in one's SM lasts only a fraction of a second; such information is made up, according to Houston, of 'very basic, unelaborated impressions of the external environment which decay rapidly unless processed into one of the other stores'. Some of the information in the SM is transferred, as the result of the process of attention, to the STS. Information may be lost from the STS in a few seconds by a process of displacement or lack of rehearsal; it is transferred to LTS as the result of rehearsal. Information in the LTS may remain there permanently, although it is subject to interference and a process of decay (Atkinson and Shiffrin 1968). A simplified diagram, illustrating this model, is given in Figure 11.1.

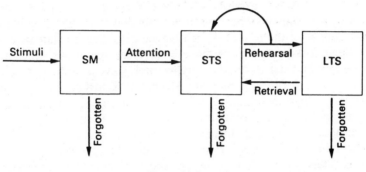

Figure 11.1

Broadbent's model comprises three stores: SM, STS and LTS *and,* between STS and LTS, an 'address register' which holds information about the items, although it does not hold the items themselves. Such information assists the student to retrieve matter from LTS by reminding him of what action is to be undertaken in the process of search (Broadbent 1958).

The concept of memory as involving the processing of information in the form of a progression through *distinct* memory stores has been criticised as failing to stress the dynamic nature of memory. It is suggested, as an alternative, that *levels of processing* be emphasised, so that there need be no clear 'terminal points' separating one store from another; memory codes should be characterised according to the degree of processing that created them. Thus, the durability of the memory trace will increase as the depth of processing increases. To retrieve deeply-processed information may require more processing capacity than that needed to retrieve shallow-processed information.

Remembering and storing information

William James commented that 'to remember' is to think about something previously experienced which we were not thinking about immediately before. To remember is to recall the consciousness. It may involve the recall of specific information (in response for example to the question: 'Who invented the Linotype machine?'); it may be the recall of experience, known as 'recognition' ('I know this melody and remember hearing Rubinstein play it! It's by Chopin!'); it may consist of the process which Gagné calls 'the reinstatement of intellectual skills', involving those intellectual operations which are necessary in order to operate a typewriter, solve a problem in geometry, or perform on a musical instrument. 'Reinstatement' may be illustrated thus: a learner faced with a problem necessitating the calculation of the length of a hypotenuse must, first, 'recall' verbal information, such as the meaning of 'triangle', 'hypotenuse'. Next, he must 'reinstate' the appropriate rules of procedure, including Pythagoras' theorem, needed to answer the problem. (The process of *remembering* has the effect of creating a relationship between past, present and future: we remember how to act so as to set a lathe in motion—knowledge acquired and stored in the *past* is recalled in the *present* so that *future* action is facilitated.) Gagné enumerates *three functions of remembering: temporary holding,* i.e. keeping something in one's mind in order to complete an action; *mediational use,* i.e. facilitating the learning of skills, for example, by the recall of verbal information; *lifetime retention,* i.e. the creation of a store of intellectual skills which can always be reinstated.

How do we 'store' information? What is the precise nature of the neurophysiological changes that occur when information is stored? Early concepts, which appeared long before the investigation of the nervous system, suggested that the human mind was a *tabula rasa* ('scraped tablet') devoid of innate ideas, upon which were imprinted concepts resulting from the senses' reactions to the external world. Aristotle and Thomas Aquinas referred to this theory, which was developed further in the writings of John Locke (1632–1704).

'Let us ... suppose the mind to be, as we say, white paper, void of all characters, without any ideas; how comes it to be furnished? Whence comes it by that vast store, which the busy and boundless fancy of man has painted on it with an almost endless variety? ... To this I answer, in one word, from experience. ... The pictures drawn in our minds are laid in fading colours; and if not sometimes refreshed, vanish and disappear. ... Impressions fade and vanish out of the understanding, leaving no more footsteps or remaining characters of themselves than do shadows flying over fields of corn ...'

This fanciful view is no longer acceptable but it continues to find an echo in the practice of those teachers who appear to act as though students' minds were 'white paper' merely awaiting the process of imprinting! Complex information is neither received nor retained as the result of a mere statement and its repetition. If that were so, remembering would cease to be a problem in the classroom. It is useful to remember here Trusted's comment that our minds are not like pieces of blank paper, ready to be written on. 'Our minds actively sort and classify sensations, they can be compared to searchlights, directed to and illuminating those parts of the world which they find particularly interesting' (Trusted 1979).

Among the many contemporary theories concerning the memory the following are of much interest:

(a) Hebb suggests that an input of information stimulates neural activity in the receptor and effector cells as a result of which there is 'reverberatory activity' in the brain thus producing a neural trace (or 'engram') which lasts for a short time—the so-called 'short-term memory' (Hebb 1949). A prolonged or repeated period of reverberation results in the modification of brain structure which facilitates the creation of connections between assemblies of cells, perhaps in the form of synaptic growths, known as 'structural traces', forming the 'long-term memory'. ('Synapses' are the functional connections between nerve cells, allowing the transmission of nervous impulses from one cell to the next.)

(b) Milner argues that during the learning process neuronic activity facilitates the release of the chemical transmitter substances which make connections between neurons. These connections may become relatively permanent as the result of modifications of the neurons, thus creating 'memory'. (His views are supported by Kandel who wrote, in 1979, of the short-term memory as residing in the persistence of a depression in 'the calcium current' in the pre-synaptic terminals (Milner 1961).)

(c)   Recent developments in cellular neurochemistry, following from the discovery of RNA and DNA, have been interpreted as suggesting that RNA may be a 'memory molecule' (i.e. the molecule which acts as some kind of 'chemical mediator' for the memory), the character of which alters with changes in learning. There is some evidence which may point to the conclusion that the concentration of RNA in the neurons tends to increase when they are stimulated during the process of learning. Further experiments have suggested, however, that the information-carrying molecule is perhaps a soluble protein rather than RDA. Many research workers now hold the view that when learning occurs, chemicals are synthesised and act so as to direct neural impulses along the circuits of the brain. The continuing research into the biochemical basis of memory promises to be of great importance for an understanding of teaching and learning.

(d)   Seligman suggests that memory is related directly to an organism's *preparedness,* so that ease of learning and remembering depends on the *meaningfulness* and *usefulness* of the learning in relation to the learner's life-style (Seligman 1970).

The complex nature of these and similar theories and the relegation of the *tabula rasa* to the museum of the history of ideas must suggest to the teacher that an explanation of students' failure to recall in terms of 'not trying hard enough' is often somewhat facile!

Why we forget

Inability to recall or recognise may range in intensity from the momentary 'slip of memory' (so that one refers to one's friend, George, as John and quickly corrects the error) to the functional disturbances of the memory such as amnesia, as a result of which the sufferer cannot recall his immediate personal history. A variety of reasons for the phenomenon of forgetting has been advanced: repression, i.e. motivated forgetting (a defence mechanism which seems to allow us to set aside and render inaccessible very unpleasant memories); disuse of information (leading, presumably, to the disappearance of the associated memory traces); trace decay; interference.

Trace decay is inferred from the phenomenon which is illustrated in Figure 11.2, i.e. the well-known 'curve of forgetting', representing a decline in the amount remembered over a period of time (if the material learned is not 'practised').

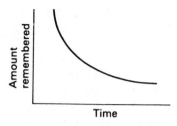

Figure 11.2

(It should be noted that the relationship is not represented as a straight line. The amount which the learner tends to forget does *not* vary in direct proportion to the passing of time—there is a gradual levelling out of the curve after an initial steep decline.) It has been suggested that traces in the learner's perceptual system tend to fade rapidly immediately after presentation. Thus, according to Thorndike (see Chapter 2), if actions fall into disuse and are not practised, they weaken and disappear from the memory. Guthrie (see Chapter 2) argued that forgetting occurs as the result of competition among responses. Many psychologists now believe that the passing of time does not in itself explain forgetting; the passing of time permits *interference* from new learning and other memories, which produces forgetting. The nature of the learner's activities between learning and attempted recall is also significant in strengthening or diminishing the capacity to remember. The relevance of this to the place of emphasis, recapitulation and revision in the planning of a lesson should be clear.

Interference refers to the inhibition of one 'piece of learning' by another. Where the learner forgets something because of something else he learns *afterwards,* the effect is known as *retroactive inhibition.* Where he forgets something because of something else he has learned *before,* the effect is known as *proactive inhibition.* Experimental groups are used to study interference in the following ways:

| Experimental group | Learn A | Learn B | Recall A |
| Control group | Learn A | Rest | Recall A |

(Here the measure of retroactive inhibition is the difference in recall.)

| Experimental group | Learn B | Learn A | Recall A |
| Control group | Rest | Learn A | Recall A |

(Here the measure of proactive inhibition is the difference in recall.)

The more similar the subject matter learned (as tasks A and B), the greater is the possibility of interference, resulting in forgetting. The importance of this finding for the management of the teaching process needs to be stressed: timetables should be arranged so as to separate as widely as is practicable subjects with a similar content, e.g. foreign languages. Further, since interference seems very powerful over short periods of time, the importance in verbal communication of leaving a short gap after a significant statement is based not on any rule of rhetoric but on the need to allow some fact to 'sink in' so that its chances of being retained by the learner are increased.

Osgood comments:

> A memory is nothing more than a response produced by a stimulus. It is merely the maintained association of a response with a stimulus over an interval of time. The question of why we forget comes down to this: what are the conditions under which stimuli lose their capacity to evoke previously associated responses? Forgetting is a direct function of the degree to which substitute responses are associated with the original stimuli during the retention interval (Osgood 1953).

There is also evidence that *trying to learn too much* may result in forgetting, since the short-term memory may have a capacity of not more than 7 ± 2 separate 'chunks'. (Miller has argued that the short-term memory is limited by its ability to handle only a limited number of 'chunks' of information. Note, however, that the amount of information contained in a 'chunk' may vary (Miller 1956).) This, too, has significance for the planning of instruction, in particular for the *timing* and *spacing* of lesson content. Failure of recall may be the result of the teacher's understandable wish to impart as much information 'as time will allow' without his taking into account the possible over-burdening of the students' short-term memory. 'Mental indigestion' may be an imprecise metaphor; it draws attention, however, to the difficulties for the student who is required to assimilate a large mass of material.

The teacher's role in aiding retention and recall

The practical experience of teachers, underpinned by some of the theory discussed earlier in this chapter, indicates that the learner can be aided in tasks of memorisation, consolidation and recall if lesson preparation takes into account certain matters. These are considered under six headings: timetabling, content, presentation, revision, practice and transfer of learning.

The *timetabling* of a course ought to take into consideration the difficulties which might arise for the learner as the result of proactive and retroactive inhibition. As mentioned previously, timetabling should 'space out' similar subjects, should allow for breaks, and should not overload the student with long, unvaried lesson periods so charged with material that acquisition and retention become impossible. (Teachers should note and consider the implications of the discovery by the Gestalt psychologist, Zeigarnik, that interrupting a task in which a learner has become involved, can lead to a higher level of recall of the material being learned.)

The *content* of the lesson ought to be presented not as an isolated unit but, essentially, as a continuation of that which has been learned previously. It ought to be *associated* clearly with the learner's existing stock of knowledge. 'The more other facts a fact is associated with in the mind the better possession of it our memory retains. Each of its associates becomes a hook to which it hangs, a means to fish it up by when sunk beneath the surface' (James 1890). (James believed that the secret of a good memory was the forming of 'diverse and multiple associations with every fact we care to retain ... All improvement in memory consists in the improvement of one's habitual methods of recording facts.') Perhaps above all, the content of the lesson must be *meaningful* to the learner if it is to lead to firm retention and swift recall. Meaningful material is usually remembered more clearly and for longer periods of time than that which has little or no relation to the student's level of learning at the time of the lesson. The statement couched in simple terms introducing new concepts in terms of those which are already known has a higher chance of acquisition than that which goes outside the student's conceptual framework, thus making comprehension and retention very difficult. 'If the material is sufficiently meaningful, there may be no forgetting whatever. Content that is not so brilliantly structured, but that still has much meaning, will be remembered in proportion to its meaning. Nonsense material is headed for extinction before the last syllable is uttered' (Stephens and Evans 1973).

Presentation of the lesson, if it is to aid retention, demands a logical, clearly-connected sequence. Where the parts of the lesson are organised coherently comprehension, acquisition and retention of the whole ought to be facilitated since patterns are usually more acceptable to the learner than disjointed fragments. (A 'warm-up period', particularly before *re-learning,* is usually beneficial to the student's recall processes.) The student should be stimulated by the presentation so that his attention remains focused on the lesson material, thus assisting assimilation and retention. Wherever possible, the presentation ought to avoid an outcome which is no more than rote-learning. (Ausubel describes rotely-learned materials as 'discrete and relatively isolated entities that are relatable to cognitive structure only in an arbitrary, verbatim fashion'.) The presenter should aim, rather, at the achievement of insight (see Chapter 4) and the understanding of principles which will facilitate retention. Principles are generally retained much more effectively than a mass of material which has been committed to memory without understanding. Note, also, the so-called *von Restorff effect,* which suggests that the teacher can assist memorisation by making ideas 'stand out', e.g. by exaggeration, under-lining, use of bold print and colour in writing.

Assimilation, consolidation and retention of lesson content require *recapitulation, rehearsal, periodic revision* and *review* (i.e. 'practice with an experimental cast'). The teacher's recapitulation at regular intervals of the lesson headings may help in their assimilation. Rehearsal—by which is meant an activity in which the student goes over the lesson material by himself after its initial presentation (which may be equivalent to a repetition of the lesson's stimuli)—can take the form of reading a handout which contains a summary of the lesson's main points, or studying and reciting one's own notes. Revision—which involves re-studying the lesson—should take place as soon as possible after the lesson has ended. (Note the work of Garcia, which throws doubt on the tenet that learning can take place *only* when stimulus and associable events are close in time (Garcia 1966).) It should be repeated at intervals and, preferably, be linked with tests which examine recall. (There is evidence to suggest that the 'distribu-tion of practice' does affect speed of learning *and* efficiency of recall. The spacing of recall tests is, therefore, of much importance in lesson planning.) The final revision ought to be planned by the class teacher and could be the occasion for a full examination which will test and assess the level of comprehension and recall.

The assimilation of material presented in class may be assisted by the process of its being applied in *practice situations.* In particular, where psychomotor skills are being taught (see Chapter 16), practice ought to walk hand in hand with theory rather than follow on its heels. The theory of the use of the navigational compass is best assimilated by the learner who is able to participate in planned projects involving the practical use of the instrument.

The concept of *circadian rhythms* should be considered by the teacher planning a programme of instruction. It is suggested that there is a daily pattern of physiological change in our bodies which affects our information-processing capacities. Short-term retention, it is argued, is better in the morning; long-term retention seems to be better when the student is learning material in the afternoon. Wing-field argues that biological rhythms have a large effect on

performance and memory—up to 10–20 per cent of a total performance score.

An aspect of behaviour from which effective retention, recall and
application may be inferred is known technically as *'transfer of learning'*. This is considered next in some detail.

Transfer of learning: its essence

In the first chapter 'education' was considered as a social process built
in large measure on the formal activities of teaching and learning.
Learning in the colleges of further education, as in other educational
institutions, may have meaning and value only if it is related to the personal development of the student as a member of society. An
important justification of the teacher's role in providing the conditions
for effective learning must be, ultimately, the value of that learning to
the student in the world outside the classroom. Training in the ability
to transfer knowledge, to generalise from learned basic principles, is,
therefore, an essential factor in the education of the student.

An important task of the teacher/manager is the planning of
instruction so that a high degree of positive transfer shall result wherever appropriate. The phenomenon of transfer may be described thus:

> Where the learning of something (A_1) facilitates the learning or per-
> formance of A_2, there is *positive transfer* from A_1 to A_2. Where the
> learning of A_1 makes the learning or performance of A_2 more difficult,
> there is *negative transfer* from A_1 to A_2. Where the learning of A_1 has no
> apparent effect on the learning or performance of A_2, there is *zero
> transfer* from A_1 to A_2.

Examples of *positive transfer* are seen in facility in the basic arithmetical processes applied successfully to the use of logarithm tables,
ability to ride a bicycle utilised in balancing on a motor cycle in
motion, dexterity in the fingering of a recorder applied to the playing
of scales on the orchestral flute. Subordinate capabilities have been
mastered (an essential factor in transfer situations) and applied successfully to more advanced and demanding tasks. An example of
negative transfer is evident in the confusion of a student trained
mechanically in the drills of denary arithmetical processes and confronted, without preparation, by an arithmetic in which $1+1=10$. A
further example is seen in the case of the young mathematician
steeped in the tradition of Euclid, which he has acquired in mechanical fashion, who meets the non-Euclidean geometry of Lobachevsky
and Riemann. *Zero transfer* exists where A_1 and A_2 have very little or
no relationship as, for example, history and shorthand.

Examples of *lateral transfer* are seen in the use of mathematics in the solution of problems in physics, the use of principles of geography in the interpretation of problems in military strategy, and the use of the scientific method in the solution of a question in applied economics. *Vertical transfer* is exemplified by the progress of the learner from the elements of arithmetic to the use of the calculus, from the knowledge of parsing to the study of semantics, from mastery of the tonic sol-fa to the writing of counterpoint.

Much early speculation on the basis of transfer centred on the 'faculty theory' advanced by those psychologists who held that there existed in the mind *separate faculties* such as learning, memory, etc. A learner's mind could be trained as a whole, it was suggested, by submitting him to a formal discipline which would 'strengthen his faculties', a process akin to the physical training of the athlete. 'Training of the mind' was often the declared objective of the traditional 'classical education', consisting largely of mathematics, Greek and Latin grammar and literature. An education of this type was held to develop the memory and the ability to think clearly—and to prepare the learner for his station in life. ('Bowling is good for the stone . . . gentle walking for the stomach, riding for the head and the like; so, if a man's wits be wandering, let him study the mathematics': Francis Bacon in *Essay on Studies* (1597). Sir Leslie Stephen's biography of his brother, Sir James Fitzjames Stephen (1829–94), the legal historian and judge, includes a statement made by their Eton tutor concerning an exercise in 'longs and shorts' (classical versification): '"Stephen Major", he once said to my brother, "if you do not take more pains, how can you ever expect to write good longs and shorts? If you do not write good longs and shorts, how can you ever be a man of taste? If you are not a man of taste, how can you ever hope to be of use in the world?"')

The concept of 'transfer of formal discipline' was discredited by the experiments of William James and Thorndike. James undertook to measure the time he spent in learning 158 lines of a poem by Hugo before spending one month memorising Milton's *Paradise Lost*. He then memorised a further 158 lines of Hugo's poem but found that it took him longer than on the previous occasion. Memory did not seem to be an independent faculty capable of being trained in this way. Thorndike showed by experiment that practice in verbal learning did not by itself improve general learning ability.

A later interpretation of transfer of learning was based on the theory of 'identical elements' associated, in particular, with Thorndike and Woodworth. Transfer occurred, they claimed, if tasks A_1 and A_2 had common elements. The amount of transfer would be a function of the number of those elements. More recent investigation suggests that the amount of transfer might be a function of the level of similarity in the situations leading to the learning events associated with A_1 and A_2.

Transfer of learning in the classroom

Transfer of learning rarely occurs spontaneously in the classroom; almost always it is the result of a teaching strategy aimed specifically at transfer. Such a strategy will generally involve direct methods of teaching and will include the practice of skills and the application of principles in *realistic situations*. Where the instructional objective is concerned with lateral or vertical transfer, the mastery of subordinate tasks is an essential prerequisite for success. Revision and recapitulation so as to ensure this mastery must have a place, therefore, in a transfer strategy. In particular, the identical elements of the transfer situations must be analysed and presented to students in detail.

Several key studies in transfer have offered the conclusion that successful transfer may depend on the ability of the learner to *generalise* by obtaining insight into the basic principles underlying his work. (The findings of the Gestalt psychologists (see Chapter 4) are of particular relevance to these studies.) Discovery by the learner of common patterns of content or technique has been said to facilitate the application of principles to novel situations. The necessity for instructional objectives to be concerned with discovery and understanding if transfer is to be achieved, implies the need for careful consideration to be given to those modes of instruction which tend to encourage the comprehension of principles. Practice in a large and varied number of stimulus situations may be essential if generalisation and transfer of knowledge are to result.

Harlow's work on transfer suggests a further principle of direct importance for the classroom. Whenever the positive transfer of learning takes place, then, according to Harlow, the student is 'learning to learn' and acquiring 'learning sets' which facilitate his performance in the situations he encounters. To teach the student *how* best to learn is to help in ensuring a fair degree of success in his task of generalisation of learned principles (Harlow 1949).

In this chapter we have considered the responsibility of the teacher/ manager for arrangement of the teaching process so that retention, recall and transfer of learning are achieved. We examine next his responsibility for the discipline necessary in class control.

12

The management of the teaching situation (3)—class discipline and student counselling

A man, viewed as a behaving system, is quite simple. The apparent complexity of his behaviour over time is largely a reflection of the complexity of the environment in which he finds himself (Simon 1969).

The aspect of the teacher/manager's role, which is considered in this chapter, concerns his responsibility for the formulation, creation and maintenance of the standards of interpersonal behaviour (involving teacher and class) which are appropriate for the reaching of objectives. The subject-matter of this chapter is *discipline in the teaching situation,* and *student counselling,* the process of helping students to learn how to solve some of their interpersonal and other problems.

The nature of discipline

Practical instruction in the handling of disciplinary problems in the classroom ought to be a part of the work of all institutions involved in the training of teachers. Too often, however, requests for advice and assistance concerning problems of class discipline (a matter of concern to many young teachers) are ignored or turned aside by the use of

138

semantic quibbles seeking to equate 'control' with 'authoritarianism', and by dogmatic pronouncements suggesting, unhelpfully and incorrectly, that 'misbehaviour in the classroom invariably reflects inadequate teaching'. The view taken in this chapter implies that discipline is not a 'thing in itself', that it reflects a number of classroom features, and that its maintenance involves a consideration of problems which *can* be solved.

The word 'discipline' is derived from *discipulus* (pupil) and *discipere* (to comprehend). Dewey warns against its confusion with 'drill'. 'Drill is conceived after the mechanical analogy of driving, by unremitting blows, a foreign substance into a resistant material; or imaged after the analogy of the mechanical routine by which raw recruits are trained to a soldierly bearing and habits that are naturally wholly foreign to their possessors.' The term is used in a variety of ways, so that one may refer to the discipline of an army, the discipline of orchestral playing, the discipline of the scholar and self-discipline (Milton's 'government of the self'). Use of the term generally implies a consciously-accepted code of conduct directed to the attainment of some desired objective. In the context of further education, it usually refers to *group conduct held to be desirable in the teaching situation.*

Discipline as a 'universally cultural phenomenon' is considered as serving a number of specific functions in the growth process of young people: it assists in their learning those standards of conduct acceptable within society; it helps them to acquire characteristics of a positive nature, such as self-control and persistence; it assists in securing stability of the social order within which the young may achieve security and maturity.

It is important not to confuse 'discipline' with 'order'. Order may indeed be 'heaven's first law'; it is not always a reliable indicator of the presence of discipline. The informality and bustle of students in a motor vehicle workshop, with its apparent lack of order but based nevertheless on a disciplined approach to the task in hand, may be contrasted with the feigned attention of a group of students apparently in a well-ordered class but, in reality, withdrawn from the teacher–student relationship which characterises discipline in its fundamental sense. The shadow must not be confused with the substance. The trappings of a superficial discipline—silent students, instant obedience to a command—have little connection with the core of the disciplined instructional process based on a voluntary partnership of teacher and class. Order, in the sense of *attention*—and without attention class teaching cannot begin—is a necessary condition for true discipline seen as a means to an end, but no more than that.

The breakdown of discipline

A variety of reasons for the breakdown of class discipline can be enumerated. Their common factor is a tendency to produce circumstances in which class management proves ineffective, so that learning for the class as a whole becomes difficult or impossible. In one way or another, lack of motivation (see Chapter 6) may be discerned at the root of the problem. Where a student has no real desire to participate in the process of instruction, he will rarely 'enter the class' in the sense of involving himself in the lesson. He may 'withdraw', expressing his action by active opposition to the teacher's demands. He does not contribute to joint teacher–class effort and his example may elicit a like response from other students. Some of the more important reasons for the breakdown of discipline are as follows:

1. *Compulsory attendance.* Some students are in attendance at college through no desire of their own. They may work in an industry in which training board or other grants are conditional on their attendance at college or they may be 'sent to college' by an enlightened employer, but against their will. This can result not only in those passive attitudes indicative of lack of motivation but in active resentment of and hostility to the college, its staff, standards and work. (This is not to suggest that the 'compulsory student' is invariably a source of discontent, for this is, demonstrably, not the case. It is to emphasise, however, the disciplinary difficulties which can stem from compulsory participation in an undesired activity.)

2. *The college seen as an 'extension of employment'.* Many young employees dislike their daily work so that any activity thought to be associated with it (such as a class held to improve skills) is also disliked. In such cases participation in college work, with its accompanying demands, may be resented and resisted.

3. *The college seen as a symbol of failure.* Attendance at a college course may reflect, for some students, their inability to obtain full-time employment. Resentment directed generally at society's failure to provide work is channelled towards the college and its classes.

4. *Frustration.* The organisation, structure, demands and external trappings of the colleges of further education may serve to fan the spark of frustration latent in some students. Frustration may emerge because they find themselves, in effect, 'back at school'

in an atmosphere which may be heavy with unpleasant memories. For some the course content may be a mere repetition of work done at school, with a consequent blow to their pride; for others the course may necessitate work at an inappropriate level and may be linked with standards and long-term goals far beyond their comprehension and ability. Some may not see the course as having any significance for their personal development; others may see it as forcing them into a pattern which has no relevance to their preferred life style. For some the course will appear unrelated to everyday work; for others the lack of a career structure in their employment can reduce to naught the significance of their efforts in college. Frustration is a fertile breeding ground for unco-operative and aggressive attitudes in education, as elsewhere.

5. *Distracting personal problems.* A student's anxiety induced by health or financial problems can result in his resenting and rejecting the demands of a course of study. (Counselling may help in a case of this nature.)

6. *Lack of confidence in the teacher.* Students' confidence has to be earned. It will vanish where, under the critical gaze of a class, a teacher is revealed as a sham. A teacher's lack of interest in a subject or poor lesson preparation, or obvious discontinuity in a programme of instruction, do not remain hidden for long. Their emergence often coincides with a weakening of confidence in the teacher which results in a weakening of class discipiline.

7. *Resentment of the teacher as catalyst.* Often, but fortunately not always, the teacher whose probing questions challenge accepted life styles may be viewed by some students as a disturber of their 'mental peace'. Far from his questions and attitudes arousing an enthusiastic response in his class, they may be resented and may lead directly to a withdrawal of co-operation. (Some psychologists discern in this situation a reaction to 'cognitive dissonance', i.e. the mental conflict said to arise when ingrained assumptions or beliefs are challenged or contradicted by new information. The resulting tensions can be relieved by defensive tactics including the deliberate avoidance or rejection of the new information so that stability is restored.)

8. *Less tolerance by the young of authority in general.* For better or worse, authority, its representatives and its symbols no longer automatically command respect. Where a college is viewed as part of a power structure linked to 'authority' resentment may build up. Co-operation with a teacher may be interpreted as 'selling out' or 'going over to the establishment'; withdrawal of

that co-operation may be equated with the assertion of 'independence'.

9. *Breakdown of communication.* Where communication breaks down, control becomes impossible. An analysis of poor discipline may often reveal a communication channel so affected by 'noise' (see Chapter 6) that teacher and class are rarely in meaningful contact. Badly-structured lesson material, inappropriate modes of instruction or failure to monitor the results of class teaching can destroy communication and, with it, class control.

10. *Immaturity and hostility.* Deliberate attempts to interfere with the conduct of a lesson often made by an immature 'odd man out', who may be aware of his inadequacies, who is hostile to teacher and class alike and who is adrift in an environment which he does not understand and therefore fears, can result in the breakdown of class control. A firm and controlled response by the teacher aimed at effectively isolating the disrupter is necessary.

An approach to the problem

The teacher in further education has almost none of the school-type sanctions with which to challenge an offender. Formal 'punishments' have no place in college life. A solution to the problems caused by a breach of discipline lies in the processes of assessment and control. Assessment demands a critical appraisal of the situation; control requires action in accordance with that appraisal. *It is essential for the teacher to try to see the circumstances surrounding breach of discipline through the eyes of the offender.* (Situations in the classroom are, for teacher and students, based on individual perceptions.) Why should a talented student prefer the role of clown to that of scholar? Why should a student of promise suddenly adopt a hostile unco-operative posture? No answer will generally be found unless an attempt is made to look at the class situation *as the student might view it.* (Personal discussions with the student, or counselling (see below), may assist in discovering the roots of non-co-operation.)

Lack of discipline arising from frustration ought to be dealt with where possible at source. The student's suitability for the particular course should be re-assessed and a detailed explanation of the objectives of the course and its relation to his career development ought to be given to him. Contact with the student's employer or training officer may be valuable on occasions such as these.

Where college rules, designed to help in the maintenance of discipline, are published they should be *unambiguous and capable of enforcement.* An important breach ought to result in prompt action. Rules which cannot be enforced, so that a blind eye has to be turned to their being broken (e.g. 'unpunctuality will lead to immediate exclusion from classes'), ought to be withdrawn.

It is extremely important, in relation to the maintenance of class discipline, that the teacher should seek to understand his class as a group with *its own* internal, informal organisation. A class is more than the mere sum of its individual students; it is a dynamic group with its own 'leaders', its internal tensions, conflicts and crises, which must be acknowledged and understood by the teacher. Mason Haire reminds us of the conflicts between personality and organisation: 'Whenever we join a group we give up some individual freedom and therefore the calculus of the balance between the individual and the group is a problem . . . As the organisation grows, the force that seems likely to destroy it is the centrifugal force arising from the fact that the members are individuals and tend to fly off on tangents towards their own goals' (Haire 1975). The teacher who is able to view his class in organisational terms and accept the inevitability of tension and occasional conflict (a task which becomes easier as comprehension of class structure becomes deeper) will find that the solution of class management problems is assisted thereby.

Hints on the maintenance of class discipline

There are no 'golden rules' for the maintenance of discipline in class; each problem requires a separate analysis and set of responses as it occurs. The following hints should be found useful, always provided that they are interpreted not in a mechanical way, but in accordance with the exigencies of specific classroom situations.

1. Ensure, as far as possible, that the classroom conditions appropriate to your lesson requirements have been prepared. Seating arrangements *are* important: thus, to seat students where they are unable to see or hear important parts of the lesson is to create an atmosphere in which order can break down quickly. Set the stage properly before the curtain rises!
2. Prepare your lesson thoroughly. Pitch it at an appropriate level,

making sure that it does not depress class morale by demanding impossible standards. Ensure, similarly, that students do not feel degraded by being asked to participate in activities which obviously require minimum standards only. Students who believe that their time is being wasted—no matter what the pretext—are unlikely to approach their tasks in disciplined fashion.

3. Where the objective of a task is not immediately obvious, be prepared to explain its significance. Discipline rarely flourishes where students are asked to engage in activities for incomprehensible ends.

4. Know your class. The tutor who has taken the trouble to learn the names of his students and to study their occupational backgrounds and academic attainments is demonstrating an interest in those for whose instruction he is responsible. Class–tutor co-operation can be intensified in this way, with a corresponding, positive effect on problems of behaviour in class.

5. Adopt an appropriate, professional style in the classroom, and keep to it. Students are rarely impressed, and often embarrassed, by a tutor who seeks to 'identify with' them by affecting an exaggerated bonhomie which, he believes, will bridge the tutor–student gap or eradicate teacher–learner distinctions. Similarly, an austere, autocratic style may have little appeal. The general rule is—as in most matters relating to class control—moderation. To be either too friendly or too remote is, almost always, to forfeit respect, with marked effects on class discipline. To 'be oneself' is probably the best guide.

6. Watch very carefully for signs of trouble. Just as a successful navigator learns to recognise and react to storm signals, so the tutor must learn to watch for those events which can presage loss of class control. The conversations which continue after the tutor has complained of their interference with the lesson, the 'clenched silence' which follows a request for co-operation, the continued failure to complete assignments, a record of unexplained absence or unpunctuality—these are signals which the tutor ignores at his peril. They demand swift assessment and action.

7. Keep up a reasonable pace of class activity. Periods of inactivity can produce the boredom which spills over easily into indiscipline.

8. Do not confuse the trivial and the important. Over-reaction to a minor breach of a rule can be counter-productive. Learn to assess swiftly the real significance of events in class. Studiously ignoring what is, in effect, a challenge to one's authority may be

perceived by students as an admission of defeat; reacting intemperately to an unimportant attempt at provocation may be perceived as evidence of unreasonableness. Neither type of response from the tutor is calculated to maintain that respect for him which is essential for class discipline.

9. Be seen as fair-minded and impartial. Favouritism of any kind, conscious or unconscious, bias and prejudice, will be interpreted by a class as an indication that fair treatment cannot always be expected. Students have a sense of justice which, when outraged, often leads to a withdrawal of co-operation.

10. When you have to issue orders, do so firmly and unambiguously. 'Be sparing of commands. Command only when other means are inexplicable or have failed ... But whenever you *do* command, command with decision and consistency' (Spencer).

11. If you feel that you have to punish, ensure that the situation really demands it and that the consequences seem worthwhile. The decision to punish (say, in the form of a severe reprimand, a warning, loss of a privilege) is in no sense a confession of failure! On the contrary, it may be a perfectly appropriate response to behaviour which critically threatens the maintenance of class control. Jones and Page, in a succinct account of the use and abuse of punishment, stress the importance of punishment being of a consistent nature, and neither random nor haphazard. They call attention also to another crucial matter: the alternative, desirable, behaviour ought to be understood by the person who is being punished and should be reinforced immediately on its occurrence.

12. Consider without hesitation the sanction of exclusion from class where the continued presence of an offender threatens the maintenance of class control. Exclusion ought to be followed by discussions with the student, and, where appropriate, his union representative and employer.

13. Follow up all important disciplinary matters. Analyse what initiated and precipitated the breakdown of discipline. Do not confuse symptom and underlying cause. Learn and apply whatever lessons you have learned from your solution of disciplinary problems.

Formal discipline can rarely be imposed on further education classes. Its existence often testifies to class motivation, the tutor's skill in instruction and his interest in the progress of his students. Its absence usually reflects a breakdown in the patterns of communication and control, the maintenance of which must be an objective of the teacher/manager. Discipline can be positive and constructive; hence it is a worthwhile objective in the classroom. Ausubel sees it in wider terms: '[Discipline] is necessary for the internalisation of moral standards and obligations—in other words, for the development of conscience' (Ausubel 1978).

Student counselling in further education: essence and objectives

The refusal by some students to accept the norms of class conduct, the deliberate obstruction of the teaching process and the failure to come to terms with the demands of the further education environment are viewed by some tutors as manifestations of psychological problems which might disappear as the result of active guidance provided by student counsellors. Shertzer and Stone define student counselling as *'an interaction process that facilitates meaningful understanding of self and environment and results in the establishment and/or clarification of goals and values for future behaviour'* (Schertzer and Stone 1980). Lewis views it as 'a process by which a troubled person is helped to feel and behave in a more personally satisfying manner through interaction with an uninvolved person' (Lewis 1976).

The objectives of counselling include, according to Hamblin, the encouragement of the growth of self-acceptance in the student, the development of internal controls within him, and his acquiring realistic, appropriate strategies of coping with his environment. The goal is the modification of behaviour reflecting insight and changed value patterns. That goal is achieved when the student understands his emotions and redirects them into new channels of behaviour among which is acceptance of the conditions necessary for effective learning (Hamblin 1980).

Counselling is much more than a mere series of unstructured inter-views in which advice is tendered to non-conforming students. The counsellor's overall strategy will determine the structure of his task, which may be considered in the light of various objectives. He must attempt, first, to discover the motives of the student's general behaviour and this, in turn, necessitates the establishing of effective communication between counsellor and student, together with the creation of an appropriate level of confidence and trust. Secondly, he has to understand the student's perception of the college environment. Next, as the result of careful questioning, he has to uncover the reasons for the precise behaviour which has created problems in class. A diagnosis should then follow, as a result of which the student should be brought to the point of voluntary acceptance of all those steps necessary to assist him.

Problems in student counselling

The major problems inherent in the counselling process derive from its very nature. It demands skills of a high order—an ability to establish a confidential relationship with students of all types, a knowledge of the techniques of eliciting and analysing information, an understanding of the prevalent, so-called, 'youth culture' and acquaintance with a variety of social environments. Its success involves patience and persistence. Above all, perhaps, it requires more than a superficial acquaintance with the principles of psychotherapy. This formidable list of desirable qualities in the student counsellor is a pointer to, and a warning against, the morass in which the well-intentioned, but ill-equipped, amateur may find himself!

Further problems may arise from the possible clash of goals and beliefs in the interviewing process which is inseparable from counselling. How is the strong-minded counsellor, possessed of a morality founded on deeply-held ethical principles, to react when faced with the 'values' of nihilism? How does the professional teacher respond to the expressions of an 'anti-culture' which denies the validity of that in which he believes? In short, how does the counsellor achieve the 'understanding neutrality' said to be required in the counselling process?

Some further education tutors who have practised as counsellors have reported their feelings of inadequacy when the complex reality of problems of classroom deviance is uncovered. Family backgrounds, financial difficulties, health concerns and emotional entanglements may have woven a web from which the student cannot be extricated, save by a long-term process of adjustment, requiring assistance which is totally beyond the counsellor's power and resources. Frustration on both sides is deepened when the counsellor's diagnosis reveals a situation from which escape seems quite impossible.

The problem of confidentiality often emerges at an early stage in student counselling. Where the interviews produce criticism of a counsellor's teaching colleagues, is it to be conveyed to them? Where an interview reveals activities of a criminal nature, are the police to be informed? What is the legal situation of a counsellor who, aware of such activities, fails to inform the authorities? Is it possible to create the conditions necessary for a successful counselling interview if the student is aware that the principle of confidentiality may be breached?

Class teachers as counsellors?

Given the desirability of student counselling, who is to act as counsellor? The student's tutor? An outside expert? The continuing controversy on this question has been reviewed by Ard. On the one side are those who maintain that *all* counsellors must be classroom teachers: they best understand the problems of behaviour in the classroom; they have experience of aberrant behaviour; they can meet their students as partners in the search for an answer to behavioural problems. On the other side are those such as Ard, who states categorically that 'the nature of the relationship to the student-client must necessarily be different from that of the teacher to the pupil'. Students, it is claimed, feel 'safer' in discussing their problems with someone who does not represent 'authority', and who seems to be neutral in matters concerning the college. Because counsellors need to be well-grounded in psychology and its applications, it is not possible for the practising teacher to move easily—even should he possess the appropriate expertise—from one role to another. Ard concludes: 'While *some* teachers might become good counsellors, *all* counsellors *need not* be classroom teachers, nor *need not necessarily have ever been* classroom teachers.'

A fusion of discipline and counselling

Williamson, in a study of what he perceives as the dichotomy between discipline ('. . . repressive, regulatory, imposed . . .') and counselling (' . . . growth-producing, self-regulating, self-initiating . . .') suggests that discipline, as such, introduces an unwanted and discordant note into an educational process intended to stimulate the growth of individuality. Discipline on its own, he says, is repressive and growth-arresting; it can be no corrective of misbehaviour in the classroom unless it emerges as the consequence of a counselling relationship. Counselling is 'our present chief prospect for changing discipline from punishment to rehabilitation . . . and for aiding the individual to achieve that degree of self-control and restraint so necessary in all members of an interdependent democratic society' (Williamson 1975).

The most important matter in affairs concerning discipline and student counselling appears to be the need to *perceive situations and problems as they are perceived by the students*. This is not a simple matter, but it has to be attempted. Erich Maria Remarque reminds us of the problem: 'There is a law of the years ... Youth does not want to be understood; it wants to be let alone ... The grown-up who would approach it too importunately is as ridiculous in its eyes as if he had put on children's clothes. We may feel with youth, but youth does not feel with us. That is its salvation' (Remarque 1931).

13

The management of the teaching situation (4)— teaching students how to study

> By not stressing learning strategies, educators, in essence, discourage students from developing and exploring new strategies, and, in so doing, limit students' awareness of their cognitive capabilities (O'Neil 1978).

It is taken for granted all too often that college students understand the techniques of effective study, that they understand 'strategies for success'. This is rarely the case: in fact, there are very few students in our colleges who would not benefit from methodical instruction in those techniques and strategies. Superstitions prevalent among students include the belief that repeated readings of a text will, in themselves, ensure learning, that long hours spent in study are not subject to the law of diminishing returns, and that forgetting is always the result of a 'poor memory'. Effective teaching involves enlightenment in these matters. Eight areas are outlined below in which instruction in techniques of study might be particularly useful: the planning of one's study time; use of the textbook; making lecture notes; project work; use of the library; retention and retrieval of learned information ('remembering'); revision; examination technique.

Instruction in study techniques

Included in the college student population will be a large proportion whose schooling will have been based solely on the formal class lesson, supplemented by homework. For this group, in particular, the pattern of much college instruction, including private study periods, attendance at lectures and producing one's own notes, presents difficulties. Explanation and demonstration of study skills becomes a task for the teacher.

Demonstrations of appropriate skills—how to take notes at a lecture, for example—ought to be given in the early days of a college course. A lecture on 'note taking' is rarely effective unless accompanied or followed swiftly by a period of supervised practice in which students test their skills by producing notes (say, of a pre-recorded lecture) which can be analysed by the tutor and compared against a standard set. The 'gutting' of a textbook so that its overall themes might be discovered requires several sessions of practice and analysis. In sum, the teaching of study skills must provide opportunities for the *practice* of those skills. Explanation, demonstration, practice and analysis of results constitute a useful framework for the attainment of skills mastery (see Chapter 16).

Planning one's time

Tutors have the task of convincing students that time is always 'of the essence'. The duration of a course and dates of examinations are fixed and students should be encouraged to draw up timetables based on a reasonable allocation of available time. Such a plan *must* allow time for revision and consolidation; these phases of study must not be viewed as 'optional extras'. Specimen study plans, illustrating impossible schemes, should be contrasted with schemes within the capabilities of most students.

In the case of part-time students, or those who can attend evening classes only irregularly, the tutor can assist in the learning process by suggesting realistic study plans based on a careful allocation of time. The importance of overall reviews, revision and consolidation must be stressed, and assistance may be needed in dealing with the competing claims on time of a full-time job and other responsibilities.

Using one's textbook

'Some books are to be tasted; others swallowed; and some few to be chewed and digested' (Bacon). Assistance to students in selecting texts can be valuable. Where texts are set by an examining body no advice on choice is needed, save to suggest supplementary or secondary texts. Where choice is a personal matter, the tutor can *demonstrate* the valuable technique of 'skimming' a text before making a choice. The student should be taught, by example, how to 'taste' a book swiftly—by obtaining an overview from the preface, by selecting a topic from the index and noting the author's method of dealing with it and, finally, by reading one or two sample chapters (always including the first).

The detailed methods of 'active reading' of a textbook should be explained and demonstrated in each case by the use of a class text. The '3R' method—read, recite, record—is worthy of consideration, but the tutor has to explain the precise purpose of each phase, in particular that devoted to reciting. Robinson's 'SQ3R' method—survey, question, read, recite, review—needs careful demonstration, particularly of the phase demanding readers' ability to 'turn headings into questions' (Robinson 1970). Pauk's well-tried 'OK5R' method—overview, key ideas, read, record, recite, review, reflect—is a valuable method of active reading for students pursuing a full-time course (Pauk 1974). Students with little time for reading should be introduced to the '3 readings' method—first (swift) reading to obtain an overview, second (detailed) reading, third (swift) reading for purposes of revision.

The marking of one's textbook, so as to assist in memorisation, should be demonstrated. Students should be encouraged to read sections or paragraphs fully before underlining, and should be shown how to use symbols in consistent fashion and in a selective manner and, above all, to mark matter requiring further study or explanation. Making one's notes from a textbook should be demonstrated; this requires from the tutor an explanation of the reasons for using one's own words rather than those used in the textbook.

Making lecture notes

Initially, the tutor may have to explain that the lecture provides a means of learning and that it is not merely an exercise in listening. The essence of notes, as opposed to complete transcriptions, should be discussed. ('The student who tries to take literal, detailed notes, can do so only by allocating capacity to this activity . . . little capacity remains for the deep processing of the information' (Wingfield 1981).)

The 'Cornell system' is worthy of consideration. It is a methodical approach based on three phases. In the first phase, before the lecture, previous lecture notes are reviewed by the student. He then prepares his note-taking material, including a margin, to be known as a 'recall column', to be separated from the 'main column' for his notes. In the second phase, which is based on the actual lecture, the student records in his main column the general ideas presented by the lecturer. Abbreviations, sketches, diagrams are used. The third phase, which follows the lecture, involves reading through the notes, underlining important points and using the recall column to note key phrases, definitions, etc., that will bring to mind the material in the main column. Recital of the lecture's main points should follow, to be prompted by reference, first to the recall column, and, secondly, to the main column.

Students should be informed of other techniques, such as Buzan's intriguing and helpful method of making 'linking' notes (Buzan 1974). A tutor's demonstration of Buzan's methods applied to a lecture is likely to be of real assistance to students. The tutor should also warn against making 'fair copies' of notes, transcribing from shorthand notes—activities of this type constitute a waste of valuable time, since none contributes in any way to the retention or recall of information presented at the lecture.

Project work

A large number of college courses demand project work from students, individually or as members of a group. The educational purpose of the project ought to be explained to students. Assistance in choosing, planning, researching and presenting the final material is often needed by students. Where projects are based on field work or laboratory findings, help may be needed by students anxious to present their material to the best advantage.

Where a project demands the use of a questionnaire, or interviews involving members of the public, tutors can assist by offering advice on the strategy of questioning, with particular reference to formulating and presenting questions and analysing results. The techniques of data analysis, of generalising and extrapolating, are rarely known to students.

Assistance in enabling students to recognise and assess what they have learned from the process of producing project material can play an important role in 'rounding off' the activity. It should be emphasised to students that presentation of the 'project folder' is not the end of the process. Tutors should demonstrate how the various activities involved in project work (obtaining, arranging and interpreting data, for example) can provide lessons of lasting significance for students.

Use of the library

The library as a 'learning centre' features all too rarely in students'
learning strategies. Concepts of the library as providing services
which facilitate study and learning should be developed at an early
stage of students' courses. The use of reference books, the study of a
variety of texts (and not merely the 'set book') before embarking upon
a written assignment, may have to be demonstrated to students if they
are to be accepted as part of learning strategy. Mere abstract statements urging students to 'use the encyclopaedia' may count for little; a
demonstration of the utility of this activity will be more to the point.

A talk and demonstration by the college library staff concerning the
range of resources should be arranged in the first days of a course. Use
of the Dewey system and the catalogue should be demonstrated and
the expertise of the library staff in recommending texts and other
sources of information should be made known. Where libraries are
used as resource centres, offering audio and video cassettes, a demonstration of these aids should be arranged for all students.

Hints concerning remembering

The concept of 'training' one's memory becomes easier for students to
accept when the fundamentals of remembering and forgetting have
been explained. A short, non-technical introduction to the structure
of the memory (see Chapter 11), concentrating on the movement of
information to the long-term from the short-term memory should be
presented to students in ways which enable them to realise the significance of *activity* in remembering.

The following suggestions might be presented to students as well-
tested hints concerning remembering. Recital, review and practice in
retrieval contribute to long-term remembering. What has been
learned should be used in the unravelling of problems; objective tests
are valuable in this process. Seek for associations within the subject
area and link the new with the old. 'The more other facts a fact is associated with in the mind, the better possession of it our memory retains'
(William James). Search for pattern and structure and do not learn
everything by rote: rote-learning has its place in study, but to *understand* what one has learned is a valuable aid in long-term

remembering. Finally, be keen to learn; in the jargon of the psychologists, 'create and maintain a positive mental set'.

Frequently, however, students encounter memorising difficulties. They should be encouraged to identify the nature of their problems and to experiment with different learning techniques (see Belbin, E. et al. 1984).

Pre-examination revision

The idea of the pre-examination revision as a 'dress rehearsal' should be explained to students, together with its implications. The revision period should be seen as wide-ranging and based on the students' own notes. Principles, illustrations and definitions should be checked. Recital of learned material, by writing out selected headings or by working out answers to problems will be a useful component of a revision period.

Advice should be given to students concerning the problems of a 'last-minute cram'. The superstition relating to the advisability of working to the very last minute dies hard among students. Nevertheless, tutors ought to comment on this practice, attempting to explain the dangers of arriving for one's examination in a state of mental indigestion!

Examination technique

There are numerous cases in which the quality of students' examination answers would have been improved significantly by the acceptance of advice on the technique of answering questions. Students must be taught to peruse questions carefully so as to discover their 'essence'. Practice in dealing with the various types of question—factual, discussion, problem—under the supervision of a tutor is very useful.

The importance of planning one's answers cannot be over-emphasised. The techniques of planning answers should be demonstrated in relation to the effective utilisation of examination time. The significance of allowing adequate time for the revision and correction of one's answers has to be explained. Finally, advice on the writing of answers in essay form is rarely wasted. The construction of the essay and its underlying structure ought not to be omitted from any discussion of examination technique at further-education level.

14

The management of the teaching situation (5)— teaching the older student

> In general, nobody under forty-five should restrain himself from trying to learn anything because of a belief or fear that he is too old to be able to learn it. Nor should he use that fear as an excuse for not learning anything which he ought to learn. If he fails in learning it, inability due directly to age will very rarely, if ever, be the reason. Adult education suffers no mystical handicap because of the age of the student (Thorndike 1928).

Teaching the older student often presents a variety of unique problems. The thirty-year old engineering supervisor attending a college-based management course requires an instructional environment which will differ from that considered appropriate for the seventeen-year old 'A' level student; the professional workers in the forty–fifty age group, who may form the majority of enrolments for an evening course on political affairs, present problems and opportunities for their tutor which differ from those related to his day-class students, whose average age is eighteen. In this chapter we comment on some important matters concerning the older student—the significance of perceptual theory, instructional strategies and the management of the learning process.

The 'older student'

The age at which a student is classified as belonging to the 'older' age group seems to be purely arbitrary. Terms such as 'young person' and 'adult' have a variety of meanings when used in the literature of educational administration. The phrase 'adult education' appears generally to mean education pursued by persons over the age of eighteen which is not primarily intended for training or career qualifications; the

Russell Committee on Adult Education seems to have had in mind classes 'for personal and social purposes' rather than 'for work-related purposes'.

The average age of students in colleges of further education seems to be under twenty-one, but the number of students aged twenty-one plus has been increasing steadily, a trend assisted by enrolments of overseas students and the growth in extra-mural classes, catering largely for older groups. It is no longer possible to speak correctly of further education exclusively in terms of the sixteen–eighteen age group. For purposes of this chapter the 'older student' is considered as a person beyond the mid-twenties age bracket; typically, he or she will be, or will have been, in full-time employment.

Perceptual theory and the older student

Perceptual theory, as adumbrated by Combs and Snygg, for example, (Combs and Snygg 1959) seems to have much relevance for the teacher of older students. The theory is built on the concept of our perceptions as the only reality we can know, and the main purpose of our activities as control of the state of our perceived world. Thus, Powers describes human behaviour as 'the control of perception' (Powers 1974). Hence, how a person views his environment—the people, things and happenings with whom and with which he is involved—will affect his behaviour in large measure. The older person's perception of his world must differ, generally, from that of the younger person; in particular, the adult's past experiences which are represented by the totality of his past and present perceptions, will be of a different quality from those of the younger person.

The determinants of the older person's perceptions include his values, beliefs, attitudes, needs and self-experiences. His feelings concerning his preferred 'way of life' and what he considers to be of lasting value, will affect his perception of the wider environment. In the same way, his view of 'reality' will be coloured by his beliefs in the worth of others and of himself. Kidd suggests that, for the adult, there may be two limits to educational growth—'the real practical limit of one's maximum ability or potential capacity and the no less real psychological limit which each man places on himself' (Kidd 1975).

Perceptions of threat from the outside world are considered by Verduin as having particular relevance for an understanding of the educational problems of older students. 'Threat is the perception of an imposed force requiring a change in behaviour, values, or beliefs.

One of the greatest threats to people is the requirement to change behaviour when beliefs, values, or needs remain unchanged.' Verduin states that the older student feels threatened when forced to alter the modes in which he attempts to maintain his self-organisation (Verduin 1978).

In the light of this theory, the teacher of the older student ought to consider, first, removal of any perceptions of threat from the teaching environment. Feelings of safety and security should not be attacked and destroyed; a mere perception of external threat to well-being will put older students on the defensive. The conservatism which often characterises the 'world-image' of the older person is peculiarly susceptible to perceived dangers stemming from suggestions of the need for fundamental change. The teacher should attempt to *modify the interpretation* of past experiences; those experiences remain the same, but the *way* in which students interpret them can be changed. Clarification of the environment, of needs, attitudes, values, and their interrelationships, is an important task for the teacher. He has to assist the older students to perceive *their* goals and their significance. They will learn 'in response to their own needs and perceptions, not those of their teachers'.

Problems of learning for the older student

The process of ageing—held by some to commence around the age of nineteen to twenty—brings problems and opportunities for the student. In the case of the older student, his experiences have multiplied, have been interpreted and re-interpreted and his perceptions of the world may have changed radically. His rate of learning—but not his efficiency of learning—may have slowed down. His intensity of motivation—but not necessarily the requisite skills and abilities—may have heightened. In sum, the older student brings to the process of learning a variety of abilities and previously-acquired skills, together with some handicaps, none of which is of an insuperable nature.

The older student will probably have experienced some deterioration in physical agility, in the acuity of his senses, in certain abilities, and in his short-term memory. Where learning tasks involve speed, the older student may be at a disadvantage: time may have acquired a particular significance for him, so that he will be more concerned with accuracy and precision and will tend to work more slowly. Problems in retrieving stored information, arising largely because of lack of rehearsal, may make tasks of memorisation increasingly difficult. (It often becomes necessary for the tutor to convince the older student by demonstration that one's long-term memory does not undergo inevitable and irreversible decline as one grows older.) His patterns of co-ordination, rhythm and fluidity, acquired during the process of skills training, may have deteriorated. His creativity and flexibility of mind, associated with discovering solutions to problems, may have apparently diminished.

The older student's awareness of a decline in some of his abilities and associated skills is often mirrored in a lack of confidence and a growth in anxieties. As his level of achievement moves to a plateau which can presage swift decline, the older learner, conscious of his self-image, becomes much more cautious, and is easily disheartened by temporary failures. He tends to resist change, is initially suspicious of novelty and does not always welcome innovation. He may be highly critical of his teachers, who are often perceived as lacking the 'practical experience' which is considered as the root of all worthwhile knowledge.

On the other hand, the older student is frequently a highly—and diversely—motivated learner. Often he will be attending a course of study simply because he wishes to do so, and because he perceives his own advancement as dependent on the acquisition of further knowledge or because he is particularly interested in the subject-matter of that course, with no thought of career advancement. He has long-range goals which may have become internalised, allowing him to perceive the college course in terms of a direct contribution to the attainment of those goals.

Experience of the outside world may result in the older student having acquired a capacity to make decisions accurately and under conditions of stress. When carried over into classroom conditions, this quality of thought can be advantageous in the processes of learning. A heightened capacity for analytical thought has been noted by many tutors of older students, who have guided them through courses involving the exercise of powers of discrimination and investigation. Further, experience may be 'the best of teachers', so that older students who have undergone and assimilated the lessons of events in the wider world outside the classroom, have acquired a 'mental set' of much value in the analysis of apparently complex situations. The contrast between a discussion on, say, trade unionism, involving, on the one hand, young 'A' level students and, on the other, industrial workers, will illustrate well the significance of experience, which comes only with age, in an understanding of social and industrial problems.

Instructional strategies

The essence of a relevant strategy for teaching the older student is the provision of a 'positive supportive-learning' climate. Verduin's investigation of appropriate strategies culminates in his advocating the techniques of 'explanation' and 'demonstration'. (It should not be assumed, however, that Verduin is advocating these techniques exclusively in relation to the teaching of the 'older' student. Explanation and demonstration are important components of instruction at *all* levels in further education. Verduin draws attention to their peculiar significance for adult learning.)

Explanation, as the central component of instruction for the older student, is described by Verduin as 'description, interpretation, analysis, direction giving, and clarification in an informal and conversational manner' (Verduin 1978). The technique has certain advantages for the older student. First, it emphasises and reinforces what he has been taught previously; additionally, it provides a review of what he has read. Secondly, it summarises and synthesises information presented to him; explanation acts, in this sense, to underline the significance of acquired information. Next, it clarifies particular points which might not have been clear to the student initially. It repeats, stresses and reinforces matter presented in outline (generally necessary in a short course). Finally, explanation assists the learner in adapting what he has learned to new situations and to other content areas.

Demonstration is described by Verduin as 'showing adults how something works and the procedures to be followed in using it'. It assists in supplementing lesson content, translates pure description into actual practice and stimulates a number of senses, with the resulting intensification of learning. The demonstration acts as a focus for attention on correct procedures and applications and assists those older students who may experience problems in reading and comprehending directions. Time, materials and equipment may be utilised economically. Finally, the demonstration constitutes a safe approach to the teaching of hazardous and expensive operations.

The management of instruction for the older learner

The 'supportive-learning' climate mentioned earlier requires careful preparation. Nothing destroys a lesson for adult students more decisively than an inappropriate environment. Wherever possible the tutor should take pains to ensure that the class environment is appropriate. The re-arrangement of furniture is, therefore, important. A 'warm-up' period before the commencement of the formal part of instruction has been found very useful for older students. During this period the tutor who knows his class (a particularly important aspect of the tutor–class relationship which plays a vital role in effective tuition at this level) can introduce the lesson in personal, informal terms and explain its significance. The objectives of the lesson should always be made clear so that students know their goals.

Sensitivity to the problems of the older student should characterise the tutor's approach. Abstraction ought to be minimised, distraction avoided and participation encouraged. Where instructional activities can be task-oriented, individual problem-solving should be encouraged. Group work has been found valuable for the older student: some educational psychologists have suggested that, as a member of the group, the older student is able to retain deeply-held beliefs until he is ready for a change. Direct criticism ought to be avoided. Achievement should be recognised; indeed, lessons should be so planned that the learner is able to see his achievement and evaluate its significance.

For the older student, no less than for all other types of learner, the tutor's style can play a decisive role in the acquisition of knowledge. In the case of the older student, however, reaction to the approach and personality of the tutor is unusually important. The teacher who is able to 'teach without seeming to do so' has a very good chance of winning the confidence of the older student, who, in most cases, would prefer to reach his destination unaided. Perhaps the words of Lao-Tze, addressed to those rulers who wish to win the hearts of their people and assist them to attain goals, are appropriate:

> A truly great ruler is one who . . . when he has accomplished his task . . .
> would hear his people say, 'We've done it ourselves' (Lao-Tze).

Continuing education for adults: BTEC policy

BTEC policy provides for the development, approval and validation of a range of vocational education courses for adults which meet the needs of business, industry and the individual, which will build on existing knowledge, skills and experience, which will be 'sufficiently flexible to respond to the changing demands of business and industry and the need for continued training throughout working life', and will develop students' potential. Conscious that adult learners may be deterred from studying because of constraints, such as difficulty in obtaining time off work, fixed times of course attendance, and limited availability of courses locally, BTEC encourages the design of courses 'using any suitable attendance pattern or form of open or distance learning'. It perceives as its target group those adults who wish to increase their effectiveness in their present jobs by undertaking further study, who wish to change direction or enhance promotion prospects or move to new posts, who intend to top-up qualifications, acquire further management or technical skills, adapt to new technologies, update expertise, equip themselves for re-employment or pursue their interests and further their own development.

Two main types of provision of courses for adults have been planned: 'post-experience units' and courses designed for the adult who may or may not have formal educational experience; and, 'post-qualification units' and courses designed to build upon students' initial education. The basic formats are 'single units'—'a single self-contained unit consisting of at least 60 hours of instructional guidance or tutorial leadership'—and a 'course'—'a complete course of study designed as a coherent whole of normally at least 240 hours'. Validation of units and courses by BTEC involves an assurance that: content has been designed to meet the identified needs of the specified audience; approach is appropriate to content and target audience; level of knowledge, skills and understanding is relevant; objectives are attainable in the prescribed time; tutorial centres have access to required resources; proposed assessment is appropriate to aims, content and target population.

Training programmes for adults: MSC policy

The Manpower Services Commission (MSC), which was founded in 1974, and consists of representatives of employers, unions and local authority and education interests, has emerged as 'the main agency through which the Government institutes action and monitors progress in training' (White Paper, 1984—*Training for Jobs*). The influence of MSC activity on work-related, non-advanced further education provided by local authorities in the colleges of further education has grown considerably. In the immediate future, courses offered to adults, which are of a technical and vocational nature, at qualification levels below those associated with degrees and higher diplomas and certificates, will be evaluated by the MSC in the context of a strategy aimed at securing a supply of workers with up-to-date skills needed to meet the demands of a changing economy. In effect, the MSC will assume and discharge the functions of a national training authority which will interest itself in the design and execution of training programmes for adults.

MSC strategy will involve the attainment of a number of long- and short-term objectives. Standards of performance are to be defined and a system of certification for vocational education is to be fashioned. (The result ought to be seen in the appearance of an element of standardisation within the large variety of college-based adult training courses.) Specialised courses for the long-term unemployed are to be designed. (It may be that such courses, particularly where they are based on retraining, will recognise the need for the acquisition of general skill patterns.) Collaboration locally between employers and colleges is to be encouraged so as to identify and meet the needs of local commerce and industry. A partnership of this nature could have beneficial effects on many adult education and training programmes. MSC's own training programmes for adults are to be re-structured so as to make 'a cost-effective contribution' to meeting the needs of industry and commerce. Attainment of these objectives is seen as necessitating the MSC taking over a significant part of the control of adult training now administered under the general heading of 'non-advanced further education'.

The recent winding-up of many industrial training boards, some of which had formulated detailed plans reminiscent of MSC objectives concerning adult trainees, should serve as a reminder to college lecturers and administrators that successful campaigns involve much more than the mere promulgation of worthy aims. Ineluctably, the fundamental problems which were so often evaded by the training boards—the relationship of training and education, and the rights (and duties) of young workers in claiming day release—will emerge and demand resolution by the MSC if the aspirations of adult trainees are to be attuned to the long-term demands of an economy in irreversible transition.

15
Modes of instruction (1)— the formal lesson

> In his teaching, the wise man guides his students but does not pull them along; he urges them to go forward and does not suppress them; he opens the way but does not take them to the place ... If his students are encouraged to think for themselves, we may call the man a good teacher (Confucius).

Although staff in colleges of further education are known as 'lecturers', they often use as modes of instruction the lecture *and* the lesson, which is defined for the purpose of this chapter as *a self-contained instructional session, designed and administered by a teacher, with the intention of attaining a learning objective through guided class activities involving a variety of teaching techniques.* The preparation of a formal lesson and its structure are considered below, together with associated matters, such as problems of questioning in class, homework and the evaluation of lesson effectiveness.

Lesson preparation

Preparation of a formal lesson demands a consideration of three major factors: the students, the subject matter, and the resources and constraints. Each factor involves a variety of problems which the teacher could examine in the following way:

1. *The students.* 'What is their academic standard?' 'Have they reached the level of attainment required for an understanding of the proposed lesson material?' ('A continuum exists in most content areas, with certain knowledge of skills prerequisite to achievement of more difficult or more complex knowledge and skills' (Hunter 1971).) 'Does my previous experience with them as

a class suggest any likely problems?' (The answers to these questions will affect the form of the *introduction* to the lesson and may necessitate a re-examination of the proposed *lesson objective.*)
2. *The subject matter.* 'How is it related to the syllabus, or scheme of work, as a whole?' 'Does the proposed behavioural objective demand a particular approach?' 'What specific teaching methods might be appropriate?' 'Will audio-visual aids be of assistance?' (see Chapter 21) 'What ought to be the general headings of the lesson?' 'What type of test should I use so as to assess and evaluate progress?' 'When ought it to be administered?'
3. *The resources and constraints.* 'How much time will be available?' 'How swiftly should I be able to make progress?' 'What time of the day will the lesson take place?' (The first hour following the lunch break may demand a very special treatment!) 'Where will I be teaching—classroom, laboratory, workshop?' 'If special apparatus is required, is it available and in good condition?'

The answers to these questions should be reflected in the teacher's *lesson notes.* The less the teacher's classroom experience, or the more difficult the lesson content, the greater should be the preparation necessary and the more detailed should be his lesson notes. Notes ought to be set out so that they include: the subject heading of the lesson; the lesson objective; the subject matter, broken down into periods of time; methods to be used; audio-visual aids; apparatus; tests. An example is given on p. 168. (Lesson notes may be requested occasionally by departmental heads, visiting inspectors, moderators, etc.)

Lesson structure

Structure reflects and is determined in part by *content.* The framework of a practical lesson on stock control, designed for part-time management-trainee students, may differ in some ways from that of a lesson on the causes of the Second World War, designed for full-time 'A' level students. Structure will also reflect *strategy,* i.e. the *objective* of the lesson, the *time* available, the use to be made of *teaching aids* and the need for *recapitulation* and *revision.*

There are three main structural components of a formal lesson: *introduction, central section* and *conclusion.* The introduction should state the object of the lesson; the central section should present, teach and test the acquisition of the lesson material; the conclusion should

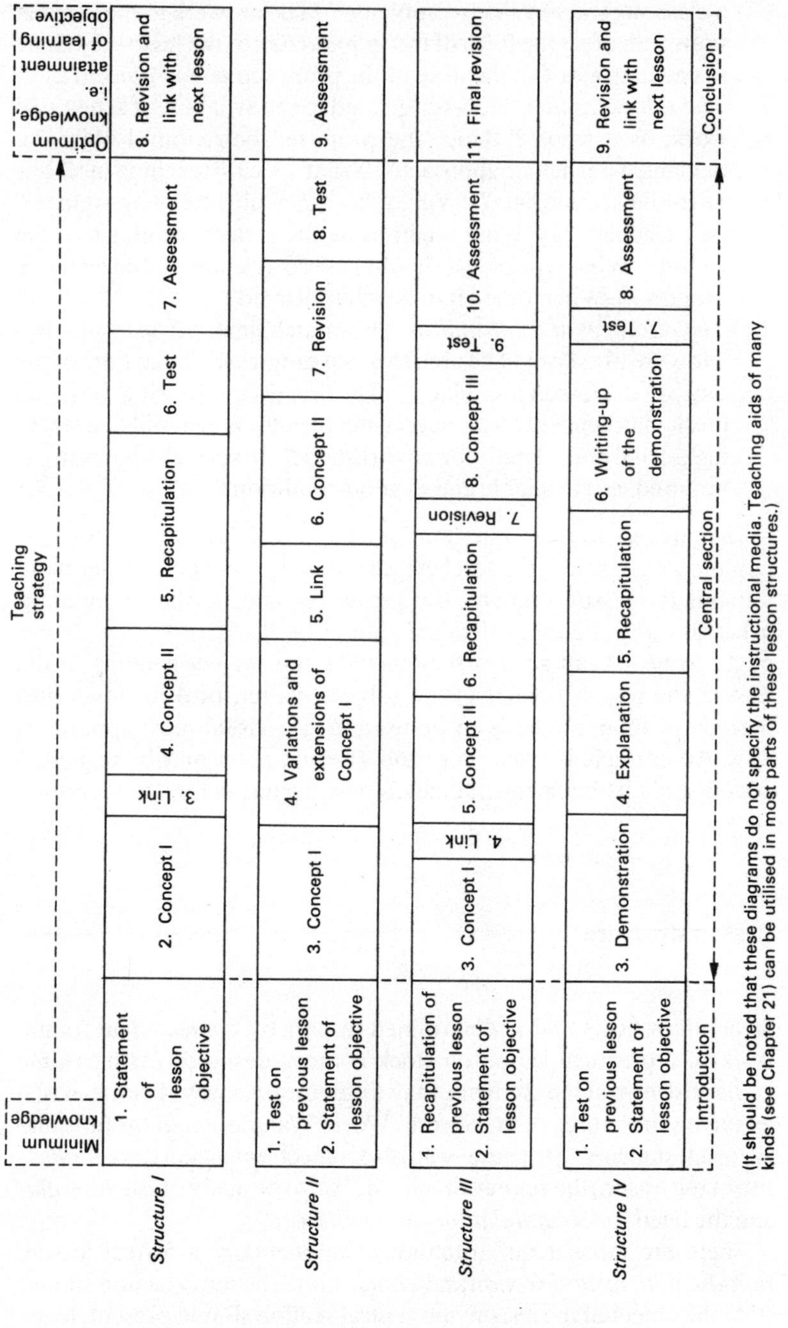

Figure 15.1 *Examples of lesson structures.*

recapitulate and revise. Variations of this basic structure are probably infinite in number. Some familiar examples are illustrated in Figures 15.1 and 16.1. (There is an obvious affinity of the basis of some of these structures with the 'introduction–exposition–development– recapitulation–second theme ... coda' of classical symphonic form in music.)

We now discuss in greater detail the main components of lesson structure.

1. *The introduction.* The arousal of interest and attention is essential in the *first minutes* of the lesson. A test on previous work should serve to focus class attention and to link the lesson with what has preceded it. (Although the lesson is a self-contained unit of instruction, it must be seen as part of a *wider sequence.*) Retention, recall and insight may be tested in these first minutes. The lesson objective should then be stated clearly, so that students are not left without an answer to their unspoken query: 'What are we about to learn?' Long, complicated statements of objective are to be avoided; a short, clear statement is preferable. For example: 'The last time we met we learned that there were three kinds of body surface through which invaders may enter—the skin, the lungs and the alimentary canal. Today we shall learn about the skin and how it guards our body. But, first, a quick test on what we learned last week ...' Another example might be: 'We begin today a new section of our work on the law affecting retailers by examining the *Trade Descriptions Act 1968*. We shall spend four lessons discussing it and today we shall ask and answer the one question, "Why did Parliament think legislation of this type was necessary?"'

2. *The central section.* The main body of the lesson may consist of the presentation of a sequence of concepts linked with previously-acquired knowledge. The sequence ought to be logical and (particularly in further education classes) should be designed, whenever possible, to elicit those responses which will develop insight (see Chapter 4). Statements of concepts, illustration by example, demonstrations, discovery by the class of underlying principles, development of concepts and their practical application, may feature prominently in the central section. Tests and assessments (see Chapter 22)—vital for the process of effective control—should also be included in this part of the lesson structure, not only as a guide for the teacher in assessing his movement to the teaching objective, but in informing students of their progress and maintaining motivation and interest.

3. *The conclusion.* The ending of the lesson ought to be planned as carefully as the introductory and central sections. It should not comprise a few hasty words, spoken when it is obvious that time has run out! A conclusion provides a final opportunity of ensuring consolidation, assimilation and retention and ought to include a revision (perhaps in the form of question and answer), a summary of which can be presented visually. A link with the next lesson in the overall scheme of work can be provided, for example, by the setting of homework which should be seen as a preparation for that lesson, or by the announcement of the next lesson's title.

Bigge outlines a widely-used type of lesson structure adopted by teachers who have been influenced by the theories of Herbart (1776–1841). Such a structure is made from five steps presented in a carefully-planned sequence: *preparation* (the utilisation of past experiences); *presentation* (the provision of new facts related in some way to the past experiences); *comparison and abstraction* (the discovery of similarities and common basic elements); *generalisation*

Date: ....Class: ....Title of course: ....
Subject of lesson: ....
Learning objective: ....
Duration of lesson: 1 hour

Time	Lesson content	Method	Aids
10 mins	Test on previous lesson	Q & A	–
5 mins	Statement and explanation of lesson objective	Exposition	o/h projector
15 mins	Concept I	Exposition; Q & A	chalkboard
15 mins	Concept II	Exposition and discussion	chalkboard
5 mins	Recapitulation	Dictation of short note	o/h projector
9 mins	Test and assessment	Q & A	–
1 min	Announcement of title of next lesson	Exposition	chalkboard

Figure 15.2

(the attempt by students to derive a principle from their abstraction); *application* (the utilisation by students of the newly-learned principle in the solving of a problem).

The best-laid plans, however, can go astray and it may be necessary to modify or even to scrap the planned structure while the lesson is actually taking place. A failure of demonstration apparatus, an unexpected difficulty in controlling assimilation of a concept, or a class test which reveals a lack of comprehension of important points exemplify some of the circumstances in which a plan may have to be altered or put aside. On occasions such as these, there is no value in 'pressing on regardless' or in going through the mere motions of completing the planned lesson. An alternative structure based perhaps on revision of a previous lesson or on the relearning of a partially-assimilated concept, ought to be readily available; it is not always easy to extemporise in a situation of this nature.

An example of outline lesson notes (which reveal lesson structure) is given in Figure 15.2.

Lesson teaching: some notes on method

The teacher's aim in a lesson must be to motivate, stimulate and communicate, to hold the attention and to achieve a defined objective through class control. The following points are of importance:

1. *The lesson must be pitched correctly.* The level of the class and its record of attainment must be the starting point for the teacher's preparation. This point cannot be overstressed. Information can *only* be incorporated in an existing scheme of thought. Ausubel is emphatic:

   > If I had to reduce all of educational psychology to just one principle, I would say this—the most important single factor influencing learning is what the learner already knows. Ascertain this and teach him accordingly (Ausubel 1978).

   In the absence of a correct appraisal (which can be made from a swift test), the probability of the lesson's success is low.
2. *The teaching objective must be realistic and clear.* This involves careful forecast and design (see Chapter 10). In the absence of an objective, the lesson can become a disjointed, pointless event. The objective must be explained to the class and its attainment ought to be accepted as a joint teacher–class aim.
3. *Exposition must be ordered, simple and clear.* Order and simplicity

of presentation are vital if the learner is to achieve mastery of a subject. This must be reflected in the teacher's exposition of his lesson material. New concepts must be linked with previously-learned material and must be shown to derive from it. New terms must be explained; it must never be assumed that they are automatically understood by the class ('. . . there's no need for me to define this, because I'm sure everyone knows what it means!'). It follows that the teacher's vocabulary must be intelligible to the class. In the absence of clear exposition effective communication is difficult to achieve.

4. *Development must be logical and consequential.* Students usually find that continuity in the development of concepts assists in assimilation and retention. Unbridged gaps, unexplained 'jumps' in exposition, make learning difficult.

5. *Presentation must be based on the essential 'social character' of the lesson.* The essence of a lesson is joint teacher–class activity, so that a 'lesson' made up of a teacher's exposition alone is a contradiction in terms. A lesson is not a solo performance; it will include periods (often alternating) in which either the teacher's stimulus activities predominate or the students' responses are paramount. Discussions, controlled sequences of questions and answers (see p. 172 below), are therefore necessary.

6. *Presentation ought to involve a variety of media.* The spoken word and the chalkboard are not the sole communication media! The many audio-visual aids (some of which are noted in Chapter 21) can be utilised so as to constitute an 'assault on the dulled senses' which can bring a lesson to life.

7. *Presentation must be related carefully to fluctuations in class attention.* Figure 15.3 generalises the well-known phenomenon of variations in the rate of class attention during a lesson sequence.

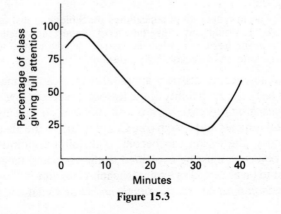

Figure 15.3

The decline of initial interest, the interference and 'noise' produced by fatigue and diminished motivation, should be recognised by the teacher in the planning and delivery of his lesson. Varied presentation, carefully-timed pauses, recapitulation and a variety of class activities may help to offset the tendency to diminishing attention. The use of the teacher's voice, often providing the central communication source in a lesson, is of great importance. Emphasis on key words, variations in pitch and tone so as to prevent monotonous delivery, and clarity at all times, aid the holding of class attention.

8. *The familiar 'sequence procedures' should be considered.* The following procedures are of relevance to lesson presentation:

   (a) *Proceed from the known to the unknown.* Students often learn by association, so that the learning of new concepts may be facilitated by their being deliberately linked with what is already known by the class. The day-release student's first-hand knowledge of his motor bicycle can be used as the basis of an introduction to theoretical lessons on the internal combustion engine; an awareness of press reports of current economic events, such as rising prices, can provide an effective lead-in to a course on the theory of price determination.

   (b) *Proceed from the simple to the complex.* A gradual shift in the level of the lesson, so that the class moves from basic principles to more advanced learning, usually necessitates an ordered sequence in the presentation of concepts, e.g. as in a lesson on design, which is based on the preliminary observation of simple, geometric patterns and which moves towards aesthetic considerations and value judgements.

   (c) *Proceed from the concrete to the abstract.* Experiments in elementary physics and chemistry are often designed and presented with this procedure in mind.

   (d) *Proceed from the particular to the general.* A lesson based on the interpretation of a specific event so that its wider significance shall emerge illustrates this principle, e.g. an examination of a country's decision to devalue its currency, from which some generalisations concerning economic policy may be deduced.

   (e) *Proceed from observation to reasoning.* This is a very important principle which draws attention to the development of the powers of reasoning and the gaining of insight as desirable lesson outcomes. To learn to reason from the 'how' to the 'why' ought to be an objective of much of the work in the colleges of further education. ('Men do not think they know a thing until they have grasped the 'why' of it, which is to grasp its primary cause' (Aristotle).)

(f) *Proceed from the whole to the parts, then return to the whole.*
     This principle is the basis of the lesson sequence which presents its subject matter initially as an entity, then proceeds to an analysis of component parts, finally returning to an overall view.

The technique of oral questioning

Davies suggests that the planned use of questions is the mark distinguishing a lesson from other modes of instruction. Oral questioning is an integral part of the joint teacher–class activity which characterises many successful lessons. It has a number of purposes. It may be used to discover the level of class knowledge so that the appropriate starting point for the presentation of new material may be determined. It can provide informative feedback, i.e. it can show what progress in teaching/learning has been achieved and what revision is needed (see Chapter 22, in which oral examinations are noted). It can be used also to gain or regain class attention, to fix facts in the memory, to develop a learner's understanding and powers of reasoning and expression, to challenge beliefs and guide consideration of values, and to develop class participation.

Questions ought not to be selected at random and asked in a perfunctory manner; they require careful preparation, timing and delivery, and should be reasonable (i.e. not impossible to answer) and relevant. Direct, precise and unambiguous phrasing which elicits equally direct and precise answers is advantageous. A long, tortuous question is likely to present the class with the added problem of attempting to understand what the questioner has in mind so that the real problem becomes secondary. The 'closed' question which demands in reply a mere 'yes' or 'no' ought not, in general, to be put, but where such a question has been asked, the reply ought to be followed by a further 'open' question, thus:

Q: 'Now that you have read this newspaper article do you consider the introduction of value added tax to have been based on a wise decision?'
A: 'Yes.'
Q: 'Would you give your reasons?'
(A more effective single question would be:
Q: 'Now that you have read this newspaper article, what do you think of the decision which was taken to introduce value added tax?')

Meaningless, rhetorical questions ('Is that clear?'—'Are you following me?'—'OK?') are of little value in class teaching. (Some communications theoreticians cite this type of question as an example of the 'blocking' of a communications channel.) Questions which demand an obvious answer, and trivial or trick questions, are also out of place in a lesson. Where possible, step-by-step questions and answers, each answer giving rise to the next question, should be utilised. (It is worth remembering Steinbeck's comment: 'An answer is invariably the parent of a great family of new questions'.)

An entire lesson consisting of questions, answers and occasional recapitulations is possible, but it would seem to require—if it is to be effective—a very efficient teacher, a very small class and subject matter which lends itself well to highly-analytical treatment. A prototype is to be found in the teaching methods attributed to Socrates and recorded in Plato's *Republic*. Socrates was famed for his skilled use of the dialectical method in teaching; question and answer dominated his mode of instruction. In his celebrated discussion with Thrasymachus, for example, a vast, complex exposition of the meaning of 'justice' emerges from the seminal question: 'You say that what is advantageous to the stronger is just. Now, what do you mean by that, Thrasymachus?' Socrates' 'heuristic method' (in which the student is enabled to discover principles for himself) is based on two phases: in the first (negative) phase, the student's ignorance is exposed by question and answer and his curiosity is aroused; in the second (positive) phase, guidance is given to the student, again through the use of questions and answers, in his search for the correct answer to problems.

Questions should be put one at a time and spread over the whole class, as far as possible, and should not be confined to a small section of 'regulars' who can be relied on to respond. Questions may be put to the class as a whole, or may be addressed to one student by name. A student's answer ought to be repeated by the teacher if it is almost inaudible. Where no answer is elicited from a named student, or from the class as a whole, the correct answer may be given by the teacher, or instructions given as to how or where it can be discovered. Credit for good answers is a useful reinforcement. Poor answers can be valuable, too, in that they provide the opportunity for further discussion and assimilation; they should not elicit from the teacher an over-critical response. Under no circumstances should a poor answer be mocked; this can destroy motivation and often lead to the student's 'withdrawal' from further participation in the lesson.

Questioning *by* the class ought to be encouraged as long as it does not degenerate into time-wasting or irrelevance. Where the class teacher does not know the answer to a question, he ought to admit this and promise that he will seek an answer, which should then be given at the earliest opportunity.

Oral questioning: further problems

Experience in the classroom suggests that the most productive question-and-answer sessions are those placed at 'strategic points' in the lesson process. Bower recommends the following practice: 'Ask questions during the course of instruction about each point that is important for students to master, rather than depend upon a general, indirect consequence from questioning.' The importance of pre-planned questions, inserted in a carefully-structured lesson sequence at vital points—where information is to be emphasised, consolidated and organised—must be stressed in answer to the teacher who asks: 'When, in my lesson, ought I to begin questioning the class?'

'Overhead or directed questions? Relay or reverse questions? Which ought to be favoured?' An *overhead question* is one asked of the class *as a whole*. It avoids the problems which may arise from singling out one student by name; it extends a challenge to the class as a whole; it allows the questioner to select the person who is to answer; it may draw from the class a variety of useful responses. A *directed question* is put to an *individual,* often *by name.* It allows the reticent or hesitant student to be drawn into discussion; it enables comment to be distributed; it draws on individual students' capacities. A *relay question* is one put by the student to the teacher; he responds by putting the question to the group as a whole. Participation is encouraged by use of this technique—and it often allows the teacher time to prepare his eventual response! A *reverse question* is one which is thrown back to the questioner by the teacher to whom it is addressed. It is said to be a valuable teaching tactic in that it encourages students to think for themselves. But its indiscriminate use can lead to embarrassment for the student and to the drying up of the flow of student–teacher questions.

'What is the value of the 'probing question' in lessons?' The *probing question* is, in contrast to the superficial query, an attempt to elicit deeper responses which, in turn, can be made the basis of further questions. It may be used to seek further information or clarification of some point made in a previous response, to encourage students to further consideration of the implications of an answer, and to stimulate students to self-criticism in relation to their previous answers. In particular, the probing question may be used for the more difficult questions in a graded series.

> 'A good questioner proceeds like a man chopping wood—he begins at the easier end, attacking the knots last, and after a time the teacher and student come to understand the point with a sense of pleasure' (Confucius).

'Is it possible to use class questioning to range over the gamut of abilities within the domains of learning?' It is not only possible, but highly desirable. Thus, Felker and Dapna have produced research findings suggesting that questions requiring higher-level thinking (e.g. in the realms of synthesis and evaluation) produce performance gains much greater than those requiring mere verbatim recall. The following sequence of questions used in the preliminary stages of an early lesson, for non-specialists, on general principles of contract law, illustrates the manner in which the abilities suggested by Bloom as comprising the cognitive domain (see p. 101) might be utilised in question-and-answer sessions.

'Let us begin with the definition of 'contract'. What would you say in response to a person with no training in law who asked you to explain to him what the term 'contract' means?' *(Taxonomy level: knowledge. Overhead question, involving recall.)*

'One of the phrases used by John in his answer to the previous question was 'legal consequences of an agreement'. What do you understand by this?' *(Taxonomy level: comprehension. Overhead question, involving understanding.)*

'Let us apply Mary's answer to the last question to the following problem. X, a student, aged 16, after finding his first job, agrees to pay his mother, Y, £15 a week to help towards his food and board. After a month, X refuses to pay Y. Has Y any remedy under the law of contract?' [After a pause] 'Fred, please.' *(Taxonomy level: application. Directed question, involving the use of principles.)*

'Fred's answer and his explanation were correct. Let's go over the points he made ... Now, remember the question I put to Fred. Suppose that X, the student, had been aged 19 at the time—would the situation, as Fred described it, have been any different?' *(Taxonomy level: analysis. Overhead question, involving ability to discriminate.)*

'Now, let's return to John's definition of 'contract'—I'll write it on the board. Note the words I'm underlining—'an agreement which the courts will enforce'. Can anyone suggest any circumstances in which the courts should insist on an agreement being carried out, even though the parties don't want the courts to interfere?' *(Taxonomy level: synthesis. Overhead question involving ability to perceive and discuss relationships.)*

'Finally, I would like you to think very carefully about the question I am going to put to you. Talk it over among yourselves for a few minutes, then I'll call on you for an answer. Here is the question: How useful is John's definition—look at it once again—for the 'man in the street', who knows no law?' *(Taxonomy level: evaluation. Overhead question, involving ability to formulate a judgement.)*

The growing awareness of the importance of effective questioning technique for the class teacher is evident in the attention being given by teacher training institutions to the use of 'micro teaching'—a process in which teaching techniques are scaled down, allowing a trainee to demonstrate particular skills, such as class questioning, in a short lesson sequence, of, say, five to ten minutes. Its objective is to isolate and study a specific teaching skill. Video and audio tapes can be utilised so as to review and analyse the trainee's performance. In this and other ways the vital technique of questioning—'the core around which most communication during the lesson is built'—can be taught effectively.

Homework and assignments

Homework and assignments may be set because of the rules of a national examination scheme or because the teacher considers it a necessary supplement to work done in class. Where set, it should be presented by the teacher as being an integral (hence non-optional) part of the course. In the case of day-release classes, meeting once a week and having to attain a high standard of work, it may be essential if the syllabus is to be covered.

The object of homework and assignments may be threefold: to extend the amount of work which can be covered in class; to revise that work; to allow the application of lessons learned in class to the solution of problems arising from new situations. Where homework is used as an extension of classwork, it should be based clearly on principles learned in class. Where its object is revision, it may consist of problems, the answers to which might form an introduction to a future lesson. Where practice in new situations is required (a precondition of transfer of learning), problems demanding recall or reinstatement of skills and insight can be valuable for home-based study.

Homework and assignments should be corrected by the teacher in a manner which is understood by the student and should be handed back as soon as possible (since feedback and reinforcement value diminish with the passing of time). They should be based on tasks which can be performed in a reasonable time and with the restricted facilities available outside the college.

Demonstrations as part of the lesson

A demonstration is not usually planned as a complete lesson in itself; it should be presented as a part of a lesson sequence, providing a stimulus situation (or 'cue') from which principles may emerge through reasoning. It requires careful planning and presentation if it is to lead clearly to the lesson objective which, in the case of the sciences, may be based on an understanding of principles, causes and effects.

Students must be prepared for the demonstration if it is to achieve its optimum effect. Certain preliminary knowledge may be essential and this ought to be tested in the lesson prior to the demonstration. The class ought to be informed of what the demonstration is intended to make clear, thus: 'Using this apparatus we shall make chlorine', or, 'We shall use this simple apparatus to learn what happens when an electric bell is activated in a vacuum.' The demonstrator ought to give an account of the pattern of events as it unfolds ('I'm now pumping the air out of the jar which contains the bell') and, in giving his description he should carefully visualise the apparatus from the students' place in the class ('Look at the bell jar, which is to *your* left').

Arrangement of the class and the apparatus is important. Michael Faraday makes this point:

> When an experimental lecture is to be delivered and apparatus is to be exhibited, some kind of order should be preserved in the arrangement of them on the lecture table. Every particular part illustrative of the lecture should be in view; no one thing should hide another from the audience, nor should anything stand in the way of the lecturer (Porter and Friday 1974).

The students should be seated as near the demonstration as is practicable.

The demonstration ought not to be too detailed; its main points ought to emerge clearly and be underlined by the demonstrator's emphasis. It should be followed by a recapitulation of the events which the students have seen and by a reasoned statement of the principles involved. The class ought then to write up the demonstration as the prelude to a test which will assess its impact.

Evaluation of lesson effectiveness

After the end of a lesson the teacher ought to attempt an evaluation of the effectiveness of the learning event for which he has been responsible. This requires an assessment of class achievement in relation to the lesson objectives. In particular, the teacher should ask himself the following questions:

1. 'Was my introduction effective in arousing interest? Did the class settle down to work swiftly?'

2. 'Was the lesson content adequate, given the amount of time available? Was the time divided adequately among the various parts of the lesson?'

3. 'Was interest maintained? Did I actively promote maintenance of that interest?'

4. 'Was my questioning adequate and how far did the answers elicited help class progress towards the lesson objective?'

5. 'Were my summaries and recapitulations adequate?'

6. 'Were my teaching aids and their use adequate? Did they really assist learning?'

7. 'Were class discipline and control adequate?'

8. 'Does the final test result indicate any specific weakness in my lesson plan or presentation?'

The teacher's answers should be as objective as possible. The result of the final test, above all, will provide an important measure and assessment of effectiveness which ought to assist his presentation and control of succeeding lessons. Gagné's enumeration of the 'components of instruction' makes a useful checklist: 1. Gaining and controlling attention; 2. Informing the learner of expected outcomes; 3. Stimulating the recall of prerequisite skills and knowledge; 4. Presenting appropriate stimuli; 5. Offering direction; 6. Providing results of feedback for the learner; 7. Appraising the learner's performance; 8. Widening the transfer of learning; 9. Ensuring retention of knowledge (Gagné 1983).

16

Modes of instruction (2)— the skills lesson

A journey of a thousand miles starts under one's feet (Lao-Tze).

The general principles relating to the teaching of a formal lesson, discussed in the previous chapter, apply also to the teaching of skills (i.e. those series of learned acts requiring simultaneous or sequential co-ordination). The successful operation of a lathe, a sewing machine or a typewriter, the correct fingering of a violin or flute, the swift and accurate representation of the spoken word in the form of shorthand symbols, involve, essentially, the acquisition of a 'practised ease of execution' in relation to the appropriate sensory-motor activities. ('Habit diminishes the conscious attention with which our acts are performed' (William James).) The principles of teaching technique are basically the same whether the subject-matter be welding or economic geography, typewriting or algebra. 'Learning by doing' tends to feature more prominently, however, in lessons aimed at skill acquisition. The objective of effective co-ordination of mind and muscle, resulting in the production of swift and meaningful, desired patterns of movement, usually requires a special arrangement of lesson content and an appropriate lesson structure.

The nature of skills

The Department of Employment's glossary of terms defines a skill as an *organised and co-ordinated pattern of mental and/or physical activ-*

ity in relation to an object or other display of information, usually involving both receptor and effector processes. Howarth regards it, in wider terms, as 'a set of strategic adaptations to the mechanical limitations of the brain and of the body, which enable human purposes to be achieved'. It is *built up gradually* in the course of repeated training or other experience. It is *serial;* each part is dependent on the last and influences the next.

Sensory-motor activity, which is at the basis of all skilled performance, is motor activity initiated and controlled by sensory input from the performer's environment and from the performer himself. The systematic motor skills which make up those activities taught in the skills lessons in the colleges of further education are based generally on a series of co-ordinated movements, the execution of which requires repeated practice. The performer must learn to be attentive to his environment, to respond to, or ignore, certain types of cue from that environment and to mark his responses by selecting immediately an appropriate and accurately-timed movement from the repertoire he has acquired as the result of previous learning. The movement of a needle on a dial, interpreted as the signal for adjustive action, the presence on a sheet of violin music of the symbol *ff*, interpreted as the need for additional pressure of bow on strings, the note in the margin of a manuscript which is being typed, which reads 'CAPS', interpreted as a signal demanding the use of particular keys on the typewriter, exemplify stimuli which ought to result in *swift, precise responses characterised by complete co-ordination of mind and muscle*. In these examples perception results in linked actions based on manual dexterity and economy of behaviour. The quality of those actions will depend, in particular, on the performer's previous experiences and learning.

Among the distinguishing features of a skilled activity are accuracy in timing, anticipation of movement, economy in appropriate movements, and, perhaps above all, a 'flow' of movement. These features reflect the general *organisation* of input data by the performer. He is able to 'make sense of' what he perceives and to 'translate' his perceptions into organised activity. It is one of the main tasks of the skills teacher to assist in the acquisition of powers of activity organisation.

The concept of 'flow' is particularly important in teaching skills. The practical significance of this concept for the teacher who is attempting to inculcate techniques is mirrored in the theoretical view, held, for example, by Smith, in which motor skills are seen as 'multidimensional behaviour patterns' rather than as 'temporal sequences of discrete responses'.

The creation and growth of skills

Among the many theories accounting for the creation and growth of skills, the following have been found to be of particular relevance to the work of teachers in the colleges of further education.

Crossman's 'selection' theory

Crossman suggests that, in acquiring skills, *the learner is refining the process of selecting the most appropriate methods from his repertoire.* Practice by the learner exerts a 'selective effect' on his behaviour, favouring those patterns of selection and action which are quickest, at the expense of others. Hence, according to Crossman, trial and error are not as effective as a process by which the teacher *guides* the learner through the selection and utilisation of the appropriate activity patterns. Speed is acquired as a result of practice based on a teacher's directions.

Adams' 'graded-movement' theory

Adams views *the learning of graded movements* as the essence of skill acquisition. The *first stage* of such learning involves the establishing of a 'perceptual trace' which the learner uses as the basis of successive movements; this is a *verbal-motor phase* in which the teacher provides verbal cues concerning the learner's actions. In the *second stage* (the *motor phase*), verbal clues are not necessary since the perceptual trace is now firmly established. In practice, therefore, skills acquisition will grow from carefully-directed teaching and practice.

Annett and Kay's 'redundancy-appreciation' theory

Annett and Kay (1956) have suggested that skills are acquired as the learner is able to understand the *redundancy in inputs of sensory information.* In the first stages of his learning he will observe that signal x is apparently followed invariably by signals y and z. With intensified perceptual understanding he will learn that the probability of signal x being followed immediately by signal y is greater than the probability of its being followed immediately by signal z. He is able to concentrate on useful cues, therefore, by learning to treat certain inputs as redundant. Skill acquisition will be determined by the selection and abstraction from the input of vital information prior to its utilisation in the form of an activity.

Fitts' 'three-phase' theory

Fitts (1967) believes that the acquisition of a complex skill necessitates the learner passing through three overlapping phases; the transition from phase to phase may take the form of a continuous rather than a sudden change. (Fitts views complex skill learning in terms of the acquisition of a number of semi-independent sub-routines which may go on concurrently or successively. Hence, he says, it is essential for success that the teacher shall identify correctly the appropriate 'executive sub-routines' concerning sequence rules in a skill.) The phases in Fitts' model are as follows:

(a) *The cognitive, early phase.* The beginner seeks to understand what has to be done and attempts to comprehend the background to the tasks he has to master. The teacher guides him towards the required sequence of actions and builds on previously-acquired part-skills, i.e. the sub-routines. Frequently-recurring errors are pointed out to the learner. As a result of this phase he acquires an 'executive routine', i.e. the required procedure.

(b) *The associative, intermediate phase.* Correct patterns of response are established in the learner's repertoire as the result of demonstrations, imitation and practice. Part-skills are 'smoothed' by the elimination of inadequate movements, and sub-skills are integrated into required total skills.

(c) *The autonomous, final phase.* Skilled acts are now performed automatically, without the learner having to stop to think of 'what comes next'. Errors have been eliminated, speed of performance has been increased, resistance to the effects of stress is built up and improvements in skill continue (although at a decreasing rate).

Miller's 'hierarchical-structure' theory

Miller (1960) views the acquisition of skills as the *progressive co-ordination of separate units of activity into a hierarchical structure.* He conducted research into 'feedback loops' of activity, using the concept of 'TOTE' units (test, operate, test, exit). The first phase of activity on which skill is based is a 'test', in which the learner assesses whether there is any difference between the actual state of the system and its required state. Any observed difference (of a significant nature) requires an 'operate' phase, followed by a further 'test phase. The cycle of 'test, operate and test again' will continue until the desired state is achieved, after which activity ends—the 'exit' phase. (Note, for example, how this sequence of activity may be observed in the tuning of a violin, the setting of a lathe or the seasoning of food.) The use of TOTEs requires a plan, defined by Miller as 'any hierarchical process in the organisation that can control the order in which the sequence of operations is to be performed'. The learning of skills is seen as the integration and ordering of units of sensory-motor activities.

The skills lesson: its essence

The skills lesson is apt to be a relatively slow process; there are very few short cuts to the permanent acquisition of procedural sequences of motor skills. Lesson preparation must take into account the necessity for careful, planned and methodical teaching and learning of the routines of sub-skills out of which mastery emerges.

The skills teacher must cover *all* the tasks which have to be learned. *What has to be done?* This involves a correct task analysis. *How is the task executed by those recognised as competent performers?* This involves a detailed analysis of criterion performance. *What senses are involved in task execution? Will they be utilised separately or together?* The selection of appropriate audio-visual aids may be determined by answers to these questions. *How shall competence be recognised and evaluated?* The answer may involve a statement of instructional objectives cast in strict behavioural terms (see Chapters 8, 9).

Lesson planning in relation to the acquisition of skills can benefit from a study of Miller's identification of the significant functions characterising that process. He notes seven functions which ought to be taken into account when skills techniques are to be taught:

1. The ability to recognise objects and symbols used in the skilled task by name and appearance.
2. The viewing, search and detection of 'task-relevant cues.'
3. The identification and interpretation of 'cue-patterns'.
4. The temporary retention ('short-term recall') of information needed to complete particular sequences.
5. The long-term recall of procedures.

6. Decision-making.
7. Appropriate motor response.

A useful categorisation of functions necessary in skill acquisition has been given by Demaree. His scheme of instruction is built on the recognition of four interrelated matters:

1. Learning of knowledge related to the task—words, symbols, rules and relationships.
2. Learning of skills and task components—perceptual identification, naming, computation, decision-taking (in the face of incomplete information).
3. Learning of whole-task performance—procedural patterns, relevant motor skills, complex decision making.
4. Learning of integrated-task performance—co-ordination and team tasks.

The following principles should be considered in the planning and execution of lessons aimed at the acquisition of skills and based on defined sensory-motor objectives.

1. *The skill ought to be demonstrated initially in its entirety as a fully-integrated set of operations* and it should be stressed from the very beginning that mastery can be acquired by those who are willing to learn; there must be no suggestion that competence can be attained only by a chosen few! The demonstration ought to be accompanied by a clear, non-technical commentary. Above all, it must be a *demonstration of mastery.* The correct movements which go to make up the skill must be in evidence from the outset. The demonstrator must not forget that what is 'second nature' to him—posture, the holding of an instrument, the guiding of a tool— must not be taken for granted; it must be seen as part of the skill to be acquired and must be analysed and taught accordingly.

2. *The skill must then be broken down into its component, subordinate activities;* each action should be demonstrated, explained, analysed and demonstrated again so as to emphasise its particular importance and its significance for the skill as a whole. The *relation* of separate activities one to the other and their *integration* into a hierarchy of complete routines which make up the skill must be stressed. *Order, sequence, pattern* and *rhythm* must be emphasised.

   (a) Learning of skills should be based initially on units which can be practised with some assurance of success. The reinforcing value of a correctly-performed action in the early days of skill acquisition cannot be over-stressed. ('Well begun is half-done.') The importance of careful and sympathetic guidance will be obvious. Praise given neither undeservedly nor indiscriminately is a valuable reinforcing agent. The beginner, who has listened with nervous apprehension to the superb musical tone produced by his instrumental teacher will be assisted by the reassurance that his first efforts, when in accordance with the teacher's directions, are the preliminary steps along the road to competence. The first successful actions of the engineering apprentice working at his lathe ought to be acknowledged and praised.

(b) There are advantages in using 'natural units' rather than unnecessarily small units which will have to be combined at a later stage if they are to be meaningful to students. Evidence has been provided by Harms to suggest, for example, that the effective learning of typing is hastened by practice based on complete words and sentences rather than individual letters and meaningless syllables (Harms 1972).

3. *Skills acquisition lessons require supervised, reinforcing, and carefully-spaced practice by students.* Technique and understanding must be linked so that the learner attains the objective of an autonomous, overall competence built from those separate activities of which the total skill is composed. Where the skill is linked closely with speed, practice must be arranged so that this feature is stressed. ('Why *must* the learner practise motor skills? What is the *basic* significance of practice?' Gagné answers that it is only by repeating the essential movements that the learner can be provided with the *exact cues regulating performance.* The movements required in the acquisition of motor skills are cued by stimuli that are only partly outside the learner; some are internal and result from feedback to his muscles. Repetition of essential movements in periods of practice allows the learner to discover the 'vital kinesthetic cues which inform him of success'.)

(a) 'Distributed practice' based on activity followed by intervals of rest (in which consolidation can take place) appears to produce better results than those emanating from one long, unbroken period. Two separated thirty-minute periods of practice are often more productive than one hour's continuous practice. In this way, 'plateaux', when practice seems to produce no improvement in performance, may be avoided.

(b) Supervision of all aspects of practice is vital if errors are to be noted, analysed and eliminated.

(c) The importance of accurate timing must emerge from

practice. Timing is not always a matter of the swift response to a stimulus; it must involve an anticipation of 'what is coming next' and a linked ability to select swiftly from one's repertoire of responses. Supervised practice should stress the significance of this concept.

(d) The 'continuous flow' of those separate actions combined into a skilled performance has to emerge from practice. This requires that the teacher shall point out the importance of acquiring a 'natural rhythm' in the performance of a task.

(e) There is evidence to suggest the importance of maintaining a minimal rate of information input in practice if the learner is to acquire efficiency in the skill. 'Underloading' may result, for example, from monotonous instruction. 'Overloading' (a more frequent occurrence in skills training) results where the learner's information channel capacity is strained. (Miller, in an analysis of much interest to teachers (Miller 1965), suggests that skilled operators tend to adopt the following 'strategies of defence' against the stresses of 'overloading': *omission* (i.e. not processing information data input); *error* (i.e. processing data input incorrectly and not making adjustments); *queueing* (i.e. delaying appropriate responses); *filtering* (i.e. omitting systematically some categories of information); *approximation* (i.e. making less-than-precise responses to data input); *escape* (i.e. cutting off the data input).) Lessenberry suggests that, in the teaching of typewriting, lessons related to the lay-out of the keyboard ought to be organised methodically so as to avoid the 'too much, too soon' danger that comes from attempting to cover the keyboard too quickly and the 'too little, too late' boredom that results if the keyboard is introduced too slowly.

(f) The pattern of skill factors making up a task appears to change progressively with practice; hence the content of a practice session must be altered regularly as that pattern is seen to change.

4. *Continuous, swift and accurate feedback must be provided for the learner* and he must be taught to interpret such information correctly. He must be reminded of criterion performance and must be informed of any gap between his achievement and the requisite standard. He must be shown how to close that gap. (Keller has suggested that the perfection of motor skills depends on the increasing refinement of discrimination between the sensory feedback of correct and not-quite-correct muscular

performance (Keller 1954). Bartlett emphasised that the old saying that 'practice makes perfect' was not true. 'But it is true to say that it is practice, *the results of which are known,* which makes perfect' (Bartlett 1954). Ammons noted that: 'The more specific the knowledge of performance, the more rapid the improvement and the higher the level of performance . . . The longer the delay in giving knowledge of performance, the less effect the given information has' (Ammons 1956).)

5. *Tests in realistic conditions ought to be administered regularly.* Insight and retention ought to be evaluated along with the capacity to transfer acquired skills to novel and demanding situations.

6. *Achievement of competence at one level ought to be accepted as a necessary preparation for movement to a higher level of skill.* It ought not to be an end in itself. The attainment of 140 w.p.m. in shorthand skill practice is one step only along the road leading to all-round competence as a secretary.

The skills lesson: its structure

Some typical skills lesson structures are illustrated in Figure 16.1. Experienced skills teachers advocate a structure planned so as to consist of 25 per cent of available time devoted to demonstration of the skill, or a component part, 15 per cent to verbal explanation and 60 per cent to guided practice. (Changes during the lesson, in both activity and pace, are said to assist in reducing student fatigue related to skill acquisition.) Lesson structure will reflect the teacher's appreciation of the role of reorganisation of sensory-input data so that the learner responds swiftly and accurately to appropriate stimulus cues in his environment. It will take into account also the nature of the ability traits essential in each phase of the skill, and the relative importance of those traits in the overall timing patterns inherent in mastery.

Structure I is derived from a lesson based on an objective concerning the correct use of engineering equipment. It begins with the creation of a link with the previous lesson. The purpose of the lesson is stated and is followed by an introductory explanation of what will be seen by the students. A complete demonstration is followed by an explanation of the principal features of what has been seen. Students then write up a record of the main features of the demonstration after which they are tested on comprehension of those features. Intensive, supervised practice is followed by a recapitulation of essential matters and further practice.

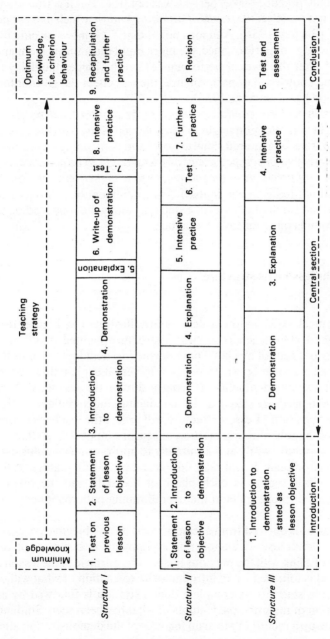

Figure 16.1 *Examples of skills lesson structures.*

Structure II is often used in the teaching of shorthand. The aim of the lesson is stated prior to an introduction which will set the scene for what is to follow. The teacher will then demonstrate the shorthand outlines which are inherent in the lesson objectives. Careful explanation is followed by intensive practice after which there is a test. Further, guided practice is the prelude to a final revision.

Structure III is commonly used in the group teaching of musical skills. A short performance by the tutor acts as a general introduction to a statement of the lesson objective. A further, intensive demonstration is followed by a technical explanation of what has been seen and heard. Intensive, guided practice is followed by the testing and assessment of individual students' performances.

In a paper presented in 1977 to the Comparative Education Society meeting in London, the Polish educationist, W. Okon, outlined an approach to skills lessons in which practical activity played an important role. He spoke of a skill as the ability to apply appropriate norms (i.e. rules and principles) to the performance of tasks facing an individual. The following stages in the process of skill formation were delineated:

1. Clarification for the learner of the name, type and significance of a given skill.
2. Formulation of rules to be applied in the activity to be performed, thus providing an appropriate theoretical foundation.
3. Presentation of a model of the activity so that the essence and value of the rules might be recognised.
4. Eliciting from students an attempted performance, under guidance, of the task, and continuous supervision designed to remedy deficiencies in performance.
5. Provision of systematic, independent practice in the use of the skill so that habits are formed that limit the amount of reflection and awareness of procedures needed by the student.

A note on 'discovery learning'

Student-participation and individual problem solving in relation to the acquisition of skills are at the centre of the method of 'discovery learning' developed by E. and M. Belbin. Some modified techniques of programmed instruction (see Chapter 20) are utilised. Learners who are under instruction in, say, the elementary principles of electrical circuits, are given a simple apparatus consisting of a board on which are mounted batteries, ammeters, switches, bulbs, wire, clips, etc. A written instruction sheet advises on how to carry out simple experiments, on what should be observed and what conclusions ought to be drawn. The learners attain their objective when they construct a circuit without receiving any assistance from the instructor. Questions to the instructor usually result in his suggesting only *how* answers might be obtained by further experiments (Belbin 1969).

The technique necessitates careful task analysis. Its advantages are said to include: total student involvement; step-by-step, intensive learning with students working at their own pace. Its disadvantages include: amount of time needed for effective task analysis and construction of experimental apparatus; possibility of certain important theoretical steps being overlooked by students. There has been criticism, too, of the role of the instructor in merely *suggesting* modes of discovering answers rather than *providing* those answers without delay. (Note Thorndike's comment: 'Refusal to supply information on the ground that the learner will be more profited by discovering the facts himself, runs the risk not only of excessive time-cost but also the strengthening of wrong habits' (Thorndike 1935).)

17

Modes of instruction (3)— the lecture

> Whatever can be said at all can be said clearly, and whatever cannot be said clearly should not be said at all (Wittgenstein).

A lecture involves a *continuous formal exposition of, or discourse on, some topic.* Verner and Dickinson define it as an instructional technique through which is presented 'an oral discourse on a particular subject' (Verner and Dickinson 1968). The Hale Committee (1964) referred to it as 'a teaching period occupied wholly or mainly with continuous exposition by a lecturer'. It exemplifies the process of 'one-way communication' and, as such, has been criticised severely. And yet the lecture persists as a common mode of instruction in colleges of further education and elsewhere. Typically, it is used to introduce course material, to give groups of students specialised information, e.g. the results of research, or to present a final revision. Its weaknesses and strengths and its peculiar difficulties for the lecturer will emerge in the consideration of lecture structure, planning and delivery which follows.

The lecture under attack

Criticisms of the lecture are often uncompromising: lecturing is said to be a negation of teaching; its autocratic form and style necessarily vitiate the partnership considered essential to the facilitation of learning; the 'intellectual passivity and weariness' of the listeners ('the lecturer is a person who talks in someone else's sleep'—an aphorism attributed to W. H. Auden) and the lack of discussion are said to be a contradiction of the process of free flow and exchange of ideas which the learning process demands. The lack of feedback (see Chapter 7) makes real class control impossible, so that the lecture is said to leave much to be desired as a mode of creating the conditions for effective learning.

Over half a century ago, Green, in a series of experiments, demonstrated that students apparently learned as much from reading passages as from hearing the same matter delivered in a lecture. More recently, Bligh, in a detailed examination of lecture techniques, concluded that lectures were not generally effective in teaching students to think (Bligh 1972). Goolkasian has found that students attending lectures do not always recognise important points better than unimportant details (Goolkasian 1979). Kintsch finds that jokes and other types of humorous, extraneous remarks made by lecturers are often remembered by students more clearly than lecturers' major statements (Kintsch 1977).

Critics of the lecture occasionally support their attacks with references to the comments of famous scholars. Thus, Dr. Johnson stated, in terms which allowed of little contradiction, 'Lectures were once useful; but now, when all can read, and books are so numerous, lectures are unnecessary.' Charles Darwin refused to attend certain lectures at Cambridge because he was 'so sickened with lectures at Edinburgh'. (His later comment tends to be overlooked: 'I attended, however, Henslow's lectures on botany, and liked them much for their extreme clearness and the admirable illustrations.') Bertrand Russell is uncompromising: 'I derived no benefit from lectures, and I made a vow to myself that when in due course I became a lecturer I would not suppose that lecturing did any good!'

It will be argued below that a well-constructed lecture which is based on an acceptance of the principles of effective instruction can, and often does, succeed in capturing students' attention and communicating information.

Structure of the lecture

As in the case of the lesson, content will play a large part in the determination of lecture structure. The *purpose* of the lecture must be reflected in the way it is constructed. A lecture on 'the effective utilisation of space in warehousing' is likely to demand a structure somewhat different from that used in an exposition of 'recent changes in the law relating to the sale of goods'; the structure of the former lecture is likely to be based on a talk illustrated by much visual display material, while the structure of the latter will probably be based on a verbal exposition only. The major determinant of structure should emerge from the lecturer's instruction strategy, based on his answers to the questions: 'What is the *purpose* of this lecture?' 'What is its *specific objective?*' 'Does the subject matter demand the use of any *visual aids* other than a chalkboard?' 'Does the subject matter necessitate a particular *approach?*'

Four typical lecture strategies are set out below: the first is often used in the presentation of a thesis; the second is designed for the posing and examination of a problem; the third lends itself well to the explanation of an aspect of systematised knowledge; the fourth can be used for the presentation, in sequential form, of material leading, by the nature of the logic of the subject-matter, to a conclusion.

Presenting a thesis

Examples of this structure might be found in a lecture to business students on an interpretation of some recent research on the location of industry, or to a general studies group on, say, the case against film censorship. The structure necessitates a careful presentation of thesis, supporting data and counter-theses. It might take the following form:

A   Statement of purpose and objective of the lecture
B   Statement of the thesis
C   Explanation of the thesis:
    1. Thesis presented as a proposition
    2. Evidence
    3. Difficulties in interpretation of the evidence
D   Restatement of thesis and recapitulation of evidence
E   Counter-thesis I:
    1. Counter-thesis presented as a proposition
    2. Evidence
    3. Difficulties in interpretation of evidence
    4. Thesis in light of counter-thesis
F   Counter-theses II, III . . . (presented as in E above)
G   Restatement of thesis and recapitulation of counter-theses
H   Conclusion:
    1. Statement of conclusion
    2. Balance of evidence
    3. Restatement of thesis

Examining a problem

Assume that the lecture form has been selected for a presentation to a group of students of some of the arguments surrounding race relations, or for the unfolding to management diploma students of the hypotheses underlying the controversial concept of worker participation in the process of industrial decision-making. Problem, data, arguments, basic hypotheses and suggested answers, can be presented in a logical, patterned structure, of which the following might serve as an example:

A   Statement of purpose and objective of lecture
B   Statement of the problem to be examined (posed in a style which is meaningful to the audience)
C   Explanation of the problem:
   1. Its history
   2. Its component features
   3. Its significance
D   Possible solutions:
   1. Solution (a): statement; argument; reasoning
   2. Solution (b) . . . . . .
   3. Solution (c) . . . . . .
E   Restatement of problem and recapitulation of suggested solutions
F   Application of suggested solutions
G   Assessment of validity of solutions
H   Conclusion:
   1. Restatement of problem
   2. Summary of valid solutions

Explanation of an aspect of systematised knowledge

This often provides suitable occasions for the use of the lecture method. Examples might be: an explanation to banking students of the organisation and functions of the money market; an analysis for a group of young managers of the use of the computer in determining project profitability. The appropriate structure will reflect the *hierarchical features* of the subject-matter, as in the following example:

A   Statement of purpose and objective of lecture

B   Point I
    1.
        (a)
        (b)
           (i)
           (ii)
        (c)
    2.
        (a)
        (b)
C   Point II
    1.
        (a)
        (b)
    2.
        (a)
           (i)
           (ii)
        (b)
D   Point III......
E   Recapitulation
F   Conclusion

Presentation of a sequence of information leading to a conclusion

This structure is valuable for an explanation of a *series* of events or other facts leading to a conclusion. It is useful in mathematics, history, logic, wherever there is a clearly-defined hierarchy of facts. Frequent recapitulation and careful definition of terms are necessary to the success of this lecture method. The following form is common in lectures on subjects such as elements of econometrics, geometry, the use of syllogisms in argument, etc.

A   Statement of purpose and objective of lecture
B   Short exposition of framework of structure to be presented
C   Point I
D   Links between point I and point II
E   Point II
F   Recapitulation
G   Links between point II and point III
H   Point III

I   Structure of points and links reviewed
J   Recapitulation
K   Conclusion

Physical environment of the lecture

Where the lecture is to be delivered in a lecture theatre, much can be done to improve arrangements so that communication is as effective as possible. Audio-visual aids (see Chapter 21) must be set out with care so that their use is not an interruption to the even flow of the lecture. The positioning of screens, blackboards and projectors requires attention prior to the delivery of the lecture.

Where the lecturer is obliged to use a general classroom, seating must be prepared so that notes can be taken with little difficulty. The positioning of the lecturer's desk should be determined by experiment; it will not always be at the midpoint of one end of the room. The literature on the subject of spatial arrangements in classrooms repays close study, particularly in relation to the suggestions that the arrangement of a lecture room may have psychological as well as physiological effects on the class as a whole.

Planning the lecture

The lecture plan will be determined most appropriately—as in the case of the lesson plan—by a consideration of three major matters: the students, the subject matter, and the resources and constraints. The problem of pitching the lecture at an appropriate level is often difficult to resolve because the audience is likely to be large in numbers, so that many different levels of learning are almost certain to be represented. This necessitates making allowance in the lecture plan for time to *define terms,* to *give examples,* to *illustrate* and to *recapitulate.* The introduction to the lecture, including a *clear statement of objective* (reinforced, perhaps, by a visual display), requires careful treatment. ('What you should do in your introduction is to state your subject, in order that the point to be judged may be quite plain ... The introduction is the beginning of a speech, corresponding to the prologue in poetry and the prelude in flute-music; they are all beginnings, paving the way, as it were, for what is to follow' (Aristotle).) Constraints include time, the nature of the lecture room, the availability of visual aids. A diagram of the lecture room ought to be studied, so that the precise position of platform, speaker's lectern or desk, chalkboard, projector, screen and other resources can be taken into account when planning the interlocking of speech and visual aids. The conclusion of the lecture requires detailed consideration; its impact is often of much significance. ('In the epilogue you should summarise the arguments by which your case has been proved. The first step in this reviewing process is to observe that you have done what you undertook to do. You must, then, state what you have said and why you have said it' (Aristotle).)

The *amount of material to be presented* in the lecture must be planned with care. (Lacking the feedback mechanisms available in the normal lesson, the lecturer cannot estimate accurately whether the points he seeks to make are being assimilated by his audience. He cannot take assimilation or comprehension for granted, no matter how carefully he plans and delivers his lecture.) He must not fail to take into account the *limits of the short-term memory* (see Chapter 11). A lecture based on relatively few concepts may have a greater chance of success in attaining its objective, therefore, than one which requires the assimilation of a large volume of information. (Miller's suggestion, noted in Chapter 11, that short-term memory capacity may be limited to approximately seven discrete 'chunks' of information at any time, is of relevance here.)

The lecture plan will reflect the necessity to *arouse and keep attention* (which may require the carefully-planned use of visual material so as to break the monotony of speech), to *present appropriate stimuli,* and to *reinforce responses* (by correctly-timed recapitulation and re-statement). The sequence of statement, elaboration and recapitulation, based on the 'sequence procedures' outlined in Chapter 15, is worth considering in the planning of a lecture.

Some writers, such as Brown, suggest that a lecture plan can be based on 'keys', i.e. 'key points' in the topic which is to form the subject of the lecture. Keys should be expressed as simply as possible, should be illustrated by examples, qualified or elaborated and, finally, re-stated in the form of a conclusion. This is a valuable mode of planning which can be used where there is little time to prepare a lecture. The planner begins by noting the subject-matter (e.g. 'inflation') in the form of a question (e.g. 'What are the causes of inflation?'). He then uses 'free association' to recall matters linked with the question (e.g. supply of money, pressure of demand), to set out certain 'keys' which are presented in logical form, and he adds, finally, an appropriate introduction and conclusion.

The lecturer's own notes to which he will refer during the course of his lecture, may take the form of a detailed, sentence-by-sentence account (useful for those teachers who have little lecturing experience), or an elaborated plan based on the framework of what is to be said. An example of framework notes is given in Figure 17.1. Note, however, that the fact that detailed lecture notes have been prepared must not result in the lecturer giving the impression of merely reading a prepared statement in mechanical fashion. Some spontaneity of expression and delivery ought to emerge in the most carefully-planned lecture.

Date:......................Group:........................Subject:........................
Lecture objective(s): ....
Time: 50 mins

Timing	Lecture content	Reference material	Aids
5 mins	Introduction and statement of lecture objectives	–	Chalkboard
15 mins	Key point I: 1. 2. 3.	Textbook, p. 100	–
5 mins	Recapitulation of Key point I	–	Chalkboard
15 mins	Key point II: 1. 2.	Textbook, p. 105 Newspaper cutting	–
5 mins	Recapitulation of Key points I and II; restatement of lecture objective(s)	–	o/h projector
5 mins	Questions. Hand out lecture summary	–	–

Figure 17.1   *Example of lecture 'framework' notes.*

How long ought a lecture to last and at what stage does it cease to have any impact? There is no golden rule, because the threshold of assimilation will vary from student to student. One will be unable to concentrate or retain data after ten minutes' unbroken speech, while another will assimilate with ease the contents of a twenty-minute talk.

In general pauses ought to be made in the interests of *concentration and assimilation* after fifteen minutes of continuous speaking. The pause may be utilised for the presentation of visual stimuli, e.g. a chart which illustrates or recapitulates a key point. (Many lecturers' experiences suggest that the entire lecture session ought to last not longer than sixty minutes. After that period attention often diminishes rapidly rapidly and assimilation becomes very difficult.)

Delivery of the lecture

A teacher's lesson style, mannerisms, speech, gestures, eye-to-eye contact with students, clarity of expression, appearance—his so-called 'personality'—can make a considerable impact on his class; positive, where it aids communication, but negative, where it acts as 'noise' which interferes with the transmission and reception of information. Impact of this kind is even more marked in the case of the lecture. It can be said with some truth that, for a lecture audience, 'the medium *is* the message'. A lecture is dependent for its success—to a marked degree—on the personality and communication skill of the lecturer. He is the sole focus of attention for most of the lecture period; his style of delivery can result in acceptance and assimilation, or rejection, of the lecture content.

Lecturing technique involves an ability to speak clearly, to modulate voice tone and pitch, to use gestures sparingly, but effectively, and to speak at a pace which does not prevent assimilation and understanding. There is evidence to suggest that 110 w.p.m. may be a 'normal' rate of delivery and that a rate beyond 200 w.p.m. results in a rapid decline in assimilation. The following general points should be considered:

1. The style of delivery ought to be neither casual, nor in the pattern of grand oratory. 'Natural delivery' requires, paradoxically, much practice! It ought to be characterised by clarity, simplicity of expression and planned timing (which may require rehearsal). Michael Faraday comments: 'In order to gain the attention of an audience (and what can be more disagreeable than the want of it?), it is necessary to pay some attention to the manner of expression. The utterance should not be rapid and hurried and consequently unintelligible, but slow and deliberate, conveying ideas with ease from the lecturer and infusing them with clearness and readiness into the minds of the audience.'

2. The emphasis of key points may require variations in the pattern and intensity of speech, a gesture, a pause, a visual illustration. (Actors and musicians, for whom communication, and rapport with one's audience, are all-important are well aware of the significance and effect of a carefully-timed pause. In a lecture it can serve as a 'signal' for a key statement, or as a kind of emphasis. For a superb example in music, consider the effect of the last bars of Sibelius' Fifth Symphony.)

3. Flamboyant, exaggerated gestures rapidly become meaningless, divert attention from the words which they accompany and may snap the thread of communication.

4. Some mannerisms (e.g. of voice, posture) may amuse initially, but in a short time may irritate, even offend and alienate, eventually creating a barrier to effective communication. (As soon as a lecturer becomes aware of them he ought to work towards their eradication.)

5. It is vital that the lecturer should convey genuine enthusiasm and interest. 'Non-verbal cues'—facial expressions, eye contact (the absence of which is often interpreted by an audience as nervousness, fear or lack of interest), use of the hands—are rapidly communicated to students, who are swift in interpretation (see below). Lecturers would do well to remember the aphorism; 'We speak with our vocal organs, but we converse with our whole bodies.'

6. Where the lecture involves the use of visual aids, they ought to be prepared and ready to hand, so that continuity in presentation is maintained.

In sum, the lecturer should remember that because he is the focal point of attention, he is communicating along a *variety of channels,* some of which are noted by implication in the preceding paragraphs. The 'linguistic channel' is, by its very nature, of great importance; choice of words, clarity in syntax, are essential features of an effective lecture. The 'paralinguistic channel', involving the lecturer's vocal tone and quality of expression, provides a vital, individual contribution to overall lecture content and delivery. The 'visual channel' involves not only the use of visual aids, but refers to the lecturer's personal appearance, which can introduce unwanted 'noise' into the communication process! The 'kinetic channel', along which the lecturer's body movements are transformed into messages and interpreted by his audience, must not be overlooked; unconscious gestures (e.g. continuous finger-tapping) may convey clear, disturbing messages.

Michael Faraday summed up the lecturer's task thus:

A lecturer should exert his utmost effort to gain completely the mind and attention of his audience, and irresistibly make them join in his ideas to the end of the subject. He should endeavour to raise their interest at the commencement of the lecture and by a series of imperceptible gradations, unnoticed by the company, keep it alive as long as the subject demands it. . . . A flame should be lighted at the commencement and kept alive with unremitting splendour to the end. (Porter and Friday 1978)

The problem of absence of feedback

Where there is no informative feedback there can be no effective control (see Chapter 7). The lecturer suffers from the disadvantage of not knowing the reactions of his audience, since he cannot generally assess the effectiveness of his efforts to communicate. He cannot periodically halt the flow of the lecture by a swift examination of the level of assimilation. To rely on the facial expressions of one's audience is of little value ('There's no art to find the mind's construction in the face'). A post-lecture discussion or test comes too late to assist assessment and control of the lecture itself. In effect, the lecturer is deprived of the means of measuring immediate class reaction and this may account for the learning difficulties of some students whose instruction is based entirely on lectures.

There has been considerable research into aspects of non-verbal communication in relation to lecture-audience feedback. Abercrombie, for example, emphasises the importance of the lecturer being trained to recognise and interpret the non-verbal elements in language and communication (Abercrombie 1960). Argyle and Kendon state: 'Movement may serve to clarify or emphasise aspects of messages transmitted through speech; patterns of looking and movement may serve to regulate the pacing of action in the encounter' (Argyle and Kendon 1967). Research of this nature has been interpreted as suggesting that an element of feedback is available to the lecturer who is able to 'read and interpret' the so-called 'body language' of his audience.

Some lecturers have used the 'buzz group' technique to provide feedback and to 'break up' the continuous exposition which characterises the formal lecture. At carefully-selected points in the course of the lecture the audience is asked to split into prearranged groups to discuss their responses to a direct question. The groups can be formed by those sitting together in various sections of the room. The lecture is resumed after some of the group comments are reported and, perhaps, discussed.

Lecture notes and handouts

What record of the lecture ought a class to possess? This is a problem which must be faced by every college lecturer. Ought he to distribute a printed version of his entire lecture, or ought he to rely on students making their own notes while he is lecturing? Ought he to give out notes (to be used as 'organisers'—see p. 64) well in advance of the lecture, or a few minutes before he begins speaking, or at the end of his talk? Ought he to dictate a short summary?

The reasons advanced in favour of students making their own notes during a lecture are varied. It is suggested, for example, that the very process of listening and recording by writing forms an important response to the stimuli presented by the lecturer, enabling new impressions to be fixed and assisting assimilation. Note-taking is the student's own work and, it is argued, represents a degree of active participation in an otherwise passive instructional process. Further, it helps to overcome the limitations of the short-term memory (see Chapter 11), thereby assisting (so the claim runs) revision, long-term retention and recall. (It is interesting to note that Hare found that those note-takers who expressed more ideas in fewer words tended to retain the information better than those who summarised the topics of the lecture in greater detail.)

Difficulties in note-taking, however, abound. Some students are quite unable to write swiftly; others may be unable to discriminate so that they fail to note an important point made by the lecturer; some may have difficulty in concentrating simultaneously on listening and writing. (The many distractions of the lecture room often do not help.) *The lecturer should not take for granted the ability of his audience to make notes.* For many in the audience it may be a new experience. A few lessons on the technique of note-taking would, therefore, be advantageous for most further education classes. They could include advice and practice relating to the construction and numbering of paragraphs, sections, subsections and cross-headings and to ways of giving emphasis to laws, definitions, formulae, by spacing, underlining, etc. For practice purposes a taped lecture can be played to the class, with prepared transparencies projected on a screen, indicating the points which ought to be noted in writing, and how they ought to be recorded. It assists students to be told by the lecturer of his cues which introduce matter that *must* be noted, e.g. 'Note carefully . . .'; 'A vital point is . . .' Students must also be shown *how to use* their notes, i.e. how to expand them (and how to space them for this purpose) and how to use them for pre-examination revision.

The lecturer should ensure that the environment and his style of delivery allow notes to be taken. The furniture of the lecture room should include note-book rests; illumination which has been dimmed to allow the showing of a slide must be increased so that students can see their notes. Short pauses during the lecture (which can be timed so as to coincide with divisions in the subject matter) are of great assistance to the note writer.

The dictation of detailed notes is generally a misuse of lecture time. The practice (fortunately rare) of dictating notes of a lecture in its entirety has been categorised as 'a passage of information from the lecturer's notes to the audience's notebooks without a sojourn in the mind of either!' The writing of the *main headings* of the lecture on a chalkboard or overhead projector transparency may help in the taking of notes and may provide a useful summary of the lecture which can be used for recapitulation and revision.

It is the practice of many lecturers to dictate short statements of principles, theories and definitions. Principles and statements of theories may constitute the essence of lectures and care has to be taken in their communication to an audience. Dictation may help to ensure that vital matter is noted correctly. Definitions can be stated in measured tones, allowing students to note them exactly, and can be repeated at intervals (perhaps by use of the overhead projector). Koestler's paraphrase of Goethe is relevant: 'When the mind is at sea, a clear definition can provide a raft!' (Teachers with a taste for philosophical disputation may be interested in Popper's refutation of the value of definitions, which leads him to the conclusion that: 'All definitions can be omitted without loss to the information imparted . . . In science, all the terms that are really needed must be undefined terms.')

Some lecturers, recognising the real difficulties of note-taking, prefer to distribute their own 'handouts', claiming that the advantage of 'participation by writing' is outweighed by the students possessing an authentic record of the lecture content. Handouts may list lecture objectives, suggest reading, give appropriate references, outline the body of the lecture in précis form and draw attention to difficult points. (Lecturers who prefer not to use handouts have claimed that their distribution prevents a lecturer changing his approach where he feels that a point has not been understood—the handout, they argue, fetters the lecturer to a prearranged, unalterable, plan.) The handouts can be distributed well in advance of the lecture, allowing for the checking of references for preliminary reading and the consideration of problems likely to emerge, or they can be given out (as is usually the case) at the point in the lecture when a final recapitulation is about to be made, or when the lecture has ended.

Structured notes which are given to the audience at the beginning of
the lecture consist of its main points stated incompletely, so that
students must listen very carefully in order to complete them. A completed version may be shown for purposes of checking and
recapitulation in the last few minutes of the lecture. An example used
in a lecture on the functions of money is given in Figure 17.2.

```
┌─────────────────────────────────────────────────────────────┐
│   1. Difficulties of barter were:   (a) ..........................  │
│                                     (b) ..........................  │
│   2. The use of money overcame                                 │
│      these difficulties by:         (a) ..........................  │
│                                     (b) ..........................  │
│                                     (c) ..........................  │
│   3. Money is, in fact, any                                    │
│      commodity which acts by                                   │
│      common consent as:             (a) ..........................  │
│                                     (b) ..........................  │
│                                     (c) ..........................  │
│                                     (d) ..........................  │
└─────────────────────────────────────────────────────────────┘
```

Figure 17.2

The lecture in further education

In spite of the weaknesses of the lecture as a mode of instruction and
of its general unsuitability for the teaching of skills, it continues to be
employed, often with great success, in the colleges of further education. Its advantages ought not to be forgotten; some were enumerated
in the *Hale Report on University Training Methods* (1964). They apply,
also, to the further education sector.

1. Students who are immature learn more readily when they listen
    than when they read.
2. The lecture is of particular value in introducing a subject.
3. The lecture is valuable where knowledge is advancing rapidly and
    up-to-date textbooks are not available. (The 'updating lecture', in
    which current developments are collated, summarised and
    explained, is of great assistance to students in areas such as eco-
    nomics, law, commerce and public administration. The lecture
    has been called 'the newspaper of teaching'; it must be kept
    up-to-date.)

4. The lecture can awaken critical skills in a student.
5. The lecture can provide aesthetic pleasure.
6. The lecture is economic of staff time, can cover more ground than a tutorial or seminar and can reach large numbers of students.

Course content delivered entirely by lectures is rare in the colleges of further education. Courses which include lectures combined with other modes of instruction are common. Thus, lectures may be used to begin a course, to provide a final recapitulation and revision, or in combination with seminars and tutorials. They also figure prominently in some types of team teaching (see Chapter 19).

Carefully prepared, well-timed and skilfully delivered with 'a touch of colour, a hint of wonder', the lecture can be a powerful and stimulating mode of communication and instruction.

18

Modes of instruction (4)— the discussion group; the seminar; the tutorial; the case study

> Though all the winds of doctrine were let loose to play upon the earth, so Truth be in the field, we do injuriously by licensing and prohibiting to misdoubt her strength and let her and Falsehood grapple; who ever knew Truth put to the worse, in a free and open encounter (Milton).

The lesson and the lecture, which were discussed in previous chapters, differ radically from the discussion group, the seminar, the tutorial and the case study, which are outlined below. The former are largely teacher-centred ('autocratic') modes of instruction; the latter are based on student-centred strategies of instruction, directed at facilitating learning within an environment in which *the teacher plays a mediating role and active class participation is the norm.* The former generally depend for their success, in large measure, on the teacher's 'solo performance'; the latter achieve success only from the continuing *collective activity* of teacher and class.

The essence and value of the discussion group

A discussion group is constituted by a class which *seeks to examine a matter by means of the free flow of argument.* Essentially, the members pool knowledge and ideas in the co-operative task of endeavouring to understand a problem by learning from one another. The discussion group is free from the relative formality of the seminar and the rigid rules of debate. Its freedom, however, necessitates careful preparation and control by the tutor if the benefits of discussion as a mode of instruction are to be realised in full.

The *purpose* of a discussion group is usually the collective exploration and 'public evaluation' of ideas. ('There must be discussion to show how experience is to be interpreted . . . Very few facts are able to tell their own story without comments to bring out the meaning' (J.S. Mill).) Two important points should be stressed; first, the discussion must have a clear *objective;* second, *prerequisite knowledge* of the elements of the topic to be discussed should be considered in the preparation of the group session.

Necessity for a clear objective

The discussion group ought not to be viewed as a stop-gap. It must be an *integral part* of the teaching programme, and ought to be accepted by students as such. It may be employed, therefore, when the tutor, in preparing his course work scheme, poses the question: 'Is there a stage in the course when interest and understanding are likely to be stimulated and when the generalisation of learned principles is likely to be aided by a collective class exchange of opinions?' and a positive answer emerges. The discussion group might then find a place in his course scheme with an appropriate, carefully-chosen objective. It might serve as a follow-up to a lecture, as a mid-course examination of ideas or as a recapitulation session.

Prerequisite knowledge

Unless there is in the group prerequisite knowledge of the topic under discussion, there can be no effective participation and the result is likely to be little more than a ritual exchange of loose thinking ('prejudices, platitudes, preconceptions and vague generalities') or of those 'irrationally held truths which may be more harmful than reasoned errors' (Huxley).

The disadvantages of the discussion group may be summarised briefly. Unless the topic is carefully chosen and the session carefully structured and controlled, there is—it is suggested—a marked tendency for the discussion to degenerate into an informal debate from which a dominant hierarchy of 'star speakers' emerges. A 'pecking order' of participants soon forms, so that the more forceful members hold the floor, while a significant proportion of the group, increasingly hesitant and unwilling to risk public contradiction, become silent observers—a negation of the very purpose of the exercise. Because groups can be easily dominated, false conclusions, presented in a facile, persuasive manner by a leader on whom the group has become over-dependent, may be accepted all too easily. A tendency for a discussion group to deteriorate into a forum for the exchange of prejudices, so that it resembles 'an athletic contest of closed mind with closed mind', is an ever-present danger. Finally, the real cost of the small discussion group makes it something of a luxury in the schemes of cost-conscious college administrators!

The advantages of the discussion group emerge, largely, from its 'democratic', permissive, collaborative nature (as contrasted with the 'autocratic' character of the lesson and the lecture). Group experience, it has been suggested, assists 'social facilitation', i.e. people tend to work more intensely when in a group. Group judgements may often be more accurate than those resulting from an individual examination of problems and membership of a group might benefit those whose thoughts can be clarified by discussion with others. Further, the conflict and disagreement which emerge in any lively discussion group may become the starting-point for new exploration, resulting in the group's increased tolerance of varying points of view—and acceptance of Wilde's dictum that 'truth is rarely pure and never simple!' Group discussion also enables a class and teacher to get to know one another's thoughts, opinions and attitudes. It provides for the teacher a useful element of feedback where the discussion has centred on the content of previous lessons.

Abercrombie reported an interesting experiment in the use of the free discussion method (Abercrombie 1960). The experiment grew out of the belief that in receiving information from a 'stimulus pattern', our selection from that information depends on our making judgements which are unconsciously influenced by many factors. More valid judgements might be made if we were conscious of those factors. Our judgement can be improved as the result of a *free group discussion* in which alternative judgements of the 'stimulus pattern' are explored and evaluated.

Preparing the discussion

The first stage in considering the mounting of a discussion group session necessitates the tutor's being quite sure as to *why* he has selected this mode of instruction. Has the course reached a stage where collective examination of a problem is essential? Can the objective which he has in mind be attained by any other form of instruction? To approach the discussion group method merely as a break in the routine of lessons or as a substitute for some other type of instruction is to weaken its chances of success. Next, the *aim* of the discussion must be clear. This is not to suggest that the discussion must be so planned and manipulated that it will reach a particular, desirable conclusion! 'Aim' implies the discussion having as its objective a reasonable examination of a specific topic.

Preparation demands that the group be active even before the discussion session. Reading lists containing suggested approaches to the discussion topic ought to be distributed and announced in advance of the date of discussion. ('When we meet in week's time we shall discuss the problem of . . . Here is a list of topics you might care to consider before that date. The college librarian has prepared a display of recent press cuttings dealing with the problem. At the end of the list you will find some statistics bearing on the matters we shall discuss.')

Boundaries, a general 'line of advance' and the overall pattern which the discussion might be expected to take should be considered by the tutor. Ought the session to begin with a short statement of the problem? By whom? Time must be allowed for swift summaries to be given. By whom? Visual material might be needed, so that basic data, maps, statistics can be presented. Is it available or does it require preparation?

Seating arrangements should be made so that the process of 'organised conversation', which typifies the good discussion group, is facilitated. Face-to-face interaction, enabling all members to communicate, is helpful. A circle of chairs, a U-shaped arrangement of tables and chairs, a chalkboard on which points can be noted and data displayed will require some rearrangement of the conventional classroom. (Abercrombie notes the importance of seating arrangements for a discussion session and comments on the significance of spatial arrangement and group behaviour during discussions.)

Controlling the discussion

The subtle art of discussion control depends largely upon the tutor's awareness of the *purpose* of the discussion method. He must ensure that all members feel free to contribute to the discussion. Members' participation should not be constrained by rigid rules, but an accepted framework of conduct is necessary if informality is not to result in mere cross-talk and gossip. (Discussion leaders learn quickly how to anticipate the side-winds which can blow a discussion totally off course.) Potentially dominant personalities must not be allowed to take over the discussion and the naturally reticent must be encouraged to contribute. Many points of view ought to find expression and the highly-unpopular, 'extremist' opinion ought not to be excluded. Three problems of control need to be solved by the teacher in his role of group leader: setting and keeping the discussion in motion; posing appropriate and stimulating questions as a part of the discussion; ending the session.

Setting and keeping the discussion in motion

Immediately the opening statement has been made, it becomes the task of the group leader to initiate and encourage the expression of varying points of view. Members ought to be invited to participate at an early stage (since the first few minutes of a discussion period can be the most difficult) with encouragement to the shy, perhaps in the form of a question (based on a common experience) which invites a direct response. The discussion ought to move around the circle of participants, briskly and pointedly. 'Wearing out' a theme, undue concentration on minor matters, ought to be politely restrained. Faulty reasoning and circular arguments ought not to remain uncorrected, 'hidden agendas' ought to be exposed, obscure statements ought to bring a request for their clarification and sweeping generalisations ought to be subjected to close examination. Interruptions, irrelevance and invective ought to elicit from the group leader a tactful rejoinder, which does not serve, however, to terminate the discussion! Occasional summaries of arguments and matters on which there is general agreement should be given and recorded on the chalkboard. The teacher must avoid, however, the type of overall control, or the too-obvious role of 'devil's advocate', which inhibits discussion because it leads the group to feel that it is being 'manipulated' so that a predetermined conclusion will result. Further, the teacher must not interpret a momentary silence as an invariable sign that discussion is flagging; it may indicate a pause for thought and may be a prelude to an improvement in the quality of the discussion.

Questioning as an aid to discussion

The discussion itself might well result from a single question, but the group leader ought to have available a number of prepared questions which can be used to provoke thought and comment, to move the discussion on to a higher level or in a new direction, or to return it to the group's general line of thought. Specific questions to individual members rather than 'overhead' questions to the group in general may serve to 'bring out' the naturally shy and prevent one or two members monopolising the session, or may be used to draw answers from members who have specialised knowledge.

Ending the discussion

Intermediate summing-up and recapitulation should occur at several stages of the discussion. The final summing-up should survey impartially the main points which have been made and should note significant areas of agreement and disagreement. It ought to link the essence of the discussion with previous lessons and should point forward to future class work in which the discussion will be seen to have played a preparatory role.

The seminar: its nature and use

The term 'seminar' is generally used in further education to refer to *a structured group discussion which may precede or follow a formal lecture or a series of lessons and which is introduced by the presentation of a thesis, often in the form of an essay.* Its specialist nature and its more formal setting differentiate it from the discussion group. Thus a course on industrial relations might include a discussion session on a topic such as, 'Can legislation assist the maintenance of industrial peace?'; a seminar on industrial law, for example, might engage in the systematic analysis of an essay presented by a seminar member on 'The history of the National Industrial Relations Court'. In general, the seminar appears to be appropriate as a mode of instruction only when the level of attainment of the group is relatively high *and* the subject matter lends itself to analytical treatment. In the colleges of further education it is often confined to advanced general and professional examination courses.

The main advantage of the seminar as a mode of instruction is its stimulation and testing of students' powers of comprehension and evaluation. The presenter of the thesis from which the seminar stems is tested, in particular, on his skill in arranging and formulating a sustained argument. The ability of a student to detect and separate principles from their context, to ponder their application and to question their relevance in certain situations, can be strengthened, it is claimed, by a critical examination of another's thoughts. A principal disadvantage of the seminar lies in the difficulties which can arise where presenter and class are unequally matched so that the group is reduced to the defensive posture of silence and non-participation.

Preparation and presentation of the seminar

The duration of the seminar must be considered by the tutor in his preparation. Often the subject matter requires discussion time ranging over several lesson periods. Seminars planned for one hour only may be of little value. Timetable rearrangement may present an initial problem.

Wherever possible, a summary of the paper to be presented ought to be made available to students two or three weeks in advance of the seminar. It should contain information under the following headings:

(a)   full title of the paper;
(b)   abstract of argument to be presented;
(c)   main headings and sub-headings of the argument;
(d)   sources; reading list; relevant statistics.

Where members have the opportunity to study a summary of the paper before it is presented, the probability of a total lack of response, which often indicates lack of preparation, is reduced. A feeling of being unequally matched with a specialist may be prevented by prior reading and consideration of a paper.

Where the presenter is a student for whom the planning and delivery of a paper are novel experiences, it should be the task of the teacher to explain and oversee its preparation and reduction to summary form. Where the presenter is a visitor to the college, the teacher has the responsibility of acquainting him with the purpose of the seminar and the level of its members. The importance of receiving the summary paper in advance of the seminar must be stressed.

The seminar timetable must be prepared and explained to the presenter. It ought to allow for the following events:

1.   introduction;
2.   presentation of the paper;
3.   discussion—part I;
4.   interim review;
5.   discussion—part II;
6.   summary of discussion (by tutor or member of class);

7. reply to discussion;
8. conclusion.

The preparation of visual aids for the presenter and planning of seating arrangements so that inter-communication is facilitated, are aspects of seminar organisation which should not be overlooked. The lecture environment, where the lecturer stands apart from his audience, is inappropriate for the seminar, which requires an environment in which the presenter's status as a member of the group is recognised.

The general principles of group discussion control (which were outlined on pp. 209–211 above) also apply to the seminar, with the important exception that the presenter is, of necessity, *primus inter pares*. Where the discussion results in criticism of his paper, he may be expected to claim—and ought to be allowed—adequate time for rebuttal, rejoinder and reply. Finally, the concluding section of the seminar should provide a link with the next section of the course scheme of work.

The essence of the tutorial

The tutorial is *a meeting between a teacher and a student, or a very small group of students, characterised by discussion and/or personal, face-to-face teaching, generally based on the content of an essay or other material written by the student(s) or on questions raised by the tutor or the student(s)*. It is a mode of tuition associated with the older English universities and requires a very generous staff–student ratio. Some few colleges of further education have been able to sustain a system of regularly-held tutorials for activities such as the following.

1. *Skills teaching groups*. Very small groups meet a tutor for the practice and refinement of psychomotor skills (see p. 102). Individual, face-to-face tuition has been found valuable in gymnastics coaching, the teaching of musical and acting skills and the practising of some machine production techniques.
2. *Remedial working groups*. In some colleges individual students are encouraged to discuss with a tutor problems arising from difficulties in classwork. Where tutorial periods are used for meetings of this nature, diagnostic and remedial work may be undertaken.
3. *Supervision tutorials*. In this type of tutorial meeting, student and tutor discuss some aspect of the student's work, often in the form of an essay which he is required to read and then to support in

argument with his tutor. This is the shape of the traditional tutorial and requires very careful preparation by tutor and student alike. Effectively prepared and handled, it can result in a heightening of student cognitive skills, in particular those involving analysis and judgement.

4. *Group discussion.* Following a formal lesson or lecture, a very small group of students will meet a tutor with whom they raise individual difficulties, problems of comprehension, etc. The tutor may choose to provide information supplementing or explaining that given in the lesson or lecture. The *shape* of the tutorial will be determined by students' queries; its *direction* must be in the tutor's hands.

Problems of the tutorial

Group size is all-important; Davies suggests 1–3 students. (He cites research pointing to a significant measure of correlation between size of instructional group and achievement.) Because the essential feature of the tutorial is a face-to-face teaching relationship, so-called tutorial groups of, say, 15–20 students are a contradiction in terms. Where a tutorial objective is the improvement of an essential motor technique or the heightening of critical skills, the tutor must insist, so far as is possible, on very small groups.

It is very easy indeed for time to be wasted during a tutorial. Lack of a clear objective, failure by tutor or students to prepare material, failure of a tutor to understand the nature of points raised by students or to comprehend the basis of their difficulties, will lead to little progress. Adequate preparation must be made the rule, so that the tutorial is neither viewed nor used as an opportunity to evade the rigours of the learning process. Where the tutorial involves a group, the tutor must ensure the involvement of all members in discussions; the general rules relating to discussions (see pp. 206–211) should be followed.

Tutorials are often criticised as 'too demanding' for students attending further education courses. The criticism misses the essence of the tutorial process. The real value of the tutorial is the intensity of tuition made possible by its very form. Its demanding nature is often its essential virtue. Properly planned and staffed, the tutorial should be capable of providing valuable assistance to college students at all levels.

The nature of the case study

The case study mode of instruction is based upon *the examination, analysis and diagnosis of a real or simulated problem so that general principles might emerge in a realistic fashion.* It is used in colleges of further education to intensify student understanding of the complex, real-world relationship embodied in law, economics, business studies, industrial affairs, social work, politics, etc. Designed originally as an aid to the study of decision-making in business, the case study is now utilised in the teaching of many of the disciplines which involve the identification and selection of a preferred course of action from possible alternatives in conditions of uncertainty. The aims of the case study may be summarised as: the creation of an active, participatory teaching/learning situation in which the subject matter closely mirrors the outside world; the improvement of the student's ability to identify underlying principles, to think swiftly under pressure and to apply his insight to the unravelling of a complex knot of relationships and events; the testing of the student's carry-over of his class learning to novel situations involving many constraints.

Three examples of the nature of case studies are given below in highly-summarised form to illustrate their use in further education courses.

An 'in-tray' exercise

Hospital administrators in training at a college of further education are presented with the contents of a typical, crowded in-tray. Their tasks are (a) to select, in thirty minutes, the items which they consider most important, to draft appropriate replies and initiate action, and (b) to justify their selection and course of action. The items of correspondence include letters of resignation from senior staff, complaints from union representatives, threats of action by former patients for alleged negligence, etc.

A 'situation' case study

Personnel managers attending a college short course are given a (simulated) letter of complaint from a retail store's graduate manager-trainees, expressing dissatisfaction with their training and career prospects. The group members are allowed a short time in which to identify the real nature of the complaint, to call for background data and to outline an immediate course of action.

The 'exercise' case study

Financial controllers responsible for very large trading accounts are asked to make a contingency plan involving a 25 per cent reduction in trading revenue. Quantitative analysis is required and a computer terminal link is made available in order to provide a simulation of the effects of decisions taken.

The case study may be used, therefore, to put flesh on the bones of theory and to emphasise to students the real costs (in terms of finance, human relations, goodwill) of decisions taken under stress. It is useful, too, in demonstrating to students, on the basis of an analysis of their errors, the dark areas of real situations which can often be lit only dimly and fitfully by the rays of untested theory! (The words of the editor of the *Harvard Business Review* (July 1981) are of relevance here: 'For the most part, only trivial management problems are neatly structured and quantifiable. All modelling and quantitative analysis directed at a decision are only preludes to subjective judgement. Vision then must transcend technique.')

Types of case study

Examples of the more widely-used types of case study, some of which may be presented by video tape, are enumerated below.

1. *The 'critical incident' study.* The penultimate event in a chain of incidents leading, say, to an industrial strike, is described. Students must decide on the additional data required in order to obtain a full picture of the circumstances. This can be a difficult exercise in analysis and comprehension.
2. *The 'next stage' study.* A case is unfolded, stage by stage. Students must suggest what is 'likely to happen next'. The exercise usually calls for a high order of ability in analysis and synthesis.
3. *The 'live case' study.* The situation presented to students leads to their being asked directly: 'What ought to be done next?' The problem, which may be based on a well-publicised event, such as a breakdown in wage negotiations in a nationalised industry, tests not only knowledge of the factual background of the situation but

the ability to think swiftly and to analyse correctly under conditions of stress.

4. *The 'business game' study.* This involves the presentation of a quantitative problem (e.g. pricing, stock control, wage bargaining, population movements). Students compete to arrive at the 'optimum solution', which may be judged in relation to a computer's solution.

5. *The 'major issue' study.* Students are given a mass of data—much of which is irrelevant to the main issue—and are asked to identify and separate that issue and to suggest remedies for the situation which is revealed.

6. *The 'role-play' case study.* On the basis of an incident which is reported to them, students are required to act out (in an improvised style) the roles of the central participants, e.g. industrial relations officer, shop steward, union official, managing director. This technique has been used with success in courses which include training in collective bargaining, arbitration, etc.

7. *The 'in-tray' exercise* (see above).

8. *The 'situation' case study* (see above).

9. *The 'exercise' case study* (see above).

Writing and controlling the case study exercise

The writing of case studies is a specialised task which may be carried out best by the course tutor using real-life material (obtained from firms and institutions with their knowledge as to its intended use and suitably disguised by the use of fictitious names and addresses). The case study should be so arranged as to call for the identification of major and minor problems and the preparation of solutions with an awareness of difficulties in their implementation. The content must be appropriate to the students' level of experience and background.

The case study material will include all the important elements of the situation to be analysed. The relevant background must be sketched in, e.g. the firm's policies, size of markets, size of labour and entrepreneurial force, etc. Appendixes setting out statistical information ought to be supplied. The material ought to be distributed to the group in advance of the study session, together with an explanation of what principle is being investigated and why, and the method of investigation which is to be adopted.

The case study session may necessitate the division of the group into syndicates, each with its secretary, chairman and reporter (who will present the syndicate's findings to the groups in the final session). The class tutor moves among the syndicates noting difficulties, providing additional information when it is requested and chairing the final session. In that session, syndicate solutions must be stated, justified by reference to principle and practice, and criticised. Where the study is based on a real situation which can be discussed without breach of confidence, an explanation and consideration of 'what really happened' can be given during a later lesson; follow-up is vital in these cases.

Advantages and disadvantages of the case study method of instruction

The case study as a mode of instruction now has a firm place in the instructional schemes of many colleges. Its links with reality are welcomed as an aid in removing the artificial barriers of the classroom situation. Its severe demands on a student's powers of analysis, synthesis and general reasoning can be balanced by the high level of interest which is sustained by his knowledge of grappling with a 'live' problem, rather than an arid, theoretical situation. The sensitive use of case studies is said to improve students' skills in the detection and rejection of irrelevance, in the consideration of the possible results of a decision and in the evaluation of alternative procedures. Case studies also accustom students to working in groups—a useful preparation for the real world of industry and commerce.

Disadvantages are said to turn on the difficulties attached to the preparation and writing of the studies. The background research, collection and interpretation of data call for much more time than is often available to the college lecturer.

In general, however, the growing bank of outline case studies in textbook form on which hard-pressed lecturers may draw should serve to assist those tutors who feel that class participation in the solution of problems drawn from the real world of industry, administration and politics has an educational value in itself.

19

Modes of instruction (5) — team teaching

> It is as important to think about the quality of teaching or the quality of the learning situations provided . . . as it is about organisation. Many of the benefits of team teaching have been lost at times because of the failure to consider this point. Individual teacher competence is the keystone of team teaching as of any other form of teaching (Lovell 1967).

The notion of an individual teacher controlling the progress of a lesson is at the heart of much current teaching practice. The concept of a sole, dominant figure accepting direct responsibility for the planning, execution and assessment of a lesson has been questioned, however, by the theory and practice of team teaching. The claims made for this practice are wide, ranging from the assertion that it makes teaching more effective, to the declaration that the teaching team is the most appropriate instructional organisation for the classrooms of a democratic society, in which co-operation at all levels and in many social activities is a worthy aim in itself. An important basic assumption made by some advocates of team teaching is that where teachers focus their collective attention on an instructional problem, the solutions at which they arrive will probably be superior to those presented by the same teachers considering the problem in isolation. Put quite simply: two heads are often better than one!

The background

The idea of team teaching seems to have originated in the USA, with the publication in 1957 of Dr J. Lloyd Trump's *Images of the Future,* written on behalf of the Commission on the Experimental Study of the Utilisation of Staff in the Secondary School. One of the conclusions drawn by Dr Trump was that the school of the future would be organised around a range of activities involving large and small groups

219

and individual instruction. Team teaching would be essential for the effective organisation of such activities and would necessitate arrangements whereby *groups of teachers* and their technical assistants would utilise their skills in planning for, and instructing in, a given subject area, involving groups of students *equivalent in size to two or more conventional classes.* Such teaching would cover groups of students organised in a variety of ways.

The basic reasoning behind Dr Trump's suggestions is not always accepted in this country, and his image of the future of American education and the appropriate institutions may not commend itself to all European teachers. Nevertheless, some of the potentialities and structures of teaching teams at which he hinted have been explored in this country, so that there now exists considerable experience of the technique in our schools and colleges.

Essential features of team teaching

Team teaching may be said to operate where *two or more teachers co-operate, deliberately and methodically, in the planning, presentation and evaluation of the teaching process.* In effect, individual teachers sacrifice some of their autonomy, pool their resources and—a vital feature of team teaching—accept joint responsibility for the teaching of groups of students.

The practice of team teaching does not necessitate a uniform teaching structure and in this country a variety of patterns has evolved. Small groups acting under a leader (perhaps a subject specialist or senior departmental member) typify a common form of structure. Large groups—entire departments—co-ordinated in their activities by a departmental head or senior lecturer exemplify another type. A group might grow spontaneously, with a loosely-knit team collaborating to deal with specific, related parts of the curriculum. Another group might be a highly-organised, centrally-directed unit, working to a planned timetable. In general, the structure of the teaching team will tend to reflect departmental objectives, strategies, and the availability of resources. Invariably, it will be based on a collective approach to the teaching situation.

A variety of student groupings may be utilised. Lectures to the entire student group, lessons, group discussions involving smaller units, and directed private study will feature in the team's programme. (Joyner suggests that the very success of team teaching reflects directly the team's ability to organise the group activity component of the teaching scheme (Joyner 1977).) The groupings to be adopted will depend on the team's responses to the questions which are posed later in this chapter under the heading 'The planning and implementation of team teaching'.

Joint responsibility for the teaching of groups, appropriate team structure and student groupings are among the most important features of team teaching, but their presence in a team plan will not necessarily guarantee its success. Of vital importance is *the team's conscious unity of purpose.* No matter how well-organised the team or how abundant the resources and teaching aids, the chances of the team's success will depend directly on the real co-operation of its members.

Behind the theory of team teaching is the assumption that teachers working together in a co-ordinated manner can produce an overall improvement in performance and that the utilisation of experts working in their specialist areas will result in a more effective employment of resources (an important advantage of the division of labour in almost any area of creative activity).

'Co-ordination' is much more than the 'working together' which characterises a college section or department in its daily activities. It involves a set of declared objectives, a common approach resulting from an examination of those objectives, an allocation of teaching tasks based on a team discussion and continuous, collective appraisal of the results of teaching.

The real value of the discussions on team teaching might be found, however, in the challenge it presents to some of the unstated assumptions which often underpin the 'traditional' approach. ('It is one of the canons of national education that a teacher is not only master in his own class but that it is understood that he will perform his function unmonitored, unwitnessed even, by a single other colleague' (Van der Eyken 1974).) The belief that the size of a learning group ought to remain unchanged no matter what the form of the teaching activity may stem from exigencies of timetable planning rather than from consideration of the conditions for successful learning. Why should class numbers of twenty be considered effective for science, engineering practice and geography? Team teaching, with its emphasis on varying sizes of groups depending on the specific educational objectives to be attained, questions this rigid approach. Why is the timetable divided into apparently immutable periods of, say, fifty minutes, or one hour? Ought the duration of the instructional period to be the same in all cases, no matter what the task? The team-teaching concept, with its varying lesson and study periods, calls into question the fixed 'slots' in the timetable. Is the typical classroom design found in many colleges of further education really appropriate to a discussion session, a large group lecture, individual study or group project? Team teaching, which makes use of many modes of instructional techniques, draws attention also to the need for experimentation in the design and furnishing of 'learning spaces'.

Structure of a teaching team

A simple team structure may be illustrated by the line chart in Figure 19.1.

In this case a small teaching team is administered by a leader who has clerical and technical assistance—vital if the team is to function adequately.

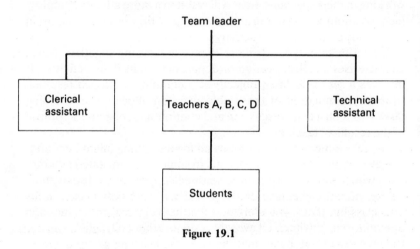

Figure 19.1

A larger operation involving the use of several teams, administered and co-ordinated by a leader, is illustrated in Figure 19.2.

The first structure (shown above) is appropriate, say, for a small team within a department; its leader may be a senior lecturer. The second structure might emerge in a department wholly committed to the team-teaching principle, with perhaps the deputy head or a principal lecturer acting as co-ordinator of the three teams.

The team leader (or, as he is known in some colleges, 'the chairman') has the complex tasks of helping to plan the team's strategy, supervising its operation, controlling clerical and technical assistants, chairing assessment discussions and participating as a teacher in the

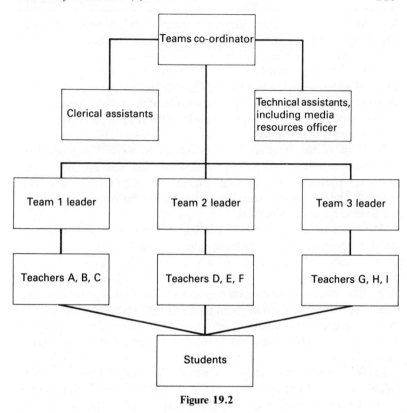

Figure 19.2

team's work. Additionally, he may have the responsibility of supervising the allocation of teaching space and audio-visual aids and of
ensuring that the team's work fits in with the general plans of a wider
section or department. In short, his functions resemble those of a
'player-manager'.

The planning and implementation of team teaching

Team teaching can be introduced into a conventional college environment as the result of a decision 'from the top', such as a resolution of
the academic board or the departmental board of studies. Often,
however, it appears to have emerged as the result of a feeling at staff
level that existing teaching patterns required revision. In some
colleges the move towards team teaching has begun with the holding
of a seminar on the topic, or the showing of a film which illustrates a

team in action. The preparatory work which then follows may include the study of reports from existing teams and an intensive discussion on the practical problems likely to arise in college.

The next stage involves the selection of an appropriate area (according to course, subject and syllabus) for the first trial. A team is then selected, having as its first task a study of the syllabus. A series of weekly meetings is planned, during which the results of the study will be reported and discussed.

Sections of the syllabus are then allocated to and examined by specialist members. Appropriate general and specific objectives couched, perhaps, in behavioural terms (see Chapter 8), are considered. The team then meets under its leader/chairman to decide on the final version of objectives.

The stage which follows is of particular importance and is characteristic of team teaching. The team's agreed objectives are used so as to pose a series of questions: 'Which of the objectives can best be attained by a large-group presentation?' 'Which by smaller groups?' 'Which by students working on their own?' The first type of objective may necessitate instruction given to the group as a whole; the second may involve lessons and discussion; the third calls for directed private study. *The team then maps out its modes of instruction on the basis of its objectives.*

Large-group instruction, perhaps in the form of a lecture, or a film followed by a lecture, may be used for the 'lead lesson', i.e. the general introduction to the course of study. It may be used, also, to end the course in the form of a 'coda', in which themes are recapitulated and the threads of discussions and lessons drawn together. Large-group instruction requires the careful preparation which should characterise a lecture (see Chapter 17) and may involve the use of a variety of audio-visual aids. Key-notes or summaries are usually distributed after instruction of this nature.

Small-group discussion and instruction is likely to follow on from the 'lead lesson'. Separate groups may examine the basis of the lesson in detail, work on individual projects and hear and discuss a number of specialist views on the course topic.

Directed private study may be interspersed throughout the course. Students may be directed by team members to read around a topic and to use the resources of the college library. Since the study is directed (and is, therefore, the responsibility of team members) it requires the careful allocation of library space and other facilities. It necessitates, also, assessment by team members of the results of private study. (The importance of furthering students' learning skills (see Chapter 13) often emerges clearly in a team-teaching programme.)

Plans for the patterns of team-teaching courses are numerous, but several tried and tested structures have emerged, some of which are mentioned below.

The 'thematic' approach

This involves one central theme which runs throughout the course, with relevant, linked topics. Thus, a team-teaching project (arranged for an advanced business studies group) on 'the location of industry' has as its central theme the specialisation of production in Yorkshire and Lancashire. The historian deals with the eighteenth- and nineteenth-century background. The economist/social scientist gives illustrated lectures on the theory of localisation and the impact on community life. The geographer (the third member of the team, and its leader) is responsible for directed private study, which involves two essays by each member of the group, selected from a list of geographical topics and related to the two counties.

The 'concentric' approach

The team arranges its syllabus of work so that, from a central thematic point, subjects 'radiate outwards'. Thus, a course on 'the legal structure of Britain' (planned by a team for the general studies component of an intermediate course) takes as its central starting point 'rights and duties' which (presented as the theme of two lectures) leads on to small-group instruction on topics such as rules of law, enforcing the law, making and changing the law, and directed private study on a chosen topic related to a current issue involving legal institutions and the public. Four team members direct the course as specialist tutors in law, social studies, history and constitutional studies.

The 'concurrently presented' thematic approach

Two or more linked themes are presented so that each member of the group is studying one theme in detail. The group meets as a whole on several occasions so that notes may be compared and links explored. A course on 'the history of scientific thought', for example, is planned by two science specialists and a historian around two central themes (the historian contributing to the study of both themes): 'the birth of modern science' and 'science and the growth of industry'. The students ('A' level science) produce a group project and individual essays. The team gives a lecture to the full group at the beginning and end of the course.

Team teaching in practice: two examples

The first example reflects the approach of a small team within a large department of general studies. The department was not formally committed in any way to team teaching; the impetus was provided by a group of five specialist tutors, three of whom had attended a course at a college of education on the theme of team teaching. With the support of the departmental head, meetings of the five were held for three hours each week over a period of two months and clerical assistance was provided for the tutor elected as team leader. The syllabus in economic history was studied and a decision was taken that the team would collectively teach that section of the introduction which was stated, baldly, as 'the Industrial Revolution, causes and results'. A list of behavioural objectives was drawn up, modified during three meetings and finally made the basis of a team-teaching scheme.

The 'lead lesson', delivered to a class of forty students, took the form of an introductory talk (thirty minutes) given by the team leader (an economist), explaining the nature of the course, the topics to be studied and the methods to be used. A second lecture took as its theme the historical context of the Industrial Revolution, which was illustrated by a film strip; notes were distributed at the end of the lecture. Members of the three small groups into which the class was divided were later given reading plans and lists of essay projects (to be made the basis of private study). Short reviews of the Industrial Revolution as seen by the economist, historian and geographer of the team were given to each of the groups. The entire group met together on four further occasions to hear a debate between two members of the team, to hear a taped BBC programme on the social results of the Industrial Revolution, to question the team members in a question and answer session and to hear the team leader conclude the course with a general recapitulation of its main themes.

A second example is of team teaching applied to a section of the economics syllabus dealing with problems of population. (This part of the course was also attended by engineering students.) Four specialists made up the team. Following agreement on objectives, the 'lead lesson' was given by the team chairman, in the form of a lecture entitled dramatically but pointedly: 'Was Malthus right?' The course was outlined by reference to notes distributed one week before the lecture. References to the doctrines of Malthus were illustrated by the use of charts and the overhead projector.

The second meeting consisted of small group discussions around points raised by the lecturer. The third meeting was used to view a video-tape programme on world population. Directed private study sessions involved work on the calculation of net reproduction rates, population forecasts and guided projects based on this material. Further large-scale instruction consisted of formal lectures by team members on food resources, desert reclamation and the work of the United Nations. The statistician member of the team led discussions in each of the small groups on some unexpected problems which arose in the interpretation of statistics. The final session consisted of each member of the team and selected students giving their specific answers to the problem posed at the first meeting. A written examination, set collectively by the team, followed one week later.

Advantages and disadvantages of team teaching

A well-co-ordinated team will attempt to use the pooled, specialist interests of its members in the best possible way—a considerable advantage of this mode of instruction. The idea of an instructional course being 'shared' among a number of specialists may be novel, but ought not to be rejected on that ground alone. There seems to be a distinct possibility, in such a situation, of members of the team learning from one another, of the widening of student horizons and the growth of a collective sense of purpose. Students may benefit from participation in a variety of teaching situations and exposure to several styles of tuition.

On the other hand, the demands on staff are said to be much heavier than those of the conventional teaching situation. (Apologists for team teaching do not deny this, but point in reply to the *raison d'être* of the technique—a more efficient mode of teaching, which, they claim, must inevitably involve greater effort.) The large student groups which meet for the lectures in team-teaching programmes are said to be difficult to control as units and, in any event, the lecture is often an ineffective mode of instruction. (Apologists will cite, in reply, the positive effects of the carefully-prepared and presented lecture.) The special arrangements of teaching space necessitated by the practice of team teaching are said to present many difficulties. (If the principle of the team be accepted, reply its supporters, few of these difficulties will prove insuperable.) The resources necessary for team teaching, it is contended, may be beyond the budgets of many colleges. (This, unhappily, may often be true but it does not weaken the case for the principle of team teaching.) It is claimed that team teaching can function efficiently only by the use of complex administrative techniques and this may result in the creation within the department of an *imperium in imperio*. (That this is an inevitable outcome may be questioned, given the experiences of teams which have functioned successfully without any radical alteration of departmental structure.)

Some reports suggest that problems have arisen in teaching teams because of interpersonal strains and general incompatibility of some members of staff. It has been suggested also that there are difficulties in bringing teachers to accept that, as part of teams, they no longer enjoy total autonomy in 'their' classrooms. Other reports hint at difficulties resulting from 'challenges' to team leaders as the course progresses; these problems have been exacerbated, it is suggested, where team leaders do not occupy appropriate positions of authority within the college hierarchy.

Team teaching is rarely advocated as a cure-all remedy. That there is room for experimentation in the organisation and deployment of teaching resources ought not to be denied. What is needed at this time, however, is more information on the *level of student attainment* in those colleges in this country in which teaching has been carried out by organised teams. Data of this nature would form a useful basis for the continuing discussions on methods of improving the efficiency of staffs in our colleges. What must be remembered, perhaps above all, is that, in Taylor's words, 'the most important resources for team teaching are sustained energy, insight and commitment on the part of the innovators.'

20

*Modes of instruction (6)—
programmed instruction;
computer-aided learning*

An educated work force learns how to exploit new technology, an ignorant one becomes its victim (Stonier 1981).

Advocates of programmed instruction, which made its appearance in Britain in the early 1960s, claim that the presentation of organised lesson material to the individual student in a prearranged sequence and at a pace determined by his responses can help in overcoming some of the deficiencies of instruction associated with conventional classroom teaching, the most serious of which is the lack of continuing feedback (see Chapter 7). Computer-aided learning is an attempt to provide effective instruction, utilising the seemingly-unlimited data-processing powers of the electronic computer in the classroom.

Skinner's theories and the linear programme

In 1954 Skinner published his seminal article, 'The science of learning and the art of teaching'. His earlier book, *Science and Human Behaviour,* and later articles on teaching machines completed the theoretical foundations of programmed instruction. Skinner applied his *reinforcement learning theory* (see Chapter 3) to the process of self-instruction. A learner's actions which are followed by rewards (i.e. which are reinforced) are likely to be repeated and learned; actions which are not followed by reinforcement will disappear from the learner's repertoire. *Behavioural patterns may, therefore, be shaped at the will of the instructor by use of a series of controlled stimuli.*

Crowder, a psychologist and statistician, writing in the late 1950s and early 1960s, suggested modifications of Skinner's process of self-instruction. He introduced alternative sequences into programmes, which would be related to the student's responses. His types of programme (which are outlined on pp. 232–233) are known as 'branching or intrinsic programmes'; Skinner's, as 'linear programmes'.

In sum, the theory of programmed instruction suggests that effective learning can result from the presentation to an individual student of a carefully-designed sequence of instructional material, eliciting responses which are reinforced in the direction of desired behavioural capabilities. A programme is, therefore, *an individual lesson, designed and presented as a sequence of relatively small units of information, which lead the student, step by step, to a level of behaviour predetermined by the programmer.*

Features of the linear programme were as follows:

(a) Material was arranged in very small, cumulative and coherent steps, so that the learner was not aware of any real difficulty in assimilation. ('The whole process of becoming competent in any field must be divided into a very large number of small steps, and reinforcement must be continuous upon the accomplishment of each step ... By making each successive step as small as possible, the frequency of reinforcement can be raised to a maximum, while the possibly aversive consequences of being wrong are reduced to a minimum' (Skinner).)

(b) The learner had to make a 'constructed response' in an overt manner to each question arising from the material.

(c) To help the learner in his responses, the material included 'cues and responses' which guided him.

(d) Immediately the response was made, the learner was informed that he was right or wrong. The learner acts as his own 'response comparator'.

(e) The programme was constructed so that a correct response would be given at least nine times out of ten. This produced satisfaction ('reinforcement') and continuous progress was made more certain.

(f) In the case of an incorrect response, the learner noted his error and moved on to the next unit of information.

A schematic representation of a typical linear programme is given in Figure 20.1.

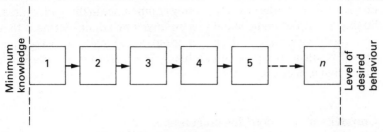

Figure 20.1

The diagram outlines the *strategy* of the lesson, i.e. the overall steps to be taken so as to achieve the lesson's objective, which is a movement from the learner's state of minimum knowledge (in relation to what is to be learned) to the level of behaviour considered by the teacher/ programmer to be desirable *at that stage of the learner's development.* Small units of information (represented by the numbered squares) are presented to the learner, who constructs his responses. His response to unit 1 is assessed and that assessment is presented to him before he responds to the stimulus of unit 2. His correct response to the *n*th unit is evidence of his having mastered the sequence.

Construction of a linear-type programme

The programmer must first *analyse the area of the subject matter* which is to be programmed. What are its boundaries? Its difficulties? Its unusual features? Does its successful teaching necessitate a particular approach? Does it involve an explanation and illustration of technical terms? (These are, of course, among the very questions which must also be posed and answered in the preparation stages of a conventional lesson.) Secondly, the precise nature of the *target population,* i.e. the students for whom the programme is to be designed, must be delineated. In this context, what relevant behaviour will be *available* at the start of the programme? What relevant behaviour is *necessary* in order to enter the programme? Thirdly, the *criterion behaviour* which should result at the end of the programme should be set out clearly in behavioural terms (see Chapter 8). Fourthly, the *sequence* of the programme and its constituent *frames* (i.e., separate items of information) must be structured in a coherent manner. Fifthly, the *terminal test* must be constructed; this ought to elicit from a student who has worked through the programme the level of behaviour which the programmer considers as constituting competence in the subject area. Sixthly, the programme should be *validated* by administering it to a representative sample of the target population. Finally, the validation should result in the programme being *re-written and re-structured,* where that is necessary.

Crowder and the branching programme

Crowder's type of programme is constructed so as to utilise the learner's responses in the determination of content and actual presentation of the material. In contrast to the linear programmer he uses multiple-choice questions (see Chapter 23). Programmes built on this basis test the learner's understanding of the materials he has studied, and allow the presentation of remedial material where incorrect responses are made.

The branching programme begins with a frame which usually contains much more information than that presented in a linear-type step. The information is followed by a multiple-choice question. A correct response results in the learner's being informed that he is correct (and why), and in the presentation of a new unit of information. An incorrect response results in the learner's being informed that he is wrong (and of the nature of his error). He may be instructed to return to the original frame, so as to 'try again', or he may be moved on to a 'remedial subsequence'. It will be apparent that *the amount of material with which the student is presented will be determined by the number of errors he makes.*

A schematic representation of a branching programme is given in Figure 20.2.

The strategy of the programme is to move the student's level of behaviour from that represented by his attainment at the beginning of the programme, through that represented by frame 4, to the level decided by his teacher as being appropriate in the circumstances. The diagram illustrates the tactical modification of the strategy which may be necessary. A student who is entirely successful moves from frame 1 to frames 2, 3, and 4. Assume that a student makes an error on frame 2. He will be directed to a remedial frame (2(i) or 2(ii), depending on the nature of the error) and will be told that he is wrong and why he is wrong. He is then directed to return to frame 2, so as to try again. Assume that he makes a mistake on frame 3. The remedial sequence (3(i), (ii), (iii)) provides further material and allows him to move on to frame 4 immediately his error is corrected. His response to the '*n*th'

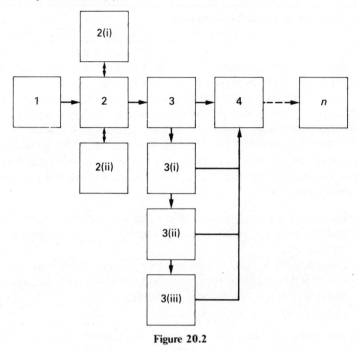

Figure 20.2

unit of information, if correct, indicates that he has mastered the material in the programme.

Construction of a branching programme

The initial stages of preparing a branching programme resemble those involved in the linear programme. Subject matter must be analysed, concepts stated and their relationships explored. The presentation technique of the branching programme, however, differs radically from that of the linear programme in the following ways:

1. A branching frame usually contains more material than that in a linear frame. It may consist of one, two, or three short paragraphs.
2. The student responds to the material by choosing *one* of several alternative answers, which appears to him to be correct.
3. The frame to which he is then directed depends on the answer he has selected. Consequently, he does not move straight through the programme, as in a linear sequence.

The use of programmed instruction

The claim of the programmers is that if a subject can be taught, it can be programmed. There is, therefore, according to this claim, no limit to the areas in which programmed instruction can be effective. It has been applied with some success to subjects as widely separated as statistics, psychology, logic, economics, operational research and computer programming. Early suspicions that its techniques were appropriate only to primary school subjects have proved groundless.

Programmed instruction seems to have been effective in the following situations:

1. The learning of a *technique* which, by its very nature, may be broken down into small steps, e.g. some processes in automobile engineering.
2. The study of a subject in which there is a *hierarchy of facts,* which lends itself to symbolic representation, e.g. symbolic logic, operational research, mathematical economics.
3. The *revision* of the outlines of a scheme of work.

In workshop instructional situations a programme which is related to psychomotor objectives (e.g. the handling of a tool) can be valuable, particularly because it allows the student to learn at his own pace. Similar situations, e.g. the stripping and reassembling of a typewriter, have provided useful opportunities for the exercise of the programmer's skill.

Criticism of programmed instruction

Fundamental criticism continues to be levelled, in particular, at the views of Skinner as they relate to the foundations of programming. Human behaviour is too complex, it is argued, to be described only in terms of his conditioning model. Further, it has been stressed that the model on which the theory of programmed instruction is based does not allow for the high probability of there being different *kinds* of learning which follow different laws. Nor has it been established beyond doubt that confirmation of a learner's correct responses is always a reinforcement, or that learning cannot proceed successfully without reinforcement.

The nature and organisation of linear programmes have also been under sustained attack. They have been held to lead, inevitably, to loss of interest and boredom because of their repetitious, small steps. In particular, their use at the higher levels of learning tends, it has been claimed, to induce a 'pall effect' which rapidly weakens meaningful assimilation. The inflexibility and restricted nature of programmes both linear and branching, fail, it is argued, to make allowances for individual differences in student attitudes and motivation.

The concept of the Socratic dialogue ('one to one') as the prototype of the successful lesson—often suggested as an advantage of programmes—is rejected by many teachers who point to the solitary nature of programmed instruction as its major defect. The excitement and stimulation of working in a group, the social importance of assisting, and being assisted by, others, in the common pursuit of knowledge, become unattainable in the programmed lesson.

In a recent survey of experiments in programmed instruction, Talyzina criticises the influence of Skinner on the principles of programming. His linear programme ignores the cognitive activities of the learner so that the probability of acquiring rational forms of 'thinking activity' is low. Nor does the linear programme require any application of already-developed rational activities. The size of instruction steps seems rarely to correspond to steps in knowledge acquisition; indeed, experiments seem to show that the best results in instruction were obtained where learners were left to regulate the size of steps. The linear programme confuses the reinforcement of responses and their confirmation, and experiments have suggested that substantial delays in reinforcement do not reduce the effectiveness of instruction. Further, the repetition of material, typical of Skinner's programmes, does not appear to yield any positive effects in instruction.

Programmed instruction remains a component feature of some few schemes in colleges of further education; its impact on industrial training has been more pronounced. It continues to provide a useful vantage point for the observation and analysis of some aspects of instruction. Some of its techniques, in particular the presentation of information in carefully-constructed, sequential steps, are of value in the development of computer-aided learning, which is considered below.

Computer-aided learning: a new technology of instruction

Computer-aided learning (CAL) refers to situations in which a computer system is used in the process of instructing students. Its introduction to colleges of further education is the direct result of three interrelated factors: the growth in the use of computers in industry and commerce, reflected in an increased demand for college-based computer courses, recent developments in computing techniques, and the vast expansion in the microelectronics field, leading to a steep fall in the price of components and the availability of relatively cheap, sophisticated computer systems.

It is important for college teachers to realise that the microcomputer, upon which CAL is based, is neither a mere automated 'page turner', nor an improved version of the teaching machines of the 1960s. It is a device which is capable of eliciting and assessing student responses to programs of instruction and of evaluating overall learning performance at prodigious speed. A typical CAL sequence might be as follows.

1. The computer presents a unit of information to the student.
2. The computer then presents a test question and waits for the student's response to be fed in by him through the keyboard.
3. The computer scans the student's textual response and categorises it as correct or incorrect on the basis of predetermined key words identified within it.
4. Where the student's response matches or approximates to anticipated incorrect answers, the computer offers corrective hints; where it does not recognise the answer it will offer general hints and/or call for a revised answer.

In total contrast to the limited, often highly-predictable, range of questions and answers provided by teaching machines, the microcomputer is able to draw on an extensive range of material from programs which can contain elements of randomness.

CAL can be used as part of an integrated instructional process. It is able to demonstrate, in very effective fashion, a variety of processes, it can be used for guided or free investigation, and it can present tutorial and coaching programs. Demonstrations and simulations of events, some of which, in reality, may be expensive, dangerous or impossible to carry out in college laboratories, can be presented and repeated as often as required. 'Guided investigation' enables the student to work through a programmed sequence, allowing him, however, to explore any 'side-issues' raised by the program. 'Free investigation' gives the student the choice of a variety of alternative paths for exploration of a topic, allowing the examination of different environments. Various modes of presentation of information—pictorial, graphical, verbal—can be linked with audio tapes into a CAL sequence.

The use of models of real-world situations, and simulations, can be extremely effective when presented in CAL. Models (the characterisation of processes and concepts in mathematical terms) and simulations (the effect of interventions on the operations of a system) have been used in CAL, for example, in the areas of company finance (to show the effects of changes in interest rates), biology (to demonstrate the results of pollution on ecosystems) and industrial management (to trace the effects on a control system of positive and negative feedback). The employment of algorithms (step-by-step procedures intended to yield optimum solutions to problems) and heuristics (exploratory methods of problem-solving) can be demonstrated very effectively by CAL programs.

Information retrieval, allowing data to be 'called up' by a student and presented within a few seconds of request is an important aspect of CAL. The technology of information retrieval has been available for some years, but the vast task of preparing and storing information in appropriate form is a never-ending process.

The evaluation of student learning has been undertaken successfully with the assistance of microcomputers. The banking of test questions, the random retrieval of past questions, the preparation of some types of objective test—all are possible with existing computer programs. The computerised recording and assessment of students' answers and the evaluation of performance in relation to previous marks and average class attainment levels, are now practised in a number of colleges.

Computer-managed learning

CAL has been extended so as to *guide* the learning process. The essence of CAL is the *tactical* assistance rendered to the student; he is assisted by the computer towards a goal of his choosing. Computer-managed learning (CML) results in decisions of a *strategic* nature; the computer suggests, on the basis of an initial interaction with the student, what ought to be the next module of instruction for him.

First, the learner is tested through the medium of a program, on his knowledge of a topic. The results of the test are checked by the computer, stored in the learner's individual file within the computer and assessed. Deficiencies are noted, unusual attainment is recorded and the computer constructs a student 'profile'. It is at this stage that the computer is able to intervene in the management function of control (see Chapter 7). The student profile is used as the basis of measurement, assessment and adjustment. Student achievement is *measured* in relation to criterion attainment (based on reference to syllabus module demands) and *assessed* in relation to course requirements as a whole. Then the computer suggests how the student's learning level might be *adjusted*. Revision of the entire unit? Practice on one or two topics only? Movement to a new topic? Movement to the next module? Remedial module? Enhancement module? The computer's decision, which, in some CML schedules is subject to further discussion by student and tutor, constitutes, in effect, the *management* of the student's conditions of instruction, so that efficient *personalised learning* is made possible.

The microcomputer in college administration

The growth in the number of courses offered by colleges, the burgeoning of MSC and BTEC schemes, have resulted in a proliferation of student records and similar data. It is possible, given time for the devising and testing of an appropriate system, to use the microcomputer for the storing and retrieval of information, such as personal and occupational data, details of attainment and examination results.

Timetable preparation is possible by means of a computer. 'Tailored', individual timetables, classroom loading schedules and the optimal use of resources, such as workshops and laboratories, can be planned swiftly and methodically by computer. Administration of the college library is providing increasing opportunities for computer control. Cataloguing, recording of loans and expenditure estimates, lend themselves readily to computerised control techniques. One of the most potentially significant areas is in the linking by computer of groups of college libraries so that the catalogue facilities of all become available on immediate demand for individual library users.

Requirements for hardware and software

The level of availability of minicomputers and appropriate software has increased dramatically in recent years; choice is now very wide. In the case of hardware (the computer and its peripherals) it is essential that it should be of strong construction—appearance is relatively unimportant. Machines selected for college use are likely to be moved from room to room and, hence, should be sturdy and portable. The availability and cost of peripherals (printers, disc drives, etc.) must be considered along with the compatibility of the chosen machine's computer languages.

The choice of software (i.e. the programs) will reflect the following requirements: first, it must meet course objectives and it should contribute much more to student instruction than a textbook can; it should be written on sound educational principles; its instruction sequence should be well-sequenced and capable of providing immediate feedback to users. Finally, the system ought to record a student's progress in terms of attainment levels.

In general, the questions to be put by a prospective purchaser of college computer software will include the following: 'What is the precise objective of the program?' 'Where, when and by whom was it compiled?' 'Are there any validated test results?' 'Is it up-to-date and otherwise factually correct?' 'What are the required level of entry, the target population and criterion behaviour at termination?'

Advantages and problems of CAL

The principal advantages and inherent difficulties of CAL will be apparent from what has been written above. The extraordinary versatility and speed of the computer allow it to be integrated into most instructional activities. It can play a specific role as demonstrator, illustrator, graphic artist, information retriever and personal tutor. It can offer assistance in learning at all the age and ability levels represented in colleges of further education. It can relieve teacher and student from the drudgery of 'unauthentic labour', such as long chains of simple arithmetical calculations, and allow both to concentrate on the real learning tasks of instructional modules.

Its disadvantages stem largely from its *real costs:* the time spent in 'debugging' programs, supervising students, analysing results and student profiles, can be considerable. The monetary costs of purchasing and maintaining the system can strain departmental budgets. Undesirable side-effects—the possible erosion of student interest in a 'print culture', concentration on the mechanics of a program, rather than on its learning objectives—have been noted. Overdependence on mediated instruction as opposed to enactive learning may also emerge as a problem. Further, the variety of administrative problems associated with the location of the computer installation within the college—the need for a specially-designed room demanding high levels of maintenance and booking schedules—can draw heavily on staff time.

CAL, CML and the future

The growth of computer technology and its use in education seem restricted only by the ingenuity of the computer engineers and designers. Devices which were, a short time ago, at the 'far end' of science fiction—screen touch activated hardware, bubble memories, for example—are now in production. The immediate future promises much: 'distance learning', in particular, in which isolated students may have access to extensive data banks, is likely to be facilitated.

But CAL and CML have yet to find acceptance within the ranks of an innately conservative teaching profession. Memories of teaching machines die hard! Arguments suggesting an 'inevitable move' of the computer into all aspects of our society make little impression on those whose definition of education emphasises its personalised operations. Nor is a profession threatened with contraction because of economic pressures likely to embrace with enthusiasm moves towards the 'automated classroom'!

Computer technology advances, nevertheless, inexorably. On the horizon (and not much more remote in time than today's microcomputer from the first computers of the 1950s) may be discerned artificial intelligence, a highly-developed science of robotics and advances in the exploration of human brain structure. Hawkridge concludes a personal forecast of the future with the expectation that education, 'insulated from many technological changes in the last century, will not be able to insulate itself from new educational technology'. But the experiences of the past three decades do not always support this optimism. Further education, in particular, illustrates the paradox of technological advance strengthening, rather than weakening, conservative institutional behaviour, so that the time lag between technological innovation and its acceptance by educational institutions seems to be increasing. It has been said that schools and colleges are 'studded with institutionalised practices which have managed to dodge the challenge of the obvious'. An exploration of the implications of new technology would appear to be essential for teachers for whom CAL and CML represent a threat rather than an opportunity.

21

Audio-visual aids

The selection, orchestration, and delivery of stimulation by means of various sources comprise a large portion of the decisions the teacher must make every day . . . The ultimate guide to decisions about the sources of instructional stimulation is the learning objective (Gagné 1983).

The object of using audio-visual material in the classroom is the communication of information incidental to the total teaching process. Selected and used skilfully—'the right aid at the right time in the right place in the right manner'—audio-visual aids (AVA) can multiply and widen the channels of communication between teacher and class. Used at random or unskilfully, so that they dominate or distort rather than assist the instructional process, or without careful consideration of their effect on the attainment of objectives, they can generate sufficient 'noise' to render those channels ineffective. The *purpose* of AVA, the *questions* which should be asked and answered before they are selected, the *selection* of appropriate AVA and the *types* generally available are considered below.

The purpose of AVA

A class acquires knowledge and skills as the result of the assimilation of responses elicited by those stimuli which create *sensory impressions*. The concept of teaching which is based on the teacher relying solely on his voice and personality stems from the belief that communication is best achieved through the medium of sound. The use of AVA in a lesson is based on the consideration of communication as related to *all the senses;* the task of the teacher in providing the appropriate stimuli for desired responses can be facilitated by his being able to engage the student's senses of hearing, seeing, touching, etc. A verbal description of the River Ganges is strengthened by a short film showing its stretches; a textbook diagram of an economy's income

241

flow takes on added meaning when a class is confronted with a working model made from transparent pipes, illustrating the interconnections and flows of the constituents of the national income, and giving an accurate impression of concepts.

Because the 'real thing' (an object or process) which is the subject matter of the lesson is unavailable, inaccessible, inconvenient or impossible to handle, or because its essential characteristics can be shown only with difficulty or not at all, AVA may be employed to provide effective substitutes. Films, three-dimensional models, characteristic sounds and enlarged microphotographs can be integrated into a teaching strategy involving the supplementation of verbal explanation, the focusing of class attention, the stimulation and maintenance of interest, the transfer of learning and the promotion of retention of information.

AVA need to be considered neither, on the one hand, frills ('optional extras') to a lesson, nor, on the other hand (and in spite of the claims of their most ardent champions) the basis of a 'total teaching technology' which may render the class teacher unnecessary. As 'mediating instruments' assisting students to achieve understanding, as components of a teaching situation requiring a combination of instructional modes, their value is beyond doubt. The use of aids such as the overhead projector, closed circuit television, the microprojector, can result in the enrichment and intensification of student learning, improvement in perception, assimilation and retention of learned material, the promotion of transfer of learning and the widening of the boundaries of insight. But a clear analysis is needed of the total situation in which they are to be used.

Aspects of the use of AVA

The class teacher who is contemplating the use of AVA should have in mind certain questions:

1. 'Does the attainment of my teaching objectives really require the employment of any AVA?'
2. 'What are the specific properties of the AVA which will enable me to attain the required lesson behavioural objectives?'
3. 'What particular responses do I require from the use of the AVA— e.g. comprehending, consolidating, remembering?'
4. 'How is my class likely to respond to the AVA?'
5. 'How shall I evaluate the effectiveness of the AVA?'

Unless the behavioural changes which the teacher seeks to bring about are hastened, intensified or consolidated by the use of AVA, he may be well-advised not to use them. Unless the teaching strategy which is appropriate at a given stage requires the transmission of information in a mode beyond the natural capacities of the teacher, AVA are unlikely to be of value.

The skills instructor, for example, must analyse course content in terms of concepts and tasks, the mastery of which constitutes criterion performance. If an aid is needed so as to demonstrate and assist the attainment of mastery, the various AVA available in the college should be considered, each in turn, in the light of the question: 'What type of aid is best suited to the purpose of evoking the specific responses necessary *at this stage* of skills learning?'

Gagné suggests that the use of visual aids contributes effectively to the growth of specific learning capabilities. Intellectual skills are enhanced by the capacity of visual aids to stimulate the recall of pre-requisite skills and to add cues for the retrieval of newly-learned skills. Cognitive strategies are assisted in their growth by a variety of visual aids adding cues for the transfer of strategies to novel circumstances. Images used in instruction broaden and add detail to contexts in which fresh information has been embedded. Motor skills can be improved by the presentation of images encoding 'executive routines and subroutines'. Attitudes are broadened by the skilful use of pictorial information in which those attitudes are encoded.

Types of AVA

The chart in Figure 21.1 indicates the principal types of AVA, most of which are now available in colleges of further education.

Each of these aids is now discussed briefly.

The chalkboard

The ubiquitous chalkboard, one of the oldest, cheapest and probably the most-used of visual aids, remains the class teacher's stand-by. It is particularly useful for building up maps, graphs and diagrams, for recording the key phrases and important definitions in a lesson or lecture, for building the scheme of a lesson as it unfolds, for recapitulating and summarising. A word or sentence recorded on the board provides an emphasis which may be lacking in the spoken, hopeful,

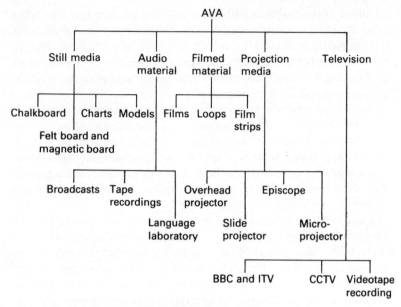

Figure 21.1 *Types of AVA.*

imperative: 'Don't forget this!' or 'Pay special attention to this . . .!' The size of the board is important; it should be large enough to allow the lay-out of a lesson in its entirety.

As the result of experiments in visual perception in the classroom the erstwhile 'blackboard' now appears in a variety of shades and is imprinted with an even greater variety of coloured chalks. White chalk on a black surface is the most widely-used combination, but many teachers prefer yellow chalk on a green surface, which is said to provide an unusually clear effect. Dark blue chalk on primrose yellow is another favoured juxtaposition of colours which is claimed to produce high clarity. Whiteboards and felt-tipped coloured markers are used in some college classrooms, but difficulties of erasure (because of the penetration of coloured inks) make special erasers necessary.

Perhaps because of the very simplicity of the chalkboard, it is often used inadequately. Chalkboard writing, which must be large and legible, and which necessitates careful spacing of words and lines, requires practice. The building up on a chalkboard of notes, or the main topics of a lesson, so that space is uncrowded and important points are emphasised, demands exercise. Cut-outs, templates, the prior preparation of diagram outlines by the use of thinly-pencilled lines, can assist the teacher in using the chalkboard to its best advantage.

The felt board and magnetic board

The felt board is usually the size of the standard chalkboard and is covered with a hairy-surfaced cloth. The backs of pre-prepared shapes are covered with lint, velvet, glass paper, or a special flock paper, and are pressed into position on the board. Diagrams, stages in the construction of formulae and equations, organisation charts can be displayed effectively in this manner.

The magnetic board is made up of a thin sheet of tinplate or iron painted with a matt surface so that it can act also as a chalkboard. Coloured magnetic material, symbols and string can be used to construct displays recording movement. (Hooks attached to the surface can be used for the mounting of heavy objects.) Geography, work study, traffic flow and control, economic structure, the construction of summaries lend themselves to displays of this nature.

Charts and models

Charts may be used so as to illustrate or emphasise verbal comment. They can be designed so as to clothe an abstraction with greater *meaning* (e.g. a visual illustration of the components of a free market, or man's family tree), to present *factual data* or *comparative information* in the form of graphs, pie-charts, histograms, to focus attention on the *characteristics* of an object (e.g. the structure of the human skeleton). Used in workshops and laboratories they can act as operational guides, illustrating handling methods and safety rules. Charts clamped together at the top and fixed to a chalkboard can be used in a 'flip' sequence so as to illustrate the structure of a topic.

The most useful charts are often those which are simple, clearly set out and which concentrate on a few points only. Colour contrasts are important and experimental evidence suggests that schemes combining blue, green and red, or blue, orange and red, have high 'attention value' when used in the construction of charts.

Three-dimensional models are valuable where students might experience difficulty in comprehending a two-dimensional diagram, e.g. as where interior views are required, or the shape of an object is too complex for adequate illustration on a page or chart, or much detail is needed for the complete communication of a concept, such as the working of a machine. The 'enlarged working model' of a micrometer or vernier is often used in the introductory phases of lessons designed to instruct in the functions of their working parts.

Broadcasts

In recent years the BBC has transmitted an excellent series of sound programmes intended for students in colleges of further education. Produced with skill and with insight into the needs of their 'target population' the programmes have ranged widely and have been heard regularly by large audiences in many colleges. Integration of the programme with departmental timetables and with the course tutor's objectives and teaching strategy is important. The timing of programmes requires careful attention—a problem which can be overcome to a large extent by the recording (with permission) of broadcasts.

The broadcast is best utilised as a teaching aid where it is preceded by an introduction from the teacher which explains its purpose and its place within the instructional scheme and where it is followed by a recapitulation given by the teacher. Used merely as a 'fill-in', unrelated to previous knowledge and attainment, it can become an irrelevancy. Used in aid of a planned scheme of work, backed by supplementary visual material, it can provide a stimulus for the student's imagination and a widening of his horizons.

Tape recordings

The tape recorder, which has revolutionised the techniques and processes of sound recording, works on the principle of imprinting magnetic variations on a tape so as to produce electric variations which can be amplified and converted into sound relayed through a loudspeaker. The tapes, which are relatively cheap and which can contain several tracks, consist of acetate strips coated with magnetic iron oxide from which recorded sound can be erased, thus providing an aid which, like the chalkboard, can be used repeatedly at a low cost.

Tapes can be 'edited' by cutting, erasing and splicing, so that sound stimuli can be made to approximate very closely to those desired by the teacher. Instant play-back and instant erasure provide flexibility of control, while the use of several microphone inputs allows the mixing of sounds. Prepared tapes may allow students to hear the views of authoritative speakers, thus adding the impact of direct sound stimuli to those presented by the printed page.

Tape recordings have been used successfully in the teaching of languages—in particular for the difficult preparatory stages of pronunciation—and in workshops, where recorded instructions on the handling of a lathe, for example, can be programmed so that the learner, to whom the sound is relayed through earphones, can play back parts of the tape and work at his own pace. In motor vehicle repair classes the recorder can be used to play back the sound of mechanical faults to students learning diagnostic and remedial techniques. Recordings can be used in conjunction with an automatic slide projector so that an entirely 'automated' presentation is made possible.

As with all other aids the effective use of the tape recorder demands careful planning. Its real value derives from its ability to augment visual with audio stimuli. Used in a casual manner its impact declines and diminishing returns set in very quickly!

The language laboratory

This apparatus allows tape recordings (usually of language drills) to be used so that a student may imitate what he hears, listen to a playback of his voice and enter upon a two-way discussion with his tutor. The laboratory attempts to create the conditions under which a language might be learned with speed. The learner is allowed to work continuously, at his own pace, on material selected to suit his standard of knowledge, and to receive individual attention from his teacher. Practice in listening and pronunciation is emphasised. Comprehension and assimilation of idiom are said to be heightened as a result of language laboratory presentations in which audio and visual material is linked. But 'leaps' in the pace of acquisition of the structure of a language do not emerge automatically from the use of devices of this nature: aptitude, intelligence and perseverance remain essential qualities in language learning. The language laboratory has provided effective aid in the presentation of linguistic drills; its value in relation to the wider problems of meaning and communication remains, as yet, unclear.

Films

Although the viewing of films has now become for many an event of little or no significance, the film properly used in the classroom remains a potent AVA, capable of bringing into the teaching situation a wide range of stimuli (including, in particular, the presentation of current affairs), of assisting in the realisation of objectives in the affective domain (see Chapter 9), and of aiding the acquisition of those skills and techniques included in the psychomotor domain (see

Chapter 9). In the influencing of attitudes, intensification of interest and, possibly increase in the retention of learned material, the film may be a highly effective AVA.

Because its use necessitates the teacher's handing over his role (since, unlike the situation in which most AVA are employed, the teacher 'disappears from view' and, therefore, must abandon class control during the showing of the film) pre-planning is of unusual importance. Choice of appropriate film from among the very large numbers now available is the first planning task. The teacher should answer the following questions in relation to the film he wishes to select:

1. 'What is its purpose?'
2. 'Has it any behavioural objective?'
3. 'How does it relate to the syllabus and to the objective I wish to achieve?'
4. 'Does it assume, and build on, the previous knowledge of the class?'
5. 'Is its content accurate, up-to-date and well presented?'
6. 'Is the commentary appropriate?'
7. 'Is the sound track clearly recorded?'
8. 'Is its length appropriate?' (Thirty minutes seems to be a maximum length of time.)
9. 'What teaching method (if any) does it employ?'
10. 'Will the class find it interesting?'
11. 'Might it act as a "trigger", generating discussion?'

When the film has been selected the teacher may consider that its value as an AVA could be improved if it were to be divided into sequences spaced, perhaps, by recapitulations and tests. In that case careful study of the timing of the film's sequences would be required.

The rearrangement of the classroom (where the college has no separate cinema) is an important part of the planning. Seating and ventilation must be considered, the projector positioned carefully and attention given to the placing of the loudspeaker (which should be, preferably, below or behind the screen). Equipment ought to be checked in detail before the showing.

The film ought to be introduced and its objectives noted on a flip-chart and explained by the teacher. In some cases, where time allows, the film can be shown twice, the second showing following a class discussion of its main points. During the second showing the sound commentary can be switched off, so that the teacher can provide his own, emphasising the important points of the film, restoring his control of the teaching situation and relegating the film to its true position as an AVA. (The film can—all too easily—become the lesson!) Follow-up study of the film is essential in the form of discussion, recapitulation or test.

The advantages of the film ought not to be forgotten. It can undoubtedly translate abstract thought into comprehensible, visual terms and, by the use of techniques such as slow motion, close up, cutting and caricature, can focus class attention in a unique fashion. Its value as an AVA with large groups is considerable. Above all, it brings into the classroom a variety of stimuli presented in an expert and attractive way, thus facilitating the learning process.

Its disadvantages include its association with the relaxed atmosphere which tends to surround the film as a mode of entertainment. The showing of a film will not automatically guarantee motivation or attention. Lack of active class participation and the loss of teacher control over the pace of presentation of information can be guarded against, to some extent, by careful planning, the use of attention-directing devices, recapitulation and testing so that the impact of the film as an AVA shall be as effective as possible.

Film loops

Loops consist of short lengths of film, the two ends of which are spliced together, thus facilitating automatic rewinding. Presented in 8 mm cassettes and allowing the projection of a 48×12.5 cm image on a translucent screen in daylight (which makes possible teacher contact, note-writing, etc.), the loop apparatus, which is easily portable, enables a student to examine repeatedly a short technical process. The picture can be stopped and retained at any frame, thus allowing detailed examination.

The 'single concept' loop, which presents one theme (and which can carry sound) is a very useful AVA, enabling a student to view an operation as seen by the performer. It can be used to illustrate those specific actions which task analysis shows to be vital for mastery of a skill and can assist in the presentation of factual data and in the formation of concepts. Class teaching can be supplemented and private study enhanced by the loop's power to convey—at the pace of individual students—information concerning complicated physical skills and criterion performance.

Sections of long instructional films can be used by the class teacher—after the requisite permission has been obtained—so as to make loops. This process has been used with success by instructors in workshop skills, athletics and games, who have isolated and edited short, relevant sequences from full-length films of factory operations, track events, international matches, etc.

Film strips

The film strip generally consists of 20–40 frames of transparencies on 35 mm film, recorded in a planned sequence. The speed of presentation is entirely in the hands of the teacher, who can select at will from the sequence. Printed notes are usually available and provide a guide for the personal commentary by the teacher which ought to accompany the showing of the frames.

The classroom need not be entirely dark, so that notes can be taken and teacher–class contact need not be lost. The frames may be used, much as charts and wall diagrams, as an aid to the normal teaching techniques. The availability of extensive libraries of film strips allows the class teacher a very large choice of material which can be related precisely to his instructional objectives.

Overhead projector

One of the most popular and versatile visual aids is the overhead projector. It consists of a horizontal window table (usually 25×25 cm) on which the material to be projected is placed. A bulb below the table provides light which is condensed by a mirror or Fresnel lens. The light then passes through the projection material, and is focused and turned through 90° by a lens mounted on an adjustable bracket attached to the window table. Little technical attention is required and recent innovations have produced compact, portable machines which project excellent images free from distortion in rooms requiring no blackout or projection screens (light-coloured walls being quite adequate).

The projector may be used as a chalkboard, the teacher writing with a special pen or pencil directly on to an acetate roll, so that his script is projected in magnified form as it is being written. The roll can be cleared and used again. Pre-drawn diagrams can be shown, blank maps can be projected and filled in as the lesson progresses, and recapitulations and prepared summaries, lecture headings (with space for detailed notes), silhouettes and objects such as transparent protractors can be shown with great clarity. In some cases polaroid moving diagrams and 'shapes' of experiments (e.g. on the electrolysis of water) can be projected.

Transparencies in many colours can be borrowed from AVA libraries or can be prepared by the teacher using photographic methods, heat process techniques, dyeline copying or xerography. 'Books' of transparencies can be put together and used on the projector as flip-charts, so as to illustrate a sequence. (Some microcomputers are able to produce transparencies from designs built up on the video display unit.)

Techniques such as 'overlay' (where additional transparencies are used so as to superimpose detail on a prepared outline) or 'reveal' (where parts of a diagram are covered by small pieces of paper attached by tape, which are removed so as to build up detail as required), help in those modes of instruction based on concept analysis in particular. Working models fixed to a perspex plate and constructed from simple Meccano metal strips can be projected so that a class may observe elementary mechanical processes.

Daylight projection and easy control are important advantages of the overhead projector. Even more important is the fact that teacher control of the class is not lost—a fully-darkened room is unnecessary and the teacher can face his class while controlling the projector. Thus the apparatus remains an aid and does not at any stage in its use 'take over' the lesson.

Slide projector

The standard apparatus, which does not require a fully-darkened room, projects a 5 cm square slide or transparency. It can be operated manually, by remote control, and by impulses from a tape recorder, thus allowing a synchronised, audio-visual presentation. More elaborate models can be loaded from a magazine which allows a prepared, fixed order of presentation and facilitates storage of slides. Careful rehearsal is advisable before presentation.

Episcope

The episcope projects the image of solid or opaque objects on a screen by means of a light which is concentrated on those objects and a mirror which reflects the image through a lens. Maps, pictures and models can be shown with clarity. It can be used to project on to a chalkboard an outline of a map or diagram which can be filled in with

chalk as the lesson proceeds. The disadvantages of the apparatus are
its size (it is rarely portable), the concentration of heat which it produces (which can destroy light maps and diagrams), and the necessity
(for most machines) of a fully-darkened room. Further, the range at
which the material can be projected adequately is very restricted.

The microprojector

This apparatus projects microscope slides and live microscopic
material, so that an entire class can view what is usually visible
through the eyepiece of a microscope. The need for a large number of
costly microscopes is reduced and teacher control, which is not
always easy where each member of a group is working with his own
microscope, remains effective. As a means of providing certain types
of visual aids for lessons in hygiene, biology, textile analysis and testing, the microprojector is unequalled.

National television broadcasts

Uncritical home viewing habits and the emergence of TV as an entertainment medium may have dulled the educational impact of a
wonderful technological achievement. The earlier fears of the
replacement of live teachers by a television screen in each classroom
have given way to anxieties that the power of this AVA has not been
exploited fully in schools and colleges. All too often the TV programme is considered as a mere intermission or 'audio-visual
wallpaper', unrelated to the syllabus or wider educational demands.

Because class teachers are generally unable to preview educational
TV programmes, difficulties arise in evaluating their suitability. The
guidance notes and leaflets which explain the nature of the programme are often of a high quality but provide no substitute for
previewing. Nor are the objectives of the programmes always made
clear. Timing of programmes must present a difficulty for teachers in
colleges which lack visual recording facilities.

Many teachers and classes, however, have derived benefit from the
wide-ranging and imaginative TV programmes which have been presented in recent years. (At a more advanced level the Open University
TV transmissions—often intended as complete lectures—arouse
much enthusiasm.) Where the programme is integrated into a lesson
scheme, i.e. where its presentation is not allowed to dominate an
instructional sequence, its impact can be remarkable. The sense of

immediacy which is conveyed by television's ability to bring important events into the classroom can be heightened by pre- or post-programme discussions. A scheme of 'introduction by the teacher—TV programme—discussion—lesson based on the programme—test and evaluation', or some similar sequence, can result in a valuable learning pattern in which TV plays a vital role as a learning aid.

As with the use of the film, TV requires a carefully arranged room and timetable. The optimum viewing period for educational programmes seems to be between 25–35 minutes, so that, where broadcasts can be recorded for later viewing, the breaking of programmes into sequences, divided by discussions or recapitulation periods, is advantageous.

Closed circuit TV

Closed Circuit TV (CCTV) has become a fast-developing teaching aid. It is essentially no more than a process whereby TV signals are received by private receivers only. It is used, therefore, within colleges to relay, say, a laboratory experiment to groups in a number of class-rooms, or, within cities, to relay programmes from an education authority's TV studio to its schools and colleges.

The basic equipment of CCTV within the college consists of a TV camera, monitoring and viewing equipment and cable connections. Extra equipment such as zoom lenses and vision mixers allows more imaginative programmes to be designed and produced. Programmes can be recorded and repeated on different days of the week, thus assisting the timetabling of day-release classes in which TV material is used.

One of the dangers of the extended use of CCTV is that it could replace practical experience and reduce teacher–student contact. It is indeed valuable for classes scattered throughout a college or city to be able to view on TV an experiment carried out by a team of experts in a central laboratory. It would be a retrograde step, however, if the viewing were to be regarded as a substitute for active class participation in a programme of practical experiments.

Video recording

Electronic video recording which enables the recording of internally-produced or nationally-broadcast visual programmes so that they can be viewed, as in TV, by electronic scanning, now has a place in the variety of AVA in use in schools and colleges. A cassette film cartridge is inserted into a tele-player linked to a TV receiver, or to several receivers at the same time. The film can be controlled so that it may be scanned slowly, held and restarted. The recording and storing of nationally-broadcast programmes enable large numbers of students to view BBC and other transmissions.

Video recording is used in some colleges to assist students who are preparing for careers which will involve them in the techniques of audio-visual presentation, such as advertising, marketing, public relations, etc. Teachers in training, too, have benefited from being able to examine video recordings of their lessons.

Research into AVA

Gagné has noted that the most important function of AVA is 'to make possible alternate modes of communication in the delivery of instruction' (Gagné 1983). Research into the delivery of instruction by means of AVA has been wide but generally inconclusive. Some research seems to suggest that students can and do learn from AVA, but that the rate and lasting quality of what is learned may be related directly to enhancement by class tutors. One feature which has emerged clearly from research is the relationship between the pictorial representation of information and 'remembering'. Hilgard and Bower cite experiments suggesting that such representation tends to facilitate retention and retrieval of information by factors of 1.5 to 3. Paivio's research findings are based on the so-called 'dual-trace hypothesis', which postulates two different forms of representation, the 'verbal' and the 'imaginal' (Paivio 1971). If a word is to be remembered, a memory trace enters the student's verbal store; if it is a 'concrete' word (rather than abstract), nodes in his imaginal system are activated, so that the student 'sees' a corresponding image, and a memory trace is laid down in the imaginal system. The double traces assist in prolonging memory and—so research appears to imply—the imaginal trace survives after the verbal trace has disappeared. It is reasonable to infer, therefore, that visual aids used in instruction produce traces that might be more resistant to the processes of 'forgetting'.

If the full impact of AVA is to be achieved, clear introductions to those parts of instruction during which the more advanced types of AVA (such as television and videotaped material) are used, statements of the general purpose and specific objectives of the presentation, summaries and recapitulations of what has been seen and heard, appear to be essential. The training of teachers in the principles, preparation and utilisation of a wide range of AVA should contribute to this end.

22

The examination and assessment of learning (1)— evaluating attainment

It is obvious that an examination can be bad in the sense of emphasising trivial aspects of a subject. Such examinations can encourage teaching in a disconnected fashion and learning by rote. What is often overlooked, however, is that examinations can also be allies in the battle to improve curricula and teaching (Bruner 1965).

Examinations loom large in the working life of the teacher in further education. Most college courses are geared to internal and external examinations so that there will be few members of staff who are not involved in the evaluation of learning as chief or assistant examiners, assessors, or members of moderating panels. Examinations in their various forms are considered in this chapter as a component of the system of control which was outlined in Chapter 7. The weighty case against the place of examinations in the life of colleges ('this veritable wound inflicted on education at all grades' (Piaget)) is also taken into account.

Examination, assessment and control

Fundamentally, the rationale of formal examinations (with which this chapter is concerned) must rest on their importance for the learning process. If that process can be effective without the use of examinations, then they have little obvious value. In Chapter 7 it was suggested that the management of teaching necessarily involves monitoring and assessment. Feedback, both to learner and teacher, was noted as being essential for the *control* of that process. If the teacher's role is accepted as involving the creation of conditions for effective learning, then the regular assessment of those conditions and their outcomes would seem to be necessary.

An examination of the learner's rate of progress towards the attainment of desired learning objectives serves a number of useful purposes. It provides the *learner* with incentive and knowledge of his achievement in relation to those objectives, thus acting as a reinforcer and enabling him to take whatever remedial action may be needed. It provides the *teacher* with a measurement of the appropriateness and effectiveness of his teaching strategy, thus enabling him to make adjustments where necessary. Therefore, an assessment which results from the monitoring of a student's achievements during a course of instruction (see, for example, the technique of 'continuous assessment', discussed on p. 266) or from the measurement of a 'terminal performance' (as, for example, the end-of-year examination for a BTEC National Certificate) forms an essential link in the chain of control, enabling the modification of teaching programmes so as to attain objectives and to improve curriculum design and presentation.

The results of formal examinations may have value, therefore, in the assessment of attainment, the diagnosis of a learner's difficulties and the evaluation and internal validation of courses and curricula. Another use of examination results which is growing in importance is the prediction of a learner's future behaviour. Thus a student's marks in the 'O' level examination may be used so as to forecast his performance in the 'A' level course; a student's performance in an 'A' level test may be accepted by some universities and polytechnics as a prediction of his likelihood of success in a degree course. This function of examinations may help to explain in part their current importance in the colleges of further education.

A case against examinations

The principal arguments presented against examinations are often not so much attacks on the necessity of assessment (although many will argue against *any* formal process of this nature), but rather against their tendency to dominate the curricula in colleges of further education. Examinations, it is claimed, often become ends in themselves and exercise repressive and restrictive influences on teachers and students. A syllabus may be determined by an external examining body, after which it becomes a central task of the teacher to work to its requirements. His freedom to decide on the treatment or weight of subject matter is unduly limited and the learner's liberty of exploring the many side paths in the subject area is curtailed. Unworthy habits such as question-spotting, the learning by rote of 'model answers', drill in reproducing the kind of material which examiners are believed to favour are fostered, while the learner's creative abilities are denied any outlet. Learning ceases to be treated as a desirable end in itself and becomes inextricably interwoven with the competitive demands of the examination system. Further, it is argued, the course of a person's future may be determined in large measure by a few anxiety-laden hours in an examination room—a practice which is not easily reconciled with those theories which draw attention to the uneven rate of development of young persons in their formative years. Attention has been drawn to the possible lasting effect on a student's self-esteem of poor performance in examinations designed for candidates with a higher level of abilities.

Examinations as modes of evaluation are, it is contended, demonstrably inadequate. They rarely produce objective assessments and reflect too often the examiner's subjective standards, so that the candidates' true levels of attainment are distorted. They place too much stress on mere memory and, it is argued, favour the uncritical regurgitation of facts (or, as has been claimed, the 'second-hand interpretation' of those facts), rather than the selective application of knowledge. Finally, they place, all too often, an unmerited premium on speed ('answer any six questions in two hours . . .') and on those special examination skills which may have little relevance to the world outside the classroom. In effect, it is urged, the examination system is 'an unmitigated blight, and the educational plant, as a result, sickens and droops'.

The value of examinations

For many teachers, the regulative functions of examinations mentioned earlier constitute a conclusive argument for their value. There are, however, other, weightier arguments. If the learner has a right to ask (and few would deny him this right): 'How am I progressing in my studies? What, at this moment, is the level of my ability? Am I ready to progress to a further stage of instruction? How do I compare with others in my group?'—then there exists, for the teacher, a related duty to answer the learner on the basis of an objective and valid assessment. If the teacher has a right to ask: 'How effective is my teaching in terms of the attainment of objectives? What, at this moment, are my students' achievements? How well do they carry over their learning into novel situations?'—then there exists a case for the process of evaluation of the kind provided by examinations.

The provision of goals for the learner and objectives for the teacher; the measurement of progress; the evaluation of merit; the uncovering of weakness and deficiencies in learning and teaching; the motivation and encouragement of students to work steadily and productively over a measured period of time; the inculcation of those communication skills needed to reproduce aspects of one's knowledge in a conventionally acceptable form—these are claimed as among the valuable results of the examination system.

Objections to the *content* of some types of examination do not, in themselves, invalidate the *value* of examinations. It may be that too many examination schemes concentrate on the mere recall of too much trivia, that too many types of question encourage the unthinking reproduction of unconsidered trifles. This may call for a change in the *structure* of examinations, in the nature of the questions set. It may demand more clarity on the part of examiners as to the very purpose of their papers. It does not, in itself, render nugatory the value of the concept of examining a learner's achievements regularly, methodically and accurately.

The allegedly cramping effects of examinations are not always immediately obvious. The extraordinary range of an 'A' level examination syllabus in physics, engineering drawing, geology, or economics and the scope provided for imaginative teaching permit one to question the validity of the argument based solely on the 'restrictive nature' of examinations of this type.

Examinations can—and often do—test the ability to penetrate to the core of a problem with insight, to marshal one's thoughts with precision and logic, to reduce those thoughts to writing within a given time and to exercise one's powers of recall and discrimination. These are important aspects of the student's personal development, the evaluation of which gives an added dimension to the teacher's record of his progress.

It should be remembered that the very act of answering an examination paper in controlled conditions can be a learning experience of some significance in that the student is obliged to recall, evaluate and integrate subject-matter. In answer to the argument which stresses the anxiety caused for many examination candidates it is important to note that the very concept of freedom from anxiety during a creative achievement may be an unrealistic goal.

The very act of aspiring to master a body of knowledge or to create something original raises the possibility of failure and depression of self-esteem, and hence is anxiety-producing by definition (Ausubel 1978).

In relation to the argument that failure in an examination has lasting negative effects on students' self-esteem, Ausubel declares that this is exaggerated; further:

> Realistic awareness of our relative intellectual status among our peers is a fact of life to which all of us must eventually adjust and the sooner the better for everyone concerned. There is no profit in sugar-coating the truth or in self-delusion (Ausubel 1978).

A case for examinations might be stated thus: *if* the objectives of a learner's course of study are worthwhile, *if* the syllabus which is to assist his attaining those objectives is sound and *if* the course of study is to result in a systematic movement to increasingly higher levels of attainment, then the repeated measuring and assessing of the learner's skills and the teacher's effectiveness become essential and therefore valuable. Without evaluation, in the form of regularly administered examinations, there is the possibility of goals disappearing from sight all too easily and of inadequate schemes of work and methods of instruction continuing unchallenged. (Additionally, employers and other members of the public who finance the work of colleges have the right to receive from time to time indicators of the progress of courses and students. Examinations act as one such indicator.) In Bruner's words, examinations can be 'allies in the battle to improve curricula and teaching'. But this is not to forget the importance of a continuous, critical review of their structure and content.

Essentials of evaluation

Bloom defines evaluation as 'the making of judgements about the value, for some purpose, of ideas, works, solutions, methods, etc. It involves the use of criteria as well as standards for appraising the extent to which particulars are accurate, effective, economical or satisfying.' Gronlund suggests that we view it as 'a process of obtaining information on which to base educational decisions' (Gronlund 1981).

Given the *purposes* of evaluation, certain essential *characteristics* of a successful process of evaluation may be considered. First, the evaluation should take place at the appropriate time, which will be determined by the rate of progress of the learner and the duration of the course. Weekly tests and end of term examinations obviously have to be administered at fixed points in the timetable, but should the learner reach the end of a unit of instruction at other times, an evaluation of his attainment ought to be made as swiftly as possible if its feedback value is to be realised. Four types of evaluation are in common use, the results providing a record of attainment and development over a period of time. A *prerequisite test* can be used to determine whether the individual student has reached the level required for entry to the course; if he has not attained that standard he ought not to commence the course without having successfully undertaken appropriate remedial work. A *pre-test* can make apparent to the teacher whether the student has, in fact, attained any of the desired objectives of the course of instruction to be followed; if he has, then his individual objectives should be changed. *Post-tests* (administered weekly or monthly, for example) can be used to measure the learner's standard of attainment following the end of lessons, or groups of lessons making up the course; the results ought to be compared with those of the pre-tests. *Retention tests,* which can include the application of that which has been learned to new situations, can follow at random intervals.

The evaluation must be in a *suitable form,* i.e. it must be structured correctly in relation to subject matter and purpose. A test in typewriting, a practical examination for motor vehicle apprentices on aspects of engine tuning, a post-test on a unit of the business studies syllabus, may call for different structures, dictated largely by *what* is to be tested, and *how.* Whether the tests will be wholly practical in nature, or theoretical, or a mixture of both, or take the form of an essay, or objective questions, or both, must depend largely upon the teacher's answer to the following vital questions:

1. 'What am I testing?'
2. 'How best can I elicit from the student those responses which will provide an unambiguous indication of what and how well he has learned?'

It follows that the test must be at the *correct level;* mere recall of facts would be quite inappropriate, for example, in an evaluation test for the final part of examinations in personnel management.

The evaluation must be in a form which is *valid.* The test should measure as accurately as possible what it purports to measure, i.e. the outcomes of the learner's study. It should gauge as precisely as possible the gap between actual and expected attainment. Further, it should range as comprehensively as possible over the content area of the syllabus. Its *predictive validity* should be high, i.e. there should be a reasonably significant degree of correlation between the learner's examination results and attainment at later stages of his development.

The examination ought to be presented to the learner as an *integral part of the course,* not as an irrelevant imposition. It has to be explained—and accepted—as a necessary step towards the next, higher level of work. The idea of the examination as a 'useful discipline', a desirable end in itself, or as a mere culmination of the learner's activities, has no place, therefore, in this concept of evaluation.

> If education is to prosper, both teachers and students must learn to welcome regular and systematic testing rather than to regard it as a threat, an intrusion, or a distraction from more important matters (Ausubel 1978).

In sum, evaluation will be worthwhile only if it assists the learner and teacher to move with assurance towards the attainment of a desired pattern of learning objectives.

The problem of the essay question

Some of the criticisms levelled against formal tests are based on doubts as to the value of the use of essay-type questions which have tended to dominate the traditional examination. First it is claimed that there can be no real uniformity in marking standards, since strict 'scorer objectivity' is impossible; standards vary, of necessity, from one examiner to another. Given the most detailed marking schemes, the responses of two or more examiners to candidates' answers to open-ended questions, such as, 'Consider the relationship between job satisfaction and productivity', or 'Estimate the effectiveness of the British Government's attempts to control the effects of inflation', must contain a subjective element and may, therefore, differ widely. It could not be otherwise, it is argued; no two examiners have the same background, experience, philosophy, or methods of interpreting and evaluating events. (In addition to variation in the standards of different examiners, it has been reported that in some experimental markings of essays, different marks have been awarded at different times to the same essay by *the same examiner!*)

Next, it is claimed that in spite of warnings issued by examining boards, examiners may be swayed unduly, and in different manner, by candidates' actual presentation of their answers. The neat, well-turned, correctly-paragraphed script may be favoured rather than the script which reaches the same standard in scholarship, but which is difficult to read and presented in a rebarbative style. The value of an assessment based on essay-type questions may be vitiated, therefore, by the so-called 'contamination factor' which clouds the central issue of an examination by the testing—often unconsciously on the part of the examiner—of matters such as style, speed of writing, punctuation, length of answer. (Ebel, who opposes the essay test because it does not usually provide valid measures of complex mental processes such as critical thinking, originality, or ability to organise and integrate, states that longer essays tend to receive higher ratings (Ebel 1979).) It is claimed, also, that the presence of a very good, well-presented script in a run of mediocre papers, or of a poor script in a group of otherwise excellent papers, may distort the general pattern of marks which the examiner awards.

The essay-type questions which make up an examination paper may not be of an equal standard of difficulty, so that they discriminate differently among candidates. Thus, where there is the possibility of choice ('answer any three questions'), and candidate X answers questions 1, 2, 3, while Y answers 2, 4, 6, and Z answers 3, 5, 7, there must be difficulties in evaluating the standard of the paper as a whole, since X, Y and Z have answered, in effect, three different papers. It is objected also that the scope of the typical examination syllabus in further education is now so very wide that it cannot be covered adequately by setting nine questions, from which a candidate may choose 'any five'. In such a case, the student is being tested on a mere portion of the syllabus. A further objection is that the time-consuming process of essay marking and evaluation makes early and effective feedback and reinforcement impossible, so that much of the purpose of the process cannot be realised.

As against these criticisms there are, however, positive features of the essay-type question to be noted. It tests not only the learner's recall and knowledge of the subject matter but also his ability to apply that knowledge in the exercise of his powers of expression in a creative and lucid manner. Tests involving the higher levels of attainment, such as comprehension, analysis, evaluation often necessitate the learner's selecting his material and presenting it with great care. For this, the essay question might seem to be suitable. The ability to select, relate and interpret facts with imagination and insight can often be tested by the writing of an essay. Indeed it has been argued that to exclude the essay question from an examination paper is to deny the student the opportunity of displaying that discipline of response and measure of perception which ought to have resulted from his course of study.

Planning and marking the examination

Members of staff of all grades in colleges of further education may be called upon to plan or mark examinations for internal purposes or for external bodies. The following matters need to be considered:

1. *The scope of the syllabus must be ascertained precisely and questions must be distributed as evenly as possible over its content.* It is unfair for the examiner to assume that any one section of the syllabus is 'less important' than another and, thus, to omit questions based upon it; its publication as part of the syllabus necessitates its being treated by teachers and examiners as material to be taught and tested.

2. *'What am I examining?'* This question must be kept in mind by the examiner. Given the level of the candidates' attainments, ought the questions to be based on mere recall, or comprehension or synthesis? Consider for example a question set to a business studies class of part-time students, aged seventeen and over. The syllabus to which they work includes a section which states, briefly: 'Money—elementary treatment of functions and characteristics.' The following questions are among those which have been set from time to time on this section:

Example A: Define money.

Example B: 'Money is as money does.' Discuss.

Example C: Which of the following would you consider to be money: (a) cheques, (b) diamonds, (c) postal orders? Give your reasons.

Example D: In a recent book recounting his experiences as a prisoner of war, the author states: 'For a time we had no money in the camp, so we used cigarettes.' Define money and use your definition to explain what the author means.

Example A is a simple recall test, of very limited value in an examination at this level; it cannot elicit from the learner any response indicating that the functions of money have been *understood*. Examples B, C and D demand an *application* of what has been learned and are to be preferred to a mere memory test.

3. *'How can I best test what has been learned?'* Essay questions? Objective tests? Data response questions? (These are based on an introductory statement and information, followed by an initial question and sequential sub-questions.) Oral examination? A

combination of several types of question? In the case of external examining bodies, the examiner may have no choice as to the type of question to be set. For the purpose of internal examinations, the teacher-examiner ought to experiment widely in the selection of forms of question.

4.   *The length of time available for the test will determine the number of questions to be answered.* In general, a minimum period of twenty minutes for an essay-type answer is considered desirable.

5.   *The draft question paper ought to be revised very carefully so as to avoid possible ambiguities.* Students tend to display a devastating 'logic' in the interpretation of examination questions and ambiguities appear where none was apparent to the examiner. Thus, in a civics paper set some years ago a question asking for the constitutional significance of 'the Queen's Speech' elicited a large number of answers dealing with the responsibility of the monarch for the setting of standards of propriety in the spoken word!

6.   *Clear instructions must be given.* If there are constraints, e.g. on the use of dictionaries or logarithm tables, these must be stated well in advance of the date of examination. (The use of pocket electronic calculators has now to be considered carefully in the design of examinations involving quantitative techniques.) The concept of the 'open book' examination, in which students are allowed the use of textbooks, atlases, dictionaries or copies of Acts of Parliament, presents an important challenge to examiners in the compiling of question papers.

Advantages claimed for the 'open book' examination include: a reduced emphasis on rote learning and the setting of questions testing recall only; reduced nervous strain on candidates; increased emphasis on skills such as selectivity and information retrieval together with the application of knowledge. Disadvantages are said to be: difficulty in framing questions which do not result in the mere copying of reference material; increased strain in examinations because of the plethora of material from which data must be carefully selected. Significantly, the Council for National Academic Awards has stated that the best performance in open book examinations tends to come from students who choose not to take in books. Open book examinations have been a significant feature of some law examinations for many years; students are allowed to refer to printed copies of statutes.

It is of interest to note the procedures used by many examination bodies in the setting of their papers. First, a chief examiner will submit his draft question paper to an assessor. The modified paper is then presented to a moderating committee, which usually includes representatives of practising teachers; it is examined for accuracy, consistency and pattern. (The importance of having the paper checked by persons other than the examiners cannot be overstressed.) Marking schemes must be submitted and checked with particular reference to their reliability and the allocation of marks.

A marking scheme will reflect the chief examiner's subjective 'weighting' of features of the test. The problem of deduction of marks for incorrect spelling, poor punctuation, grammatical inaccuracy must be studied carefully. Are marks to be deducted for each repetition of an error in spelling, for example? What are the criteria on which pass or fail in an essay answer will be determined? Is the pass mark or grade to be publicised? In the case of internal examinations these matters will call for a full discussion between the teacher-examiner and his head of department.

Continuous assessment

Opposed to the concept of a once-for-all evaluation in the form of an 'end-of-course' examination, is the principle of continuous assessment. In practice, this substitutes for the single examination a series of continuously-updated judgements by the teacher of the learner's attainments. These judgements may be based on, say, weekly tests of the learner's performance in a variety of situations. His written and practical work, his contribution to the work of the class as a whole may be taken into account and assessed. (An 'objective-related assessment' is based on a checklist of instructional objectives which the student should have attained by the end of the course.) As a result, there is produced a record of changes in the learner's performance. This cumulative judgement, rather than the result of a single examination, forms the basis of the final assessment of his capabilities.

It has been claimed that an assessment of this nature may provide a much 'fairer' picture of a learner's level of achievement than that given by a traditional formal examination. The strain and anxieties induced by a three-hour test may produce, it is suggested, a distorted reflection of that achievement. The relatively relaxed atmosphere surrounding a test which is administered as a regular feature of classroom activity, it is argued, may allow the learner to give a much more reliable account of his abilities. The ability to work swiftly in a short period of time and the importance of memory, both of which characterise standard formal examinations, are not emphasised in continuous assessment.

Further, the student is supplied with feedback relating to his achievements and is able to plan immediate remedial action. Finally, and perhaps of the greatest importance, the future of the student is not determined by his performance in one examination only.

On the other hand, it is contended that for the strain of one examination is substituted a continuing anxiety spread over an entire term or year. Further, the heavy demands made on teaching staff in relation to the large number of assessments to be made throughout a course may be counter-productive. For some critics the dependence of continuous assessment on the subjective judgement of teachers and the lack of external moderation of test assessment are the most cogent arguments against its acceptability. Much research on the effectiveness of continuous assessment as a measure of learning remains to be carried out.

The use of projects in assessment

A 'project' is part of the learning process, based on tasks carried out by students working individually or in groups and generally culminating in the presentation of a report (which may be assessed as part of an overall course evaluation) resulting from personal investigation of a topic, the choice of which has been approved by the course tutor.

An example of the use of the project is seen in the highly-imaginative syllabus for 'A' level communication studies set by the AEB. The subject-matter of the examination is defined as 'a study of the arts, practices and media of communication, including the formulating, gathering, presenting, receiving and interpretation of ideas, information and attitudes'. Candidates are expected to prepare a project selected from six topic areas. The aim of the project is the presentation of work indicating the candidate's ability to find and use sources of information, classify material, communicate factually, clearly and concisely, prepare a synopsis and write for specified levels of readers, etc. Choices of topics may be made from a list including the writing of a factual report on a current situation, preparation of an instruction manual, drawing up a guide to the workings of an institution or organisation and the constitution of a broadcast programme. The project (which includes an oral examination—see below) carries thirty per cent of the total examination marks.

Project work is said to motivate students and to raise their general level of interest in the course. It allows for creativity, decision-making and independent work, and may lead to 'the personal development which stems from the acceptance of responsibility.' It is important, however, that the precise purpose of the project be explained to students, so that it will be seen as an essential feature of the course, and not merely as a shifting of work from teacher to student, and that it be accorded due recognition in the overall evaluation of students'· course work.

The use of oral examinations

The oral examination, traditionally used in the testing of skills in foreign languages and as a supplementary test in certain types of university course (e.g. in medicine), has been strangely neglected in further education examination schemes, in spite of the fact that oral communication skills are essential for many areas, such as business and management. Its advantages are: verbal fluency and confidence in a stress situation can be assessed; a student's weaknesses and strengths in expression can be revealed swiftly. Its disadvantages are said to include: reliance on an essentially subjective assessment can create difficulties; real costs of administering the tests are often high; restrictions on the amount of learned material that can be examined have to be taken into account. Of crucial importance in oral tests is the role of the examiner and very careful training for examiners in this mode of assessment is essential.

An oral examination forms part of the project in communication studies referred to above. It is conducted by the course tutor and is moderated by a representative of the AEB. The purpose is to allow the candidate to demonstrate his ability to communicate the objectives of his project by some method other than writing, to clarify points in his written project and to expand on points therein.

Assessment for BTEC awards

BTEC policy in relation to evaluation and assessment is derived from that of the former BEC and TEC. The terminology used in the Council's publications is significant for a consideration of its attitude towards the formal processes of assessment. Three important terms are defined in Council documents as follows:

(a) *Examination:* a formal, written, time-constrained assessment which is set on completion of work for a particular module or modules.

(b) *Test:* a method of testing objectives as part of an in-course assessment, by which students are required to answer unseen questions, or to perform an activity or apply a skill on previously unseen material, within a time-constrained period. Used only where required by objectives in certain modules.

(c) *Assessment:* any Council-moderated assessment which counts towards an award. Such an assessment may be a formal end-of-year examination or an in-course assignment; in the latter case it may be made up of assignments or a combination of assignments and tests.

The general objectives of the assessment methods adopted by BEC and TEC, and now carried over into BTEC practice, are as follows:

(a) Assessment must be related to the aims of the course as a whole and must also reflect the need to measure the extent to which the student can interrelate and apply the knowledge and skills gained from the study of a number of modules.

(b) Assessment must include an adequate recognition of the student's work during the course.

(c) Assessment must include a significant emphasis on written examinations.

The attitude of BTEC to the relationship of assessment and overall quality of examinations is outlined in the Council's *Discussion Document on Education Policy,* published in 1984.

> It is superficially tempting to seek to maintain educational standards through the provision of national examinations; BTEC does not propose to do this . . . BTEC remains committed to a balance between intermediate and final assessment, and to assessment being not a means of determining academic status but of confirming a student's mastery of competence (BTEC 1984).

Grading scales and examination records

Student X scores 58 marks out of a possible 100 in an examination. Has he 'passed' or 'failed'? The dividing line between success and failure in an examination must be drawn on the basis of a decision which, inevitably, is somewhat arbitrary in nature. X's mark of 58/100 must be interpreted by the examiner so that it can be evaluated with reference to a variety of criteria. What does this mark tell us of X's level of attainment? How does it compare with the level accepted by the examiner as indicating proficiency or mastery? How does it compare with the level of average attainment? Has it any real predictive value? How does it compare with marks obtained by other candidates in the same group? Does it indicate whether X should move to the next unit of study? In deciding, therefore, whether the pass mark shall be 60, 58, 50, etc., the examiner must consider with care his assumptions as to the precise purpose of the test. The basic question: 'What am I examining?' has to be considered afresh on this occasion.

Where members of the class are to be assessed in order of merit, a grading procedure is needed. Where the test has been sufficiently 'discriminating', so that it results in a general spread of marks, standards can be graded with relative ease. A simple scale of 'good, average, poor' might suffice. A five-point scale, based on 100 students, might produce a pattern related to the following distribution:

> 3 'very good'
> 22 'good'
> 50 'average'
> 22 'weak'
> 3 'poor'

A finer, seven-point scale might produce, typically, the following spread:

> 5 'excellent'
> 10 'very good'
> 20 'good'
> 30 'average'
> 20 'fair'
> 10 'poor'
> 5 'very poor'

The so-called 'normal distribution curve' (the area under which represents the total number of candidates) tends to resemble Figure 22.1.

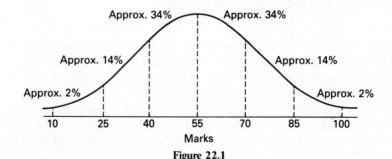

Figure 22.1

The recording of examination results is of great importance in colleges of further education, particularly where the career development prospects of part-time students are linked with the attainment of specified levels in examinations. Ideally, a record card ought to contain all the information necessary for accurate extrapolation, thus enabling a pattern of development to be deduced. Such information would include, in addition to personal details relating to the student, statistical data such as:

(a) intelligence quotient, where known;
(b) grades in examinations taken before entry to college;
(c) pre-test grades;
(d) post-test grades (which, in the case of continuous assessment, must be up-dated regularly).

23

The examination and assessment of learning (2)— objective tests

If we are really serious about education, we must have precise ways both of measuring learning outcomes in individual students and of ascertaining whether they are consonant with our educational objectives (Ausubel 1978).

Earlier chapters have drawn attention to the necessity for swift and accurate assessment and feedback of a learner's level of achievement. The previous chapter considered examinations as a mode of assessing attainment and noted some of the criticisms levelled against them, in particular those based on the alleged deficiencies of the essay-type question. Objective tests, which are explained in this chapter, are presented by some of their advocates as feasible alternatives to the subjectively-assessed essay questions which so often dominate the conventional examination paper.

Essence of objective tests

An objective test has been defined by the Department of Employment as: 'a test or examination in which every question is set in such a way as to have only one right answer. That is, the opinion of the examiner or marker does not enter in judging whether an answer is good or poor, acceptable or wrong; there is no subjective element involved.' The definition emphasises the fact that the term 'objective' relates to the marking of the test. Whether subjective elements have been eradicated from tests of this type remains undecided. The syllabus content to be covered by the test, the choice of questions, the construction of

272

the alternative answers between which the candidate must discriminate, the abilities to be tested, involve examiners' decisions which must be, to a large extent, subjective in their nature.

A test of this type may be made up of 'items' which are so constructed and presented that for each item there is *one, pre-determined, correct answer.* Candidates select the one answer which they consider to be correct from a list provided by the examiner. It is claimed that the objective test, by its nature, design, form and administration, removes from the process of assessment many of the disadvantageous features of the essay-type examination.

Types of objective test

There are several types of test, so that it is not necessary to make up an examination paper from one type only. Indeed, some students who have been tested by objective questions state a preference for a variety of types of question, rather than a paper made up of only one form of item. Five of the more usual types are considered below.

The multiple choice item

This is made up of a *stem* and several (usually four or five) *choices of answer* (often called 'responses' or 'options'). One of the options—the *key*—is correct; the others—the *distractors*—are incorrect. The stem of the item may be constructed so as to present an incomplete statement, or so as to pose a question.

Examples of multiple choice items are given in Figures 23.1 and 23.2.

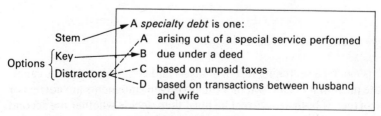

Figure 23.1

The following figures are based on the National Income Accounts:

Gross domestic income at factor cost   £25 000m
Net property income from abroad   £500m
Capital consumption   £3000m

Gross national income at factor cost is:
A   £28 500m
B   £28 000m
C   £25 500m
D   £24 500m
E   £22 000m

Figure 23.2   *From Curzon, L.B. (1971)* Test Your Economics. *Harmondsworth: Penguin.*

The multiple response item

In this type of item more than one of the given possibilities is correct. Figure 23.3 is an example:

Which of the following would be included among the functions of a bill of lading?

   I   it is a receipt for goods shipped
  II   it is evidence of a contract of carriage
III   it is a document of title to goods
IV   it is evidence of insurance

A   I only
B   II and III
C   III and IV
D   I, II and III
E   I, II, III and IV

Figure 23.3   *From Curzon, L.B. (1981)* Objective Tests in Commerce. *Plymouth: Macdonald and Evans.*

The assertion-reason item

This can be a searching test of analysis and comprehension. A candidate must first decide whether the two given statements are correct or incorrect. If both are correct he must then decide whether the second statement explains the first. (See Figure 23.4.)

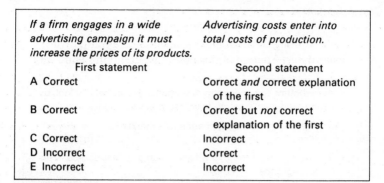

	First statement	Second statement
A	Correct	Correct *and* correct explanation of the first
B	Correct	Correct but *not* correct explanation of the first
C	Correct	Incorrect
D	Incorrect	Correct
E	Incorrect	Incorrect

If a firm engages in a wide advertising campaign it must increase the prices of its products.   *Advertising costs enter into total costs of production.*

Figure 23.4 *From Curzon, L.B. (1979)* Objective Tests in Economics. *Plymouth: Macdonald and Evans.*

The matching list item

Two lists are presented and candidates are required to match the contents of one list with those of the other. It will be noted that in the example given in Figure 23.5 a candidate cannnot use a process of elimination in order to obtain a correct last item, since List II contains more topics than List I.

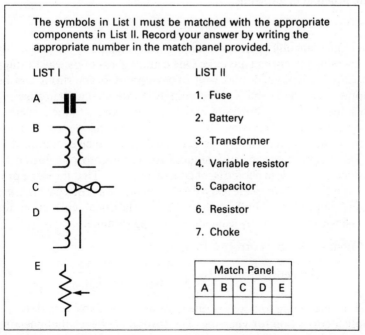

Figure 23.5 *From* Objective Testing *(1970) (City and Guilds of London Institute).*

True/false item

Statements forming the item must be evaluated as either true or false by the candidate. (An item of this nature is set out in Figure 23.6.)

State whether the following statements are correct or not by deleting the word 'true' or 'false' (so that your choice remains).

(i) The London Stock Exchange is a market for new shares.

TRUE/FALSE

(ii) The higher of the two prices which a jobber quotes is his selling price.

TRUE/FALSE

(iii) The fee which must be paid for postponing payment for shares is known as 'contango'.

TRUE/FALSE

(iv) A 'bull' is a speculator who purchases shares which he does not intend to take up.

TRUE/FALSE

Figure 23.6

The problem of guessing

An immediate objection to this kind of test is raised by the possibility of guessing the correct answers. One cannot guess one's way through an essay, it is argued, and wild or unsupported assertions can be spotted easily and penalised accordingly in extended written answers. This does not apply, however, in the case of answers to the questions in objective tests. Guessing—by which is meant making 'snap' judgements based on uncertainty—is, presumably, not to be encouraged!

That a candidate can arrive at the correct answer to a single item by a process of random choice is, of course, possible. That the same process applied to a complete test will result in the award of a pass mark is highly improbable. In fact, however, a statistical correction for guessing can be made by using the following formula:

Candidate's score corrected for guessing =
$$\text{Total correct answers} - \frac{\text{Total incorrect answers}}{\text{Number of alternatives} - 1}$$

(It is interesting to note that the City and Guilds Institute does not apply a correction for guessing. The Institute believes that guessing has no significant effect on the rank order of candidates.)

Preparing an objective test

Where possible, the preparation of an objective test ought to be based on *teamwork*, i.e. the combined operations of a group of teachers acting as item writers, revisers, testers and editors. The steps which these operations involve are outlined below.

First, a *test specification* should be constructed. This necessitates discussion by course tutors and examiners concerning the syllabus content which is to be covered by the test, the total number of items to be included (with reference to the time available) and—of much importance—the abilities which are to be tested. A 'grid' can be constructed so as to 'weight' those abilities in relation to the various sections of the syllabus.

Next, the *item must be written*. This involves a consideration of the rules set out on pp. 278–279.

The *items should then be edited*. The editor should keep in mind two questions: 'Are the items set out correctly?' 'Are they free from error?' The items ought to be checked so as to ensure that the suggested 'key' *is* the correct answer and that none of the 'distractors' provides an alternative which *could* be correct in circumstances not envisaged by the item writer. Information in the 'stem' ought to be checked for accuracy. The wording of the 'stem' and the 'options' should be free from ambiguity.

The *pre-test and analysis of results* follow. The object of the pre-test is the ascertainment of the difficulty of items, of their discriminating power and of the time necessary for completion of the test. As large a group of students as can be made available ought to be used for the pre-test and they should be representative of those for whom the examination is designed. There is little value, therefore, in using a sample of 'A' level students in a pre-test of items designed for 'O' level groups.

The results of the pre-test may be analysed so as to yield the following statistical measurements: *item facility* (known also as 'facility value', or FV); *item discrimination* (known also as 'index of discrimination' or ID); *distractor plausibility*.

(a) *FV* is expressed as the percentage of candidates attempting the item who give the correct answer. Thus:

$$FV = \frac{\text{Number giving correct answer}}{\text{Total number of candidates}} \times 100$$

As a general rule, a FV of 90 per cent suggests a very easy item;

70–89, an easy item; 30–69, an item of medium difficulty; below 30, a difficult item. The average FV of the items to be included in the test should be selected on the basis of an evaluation of the nature of the subject matter, the purpose of the test and the level of attainment of the candidates.

(b) *ID* will indicate how an item differentiates between candidates who are at different levels of competence in the subject which is being tested. It can be measured, in simple fashion, by the following formula:

$$ID = \frac{\begin{array}{c}(\text{No. in top 27\% of} \\ \text{candidates} \\ \text{giving correct answer})\end{array} - \begin{array}{c}(\text{No. in bottom 27\% of candidates} \\ \text{giving correct answer})\end{array}}{27\% \text{ of total number of candidates}}$$

The ID will range from −1.0 to + 1.0. In general, the higher its value in the case of a particular item, the greater will be the probability that those answering that item correctly will score well on the test as a whole. An ID of 0.4 or above usually suggests that an item discriminates very adequately; below 0.2 suggests weak discrimination (and points to the necessity of rejecting the item).

(c) *Distractor plausibility* (i.e. the measure of how plausible a distractor was) is calculated by counting the number of candidates who selected it, and converting that number to a percentage of the total number of candidates.

Finally, after measurement and assessment of the results of the pre-test, the structure is adjusted and *the test is given its final shape*. Items are selected from those used in the pre-test, and suitable items which are not included may be 'banked' for use on other occasions. The number of items to be used will reflect the time available for the examination, and its level.

Writing items

Several 'rules' have emerged from the practice of writing multiple-choice items and from the administration of objective tests, the most important of which are set out below:

(a) The question must arise from the syllabus of study.
(b) Only relevant abilities should be tested.
(c) The question to be answered must emerge clearly from the stem.

Some item writers work according to the rule that a good candidate ought to be able to anticipate the correct answer even before looking at the various alternatives presented.

(d) The correct option (or options, in the case of multiple response items) should be unequivocally correct. None of the distractors should be potentially correct, but they should be plausible.

(e) The position of the correct options in a series of items should be based on a random pattern.

(f) The stem and each option should be unambiguous and as brief as possible.

(g) Positive, rather than negative, stems are preferable. A negative stem should be emphasised, if used.

(h) The stem must be relevant to the options.

(i) Stem and options must be linked grammatically.

(j) There should be no unintentional clues to the correct answer in the stem or in any of the options, e.g. by the use of key words, or by the construction of an option which 'looks correct' because it is longer than the others. Another kind of unintentional clue, which should be avoided, can be given by 'the self-evident implausibility of the wrong alternatives'. (To give unintended clues is, in effect, to test a candidate's ingenuity and his 'test wisdom' rather than his knowledge of the subject matter.)

(k) Items of a trivial nature ought not to be written. (How important, for example, in the testing at 'O' level of an understanding of the functions of the Bank of England, is an item which merely tests recall of its geographical location?)

Reviewing the objective test

Following the administration, checking and marking of an objective test, a general review and evaluation of its utility ought to be undertaken, preferably by a small panel drawn from those who wrote, edited and chose the items. The review should have as its objectives: the discovery of information concerning the overall suitability of the test; the exclusion from future tests of unsuitable items; the banking of suitable questions for use in future tests.

The review should elicit answers to the following questions: Did any administrative problems arise? (For example, was the time allowed adequate? The answer can be discovered by checking the number of those who failed to complete the test.) Were all questions attempted by the majority of candidates? Were some items based on material outside the syllabus? Were any questions too easy? Were any distractors insufficiently misleading? Was average performance satisfactory? What is the relationship between the mean mark in this and previous tests taken by the candidates?

Advantages and disadvantages of objective tests

The advantages claimed for objective tests appear to derive from the nature and form of their presentation, e.g. their comprehensive coverage of the syllabus, unambiguous style and ease of assessment. It is argued that the large number of items which can be included in, say, a half-hour test, makes it possible to cover very wide areas of the examination syllabus. Choice of questions is eliminated, so that a candidate's answers are not confined to his 'favourite topics' in the syllabus. Question-spotting, too, becomes very difficult. Next, questioning of an exact nature is made possible, so that depth and precision of knowledge can be tested in a way not always possible in the discursive essay paper. Overlap of questions can be avoided completely. Further, the effect of some features of a candidate's work (e.g. 'penmanship' or 'powers of expression') which may not be relevant to the ability which is being tested, is reduced.

The pre-testing of items provides the teacher with a highly selective type of feedback—an added advantage of this mode of assessment. Levels of attainment, gaps in the teaching programme, effectiveness of types of instruction and unforeseen difficulties in comprehension may be discovered by evaluating the results of the pre-test. An important advantage of the test which is eventually administered (after revisions resulting from evaluation of responses to the pre-test) is its capacity to supply candidates with feedback in a relatively short time, as compared with the time required for the assessment of an essay question paper.

A further advantage of objective tests is their standardisation in relation to their preparation, checking and the circumstances of their administration: instructions, time limits, etc., are the same for a large number of examining centres, so that meaningful comparability of scores is ensured. Subjectivity and variability in scoring procedures are eradicated and, finally, there is very high 'scorer reliability'—one hundred per cent where the test is marked by a document-reading machine or computer!

The disadvantages of objective tests also derive, not unexpectedly, from their nature and form. The ability to express oneself coherently in writing, considered by many teachers to be vital at any stage of education other than the most elementary, cannot be tested properly, it is argued, by objective items. Originality, communication skills, powers of critical analysis and sustained argument, and clarity of expression do not seem capable of appraisal by objective testing. Whether synthesis, comprehension and similar high-order abilities are amenable to assessment in this manner is, it is argued, very doubtful. Many teachers remain unconvinced by Ebel's claim that the multiple-choice test can be used 'with great skill and effectiveness to measure complex abilities and fundamental understanding' (Ebel 1979). Teachers' suspicions, in spite of assurances to the contrary, that guessing of answers plays too great a role in objective testing, that students may retain some of their errors of choice in response to distractors, and that the tests make no allowance for the intelligent student who sees alternatives which the test writer has not offered, remain unallayed.

Ausubel criticises the great emphasis placed by objective testing on time pressure.

> It tends to favour the glib, confident, impulsive, and testwise student, and to handicap the student who is inclined to be cautious, thoughtful, and self-critical, or is unsophisticated about testing. . . . The current emphasis on speed in most standardised tests of achievement detracts from their validity by placing a premium on factors that are intrinsically unrelated to genuine mastery of subject matter.

He emphasises, additionally, the limitations of objective testing:

> . . . by definition, the tests cannot measure students' ability spontaneously to generate relevant hypotheses . . . to marshal evidence in support of a proposition, to design an original experiment, to structure a cogent argument, or to do creative work (Ausubel 1978).

The processes involved—pre-tests, collection and interpretation of results, re-writing and editing—are said to place a heavy burden on the teacher who has little time to spare for activities of this nature. The expense of objective testing in terms of time, intensity of effort and real costs of administration can be very high.

The most serious of the charges brought against objective testing would seem to be that it has a tendency—because of its very nature—to encourage a 'fragmentary' approach to teaching and learning. The whole *is* greater than its parts, and a test of subject mastery which concentrates on detail while apparently ignoring the overall significance of that which has been learned, which seems to examine the components while neglecting the totality, may have undesirable effects on the manner in which teacher and students set out to achieve their objectives.

Ausubel's reminder is of importance:

> Despite considerable improvement in this respect . . . many objective tests still measure rote recognition of relatively trivial and disconnected items of knowledge rather than genuine comprehension of broad concepts, principles and relationships, and ability to interpret facts and apply knowledge (Ausubel 1978).

The history of objective testing is too brief and research too limited to pronounce with confidence on its suitability as a mode of assessment. Further research is needed in order to discover whether objective testing can effectively examine more than factual recall and simple application. If it can be demonstrated clearly that the higher abilities, such as the perception and analysis of relationships and synthesis, can be tested by this method, much of the opposition to its use may disappear. There are indications at the present time, however, of a willingness by teachers to experiment in the application of a variety of examining techniques, so that it is possible to foresee in the immediate future an increase in the use of those forms of examination papers consisting of a mixture of essay-type and objective questions.

Bibliography

Chapter 1

Bandura, A. (1969) *Principles of behaviour modification.* Holt, Rinehart & Winston.
Biehler, R.F. (1978) *Psychology applied to teaching.* Houghton Mifflin.
Dembo, M.H. (1981) *Teaching for Learning.* Goodyear.
Dewey, J. (1940) *Experience and Education.* Macmillan.
Eisner, E.W. (1979) *The Educational Imagination.* Macmillan.
Galperin, P.Y. (1965) *Psychology and Teaching.* USSR Publishing House.
Gage, N.L., & Berliner, D.C. (1979) *Educational Psychology.* Rand McNally.
Gagné, R. (1983) *The Conditions of Learning.* Holt-Saunders.
Goodwin, W.L., & Klausmeir, H.J. (1975) *Facilitating Student Learning.* Harper & Row.
Groves, P., & Schlesinger, K. (1979) *Biological Psychology.* Brown.
Hebb, D.O. (1949) *The Organisation of Behaviour.* Wiley.
Hilgard, E.R., & Bower, G.H. (1981) *Theories of Learning.* Prentice-Hall.
Hulse, S.H., et al. (1980) *The Psychology of Learning.* McGraw-Hill.
Kimble, D.P. (1963) *Physiological Psychology.* Addison-Wesley.
Mackintosh, N. (1974) *The Psychology of Animal Learning.* Academic Press.
Manning, A. (1979) *Animal Behaviour.* Arnold.
McClelland, V.A. (ed.) (1980) *Educational Theory in a Changing World.* University of Hull.
Michelet, J. (1846) *The People.* University of Chicago Press.
Polanyi, M. (1958) *Personal Knowledge.* Routledge & Kegan Paul.
Popper, K.R., & Eccles, J.C. (1979) *The Self and Its Brain.* Springer.
Ryle, G. (1983) *The Concept of Mind.* Penguin.
Skinner, B.F. (1938) *The Behaviour of Organisms.* Appleton-Century-Crofts.
Skinner, B.F. (1968) *The Technology of Teaching.* Prentice-Hall.
Smith, K. (1966) *Cybernetic Principles of Learning and Educational Design.* Holt, Rinehart & Winston.
Solow, R. (1965) 'A contribution to the theory of economic growth', in *Quarterly Journal of Economics* **70.**
Thorpe, W. (1975) *Animal Nature and Human Nature.* Eyre-Methuen.
Williams, C.R. (1982) 'Teaching', in *Theory into Practice.* Ohio State University, **2.**
Young, J.Z. (1981) *Programs of the Brain.* OUP.

Young, J.Z., & Boycott, B. (1950) 'The comparative study of learning', in *Symposia of the Society for Experimental Biology.* Academic Press.

Chapter 2

Babkin, B.P. (1949) *Pavlov, a Biography.* University of Chicago.
Bigge, M.L. (1983) *Learning Theories for Teachers.* Harper & Row.
Bolles, R.C. (1979) *Learning Theory.* Holt, Rinehart & Winston.
Bourne, L.E., & Ekstrand, B.R. (1982) *Psychology—its principles and meanings.* Holt, Rinehart & Winston.
Chaplin, J.P., & Krawiec, T.S. (1979) *Systems and Theories of Psychology.* Holt, Rinehart & Winston.
Cohen, D. (1979) *J.B. Watson.* Routledge.
Cross, G. (1974) *The Psychology of Learning.* Pergamon.
Davidoff, L. (1980) *Introduction to Psychology.* McGraw-Hill.
Fontana, D. (1981) *Psychology for Teachers.* BPS Macmillan.
Gagné, R. (1983) *The Conditions of Learning.* Holt, Rinehart and Winston.
Gray, J.A. (1979) *Pavlov.* Fontana.
Guthrie, E. (1930) 'Conditioning as a principle of learning', in *Psychological Review,* **37.**
Guthrie, E.R. (1952) *The Psychology of Learning.* Smith.
Guthrie, E.R. (1959) 'Association by contiguity', in *Psychology,* ed. Koch, S. McGraw-Hill.
Harris, B. (1979) 'Whatever happened to little Albert?', in *American Psychologist,* **34.**
Hilgard, E.R., & Bower, G.H. (1981) *Theories of Learning.* Prentice-Hall.
Hill, W. (1973) *Learning.* Methuen.
Hubel, D. (1979) 'The Brain', in *Scientific American,* **3.**
Joncich, G. (1968) *The sane positivist—a biography of Thorndike.* Wesleyan U. Press.
Marx, M.H., & Bunch, M.E. (1977) *Fundamentals and Applications of Learning.* Collier-Macmillan.
Marx, M.H., & Hillix, W. (1979) *Systems and Theories in Psychology.* McGraw-Hill.
Morris, P. (1974) *Behaviourism.* Open University.
Murphy, G., & Kovach, J. (1978) *Historical Introduction to Modern Psychology.* Routledge.
Pavlov, I. (1932) 'Reply of a physiologist to psychologists', in *Psychological Review,* **59.**
Popper, K.R., & Eccles, J.C. (1979) *The Self and Its Brain.* Springer.
Robinson, D.N. (1981) *An Intellectual History of Psychology.* Collier-Macmillan.
Sahakian, W.S (1976) *Learning—systems, models and theories.* Rand McNally.
Talyzina, N. (1981) *The Psychology of Learning.* Progress Publishers.
Tomlinson, P.D. (1981) *Understanding Teaching.* McGraw-Hill.
Watson, J.B. (1919) 'The behaviouristic orientation', in *Psychology from t Standpoint of a Behaviourist.* Lippincott.
Watson, J.B. (1925) *Behaviourism.* Norton.
Watson, J.B. (1928) *The Ways of Behaviourism.* Harper.

Watson, J.B., & Raynor, R. (1920) 'Conditioned emotional reactions', in *Journal of Experimental Psychology,* **3.**
Wetherick, N. (1978) 'Behaviourism', in *Thinking in Perspective,* ed. Burton, A. Methuen.

Chapter 3

Blackman, D. (1974) *Operant conditioning—an experimental analysis of Behaviourism.* Methuen.
Breland, K., & M. (1961) 'The misbehaviour of organisms', in *American Psychologist,* **16.**
Chomsky, N. (1978) 'Psychology and Ideology', in *The Philosophy of Society,* ed. Beehler, R. Methuen.
Dembo, M.H. (1981) *Teaching for Learning.* Goodyear.
Gagné, R. (1968) 'Contributions of learning to human development', in *Psychological Review,* **75.**
Gagné, R. (1974) 'Learning Hierarchies', in *Contemporary Issues in Educational Psychology,* ed. Clarizio, H., & Craig, R. Allyn & Bacon.
Gagné, R. (1974) *Essentials of Learning for Instruction.* Dryden.
Gagné R. (1983) *The Conditions of Learning.* Holt, Rinehart and Winston.
Gagné, R., & Briggs, L.J. (1979) *Principles of Instructional Design.* Holt, Rinehart and Winston.
Koestler, A. (1970) *The Ghost in the Machine.* Paladin.
Mackenzie, B. (1977) *Behaviourism and the limits of Scientific Method.* Routledge and Kegan Paul.
Rachlin, H. (1980) *Introduction to Modern Behaviourism.* Freeman.
Skinner, B.F. (1950) 'Are theories of learning necessary?', in *Psychological Review,* **57.**
Skinner, B.F. (1969) *Contingencies of Reinforcement.* Appleton-Century-Crofts.
Skinner, B.F. (1971) *Beyond Freedom and Dignity.* Penguin.
Skinner, B.F. (1972) *Cumulative Record.* Appleton-Century-Crofts.
Skinner, B.F. (1974) *About Behaviourism.* Knopf.
Skinner, B.F. (1979) *The shaping of a behaviourist.* Knopf.
Tolman, E.C. (1949) *Purposive behaviour in animals and men.* U. of California.
Tolman, E.C. (1949) 'There is more than one kind of learning', in *Psychological Review,* **56.**
Tolman, E.C. (1951) *Behaviour and psychological man.* U. of California.
Tolman, E.C. (1959) 'Principles of purposive behaviour', in *Psychology,* ed. Koch, S. McGraw-Hill.

Chapter 4

Allport, F. (1955) *Theories of Perception and the Concept of Structure.* Wiley.
Bell, D. (1980) 'The information society', in *The Computer Age,* ed. Dertouzos, M. MIT Press.

Boyer, C. (1968) *History of Mathematics.* Wiley.

Burton, E. (1978) 'The whole idea in Gestalt psychology', in *Thinking in Perspective,* ed. Burton, A. Methuen.

Duncker, K. (1945) 'On problem solving', in *Psychological Monographs,* **58.**

Eigen, M., & Winkler, R. (1981) 'Structure, pattern and shape', in *Laws of the Game.* Penguin.

Ellis, W.D. (ed.) (1950) *Source Book of Gestalt Psychology.* Humanities Press.

Gruber, H. (1974) *Darwin on Man.* Wildwood House.

Hadamard, J. (1954) *The Psychology of Invention in the Mathematical Field.* Dover Books.

Harlow, H. (1949) 'The formation of learning sets', in *Psychological Review,* **56.**

Hartmann, G.W. (1974) *Gestalt Psychology—facts and principles.* Greenwood.

Henle, M. (ed.) (1961) *Documents of Gestalt Psychology.* U. of California Press.

Hilgard, E.R., & Bower, G.H. (1981) *Theories of Learning.* Prentice-Hall.

Hofstadter, D.R. (1980) 'Figure and ground', in *Gödel, Escher, Bach—an eternal golden braid.* Penguin.

Katona, G. (1940) *Organising and Meaning.* Harper & Row.

Katz, D. (1979) *Gestalt Psychology—nature and significance.* Greenwood.

Koestler, A. (1982) 'Creativity and the unconscious', in *Bricks to Babel.* Picador.

Koffka, K. (1924) *The growth of the mind.* Kegan Paul.

Koffka, K. (1935) *Principles of Gestalt Psychology.* Harcourt, Brace.

Köhler, W. (1925) *The Mentality of Apes.* Harcourt, Brace.

Köhler, W. (1970) *Gestalt Psychology.* Liveright.

Meese, C.E. (1946) *The Path of Science.* Wiley.

Philoponos, J. (*c.* AD 500) *Commentaries on Aristotle.* Zurich.

Prentice, W.C. (1959) 'The systematic psychology of Köhler', in *Psychology,* ed. Koch, S. McGraw-Hill.

Robinson, D.N. (1981) *An Intellectual History of Psychology.* Collier-Macmillan.

Taton, R. (1957) *Reason and Chance in Scientific Discovery.* Hutchinson.

Wallas, G. (1926) *The Art of Thought.* Harcourt.

Wertheimer, M. (1959) *Productive Thinking.* Harper & Row.

Yerkes, R.M. (1927) 'The mind of a gorilla', in *Psychological Monographs,* **2.**

Chapter 5

Archambault, R. (ed.) (1974) *John Dewey on Education.* U. of Chicago Press.

Ausubel, D.P. (1960). 'The use of advance organisers', in *Journal of Educational Psychology,* **51.**

Ausubel, D.P., et al. (1978) *Educational Psychology—a Cognitive View.* Holt, Rinehart and Winston.

Ausubel, D.P. (1978) 'In defence of advance organisers', in *Review of Educational Research,* **45.**

Bindra, D. (1978) 'How Adaptive Behaviour is produced', in *Behavioural Sciences,* **1.**

Bruner, J.S. (1957) 'On Perceptual Readiness', in *Psychological Review*, **64.**
Bruner, J.S. (1961) 'The act of discovery', in *Harvard Eductional Review*, **31.**
Bruner, J.S. (1965) *The Process of Education*. Harvard U. Press.
Bruner, J.S. (1966) 'Some elements of discovery', in *Learning by Discovery—a critical appraisal*, ed. Shulman, L.S., & Keislar, E.R. Rand McNally.
Bruner, J.S., et al. (1957) *Contemporary Approaches to Cognition*. Harvard U. Press.
Bruner, J.S., & Anglin, J. (1974) *Beyond the Information Given—Studies in the Psychology of Knowing*. Allen & Unwin.
Butterfield, H. (1980) *The Origins of Modern Science*. Bell & Hyman.
Davies, I.K. (1976) *Objectives in Curriculum Design*. McGraw-Hill.
Dembo, M.H. (1981) *Teaching for learning*. Goodyear.
Dewey, J. (1940) *Experience and Education*. Macmillan.
Dewey, J. (1966) *Democracy and Education*. Free Press.
Dewey, J. (1971) *Philosophy of Education*. Littlefield.
Dewey, J. (1971) *The Way out of Educational Confusion*. Greenwood.
Dewey, J. (1974) 'My pedagogic creed', in *John Dewey on Education*, ed. Archambault, R. U. of Chicago Press.
Hartley, J. and Davies, I. (1974) 'Introducing new materials—the role of pre-tests, behavioural objectives, reviews and advance organisers as pre-instructional strategies', in *Review of Educational Research*, **46.**
Joyce, B., & Weil, B. (1972) *Models of Teaching*. Prentice-Hall.
Morgenbesser, S. (ed.) (1977) *Dewey and his critics*. Hackett.
O'Neil, H.F. (1978) *Learning Strategies*. Academic Press.
Popper, K.R., & Eccles, J.C. (1979) *The Self and Its Brain*. Springer.
Radford, J., & Burton, A. (1978) *Thinking—its nature and development*. Wiley.
Russell, B. (1964) 'John Dewey', in *A History of Western Philosophy*. Allen & Unwin.
Taba, H. (1963) 'Learning by discovery', in *School Journal*, **3.**
Tyler, F.T. (1964) 'Issues related to readiness', in *Theories of Learning and Instruction*. U. of Chicago Press.
Whitehead, A. (1929) *The Aims of Education and Other Essays*. Macmillan.

Chapter 6

Adler, R.B., & Rodman, G. (1982) *Understanding Human Communication*. Holt, Rinehart and Winston.
Alderfer, C.P. (1972) *Existence, Relatedness and Growth*. Free Press.
Atkinson, J. (1980) *Introduction to Motivation*. Van Nostrand.
Ausubel, D.P., et al. (1978) *Educational Psychology—A Cognitive View*. Holt, Rinehart and Winston.
Barnlund, D.C. (1968) *Interpersonal Communication*. Houghton Mifflin.
Beard, R., & Senior, J. (1980) *Motivating Students*. Routledge.
Beck, R.C. (1978) *Motivation—theories and principles*. Prentice-Hall.
Berlo, D. (1960) *The Process of Communication*. Holt, Rinehart and Winston.
Bernstein, B. (1971) 'Social class and linguistic development in a theory of social learning', in *Class, Codes and Control*. Routledge.
Bormann, E.G. (1980) *Communication Theory*. Holt, Rinehart and Winston.

Bormann, E.G., et al. (1982) *Interpersonal Communication in the Modern Organisation*. Prentice-Hall.

Bradley, B.E. (1981) *Fundamentals of Speech Communication*. Brown.

Budd, R.W., & Ruben, B.D. (1978) *Interdisciplinary Approaches to Human Communication*. Hayden.

Dance, F.E. (1977) 'The concept of "communication"', in *Communication in Organisations,* ed. Porter, L.W., & Roberts, K.H. Penguin.

Davies, I.K. (1971) *The Management of Learning*. McGraw-Hill.

Ehninger, D., et al. (1982) *Principles and Types of Speech Communication*. Scott, Foresman.

Fisher, A.B. (1978) *Perspective in Human Communication*. Macmillan.

Herzberg, F. (1959) *Motivation to Work*. Wiley.

Hilgard, E.R., & Bower, G.H. (1981) *Theories of Learning*. Prentice-Hall.

Hills, P. (1971) *Teaching and Learning as a Communication Process*. Croom Helm.

Knapp, M.L. (1978) *Nonverbal Communication in Human Interaction*. Holt, Rinehart and Winston.

Koehler, J.W., & Anatol, K.W. (1981) *Organisational Communication— Behavioural Perspectives*. Holt, Rinehart and Winston.

Kolesnik, W.B. (1978) *Motivation*. Allyn & Bacon.

Labov, W. (1976) *Language in the Inner City*. U. of Pennsylvania Press.

Maslow, A.H. (1970). *Motivation and Personality*. Harper & Row.

Mehrabian, A. (1981). *Silent Messages*. Wadsworth.

Mondy, R.W., et al. (1983) 'Motivation', in *Management—concepts and practices*. Allyn & Bacon.

Mortensen, C.D. (1979) *Basic Readings in Communication Theory*. Harper & Row.

Paisley, W. (1980) 'Information and Work', in *Progress in Communication Sciences*. Ablex.

Parry, R. (1966) *The Psychology of Human Communication*. ULP.

Shannon, C., & Weaver, W. (1949) *The Mathematical Theory of Communication*. U. of Illinois Press.

Stoner, J. (1982) 'Communication', in *Management*. Prentice-Hall.

Taylor, A., et al. (1980) *Communicating*. Prentice-Hall.

Tortoriello, T.R. (1978) *Communication in the Organisation*. McGraw-Hill.

Treece, M. (1983) *Communication for Business and the Professions*. Allyn & Bacon.

Vroom, V.H., & Deci, E.L. (eds.) (1981) *Management & Motivation*. Penguin.

Weiner, B. (1980) *Human Motivation*. Holt, Rinehart & Winston.

Williams, R. (ed.) (1981) *Contact—Human Communication and its History*. Thames & Hudson.

Wlodowski, R.J. (1978) *Motivation and Teaching—a practical guide*. National Educational Association, Washington.

Wolff, F., et al. (1983) *Perceptive Listening*. Holt, Rinehart and Winston.

Chapter 7

Annett, J. (1969) *Feedback and Human Behaviour*. Penguin.

Anthony, R., & Dearden, J. (1980) *Management Control Systems*. Irwin.

Boulding, K. (1956) 'General systems theory', in *Management Science*, **3.**
Drucker, P. (1974) *Management-Tasks, Responsibilities, Practices.* Heinemann.
George, F.H. (1979) *Philosophical Foundations of Cybernetics.* Abacus Press.
Holloway, C. (1974) *Human Information Processing.* Open University.
Katz, D., & Kahn, R. (1980) *The Social Psychology of Organisations.* Wiley.
Lawler, E., & Rhode, J. (1976) *Information and Control in Organisations.* Goodyear.
Miller, J. (1955) 'Towards a general theory for the behavioural sciences', in *American Psychologist*, **10.**
Pask, G. (1975) *The Cybernetics of Human Learning and Performance.* Hutchinson.
Powers, W.T. (1975) *Behaviour—the Control of Perception.* Wildwood House.
Smith, K. (1966) *Cybernetic Principles of Learning and Educational Design.* Holt, Rinehart and Winston.
Talyzina, N. (1981) *The psychology of Learning.* Progress Publishers.
Tustin, A. (1952) 'Feedback', in *Scientific American*, **3.**
Wiener, N. (1948) *Cybernetics.* MIT Press.
Wiener, N. (1954) *The Human Use of Human Beings.* Houghton Mifflin.

Chapter 8

Armstrong, R.J., et al. (1970) *Development and evolution of behavioural objectives.* Brown.
Atkin, J. (1968) 'Behavioural objectives in curriculum design—a cautionary note', in *Science Teacher*, **35.**
Bloom, B.S. (ed.) (1956) *Taxonomy of Educational Objectives: Handbook I—the Cognitive Domain.* Longmans.
Bloom, B.S., et al. (1981) 'Formulating and Selecting Educational Objectives', in *Evaluation to Improve Learning.* McGraw-Hill.
Davies, I.K. (1976) *Objectives in Curriculum Design.* McGraw-Hill.
Eisner, E.W. (1967) 'Educational Objectives—help or hindrance?', in *The School Review*, **75.**
Flanagan, J.C., et al. (1971) *Mathematics Behavioural Objectives.* Westinghouse.
Gagné, R. (1965) 'Educational objectives and human performance', in *Learning and the educational process.* Rand McNally.
Gagné, R., & Briggs, L.J. (1979) *Principles of Instructional Design.* Holt, Rinehart and Winston.
Gardner, L. (1977) 'Humanistic education and behavioural objectives', in *School Review*, May.
Gronlund, N. (1981) 'Preparing instructional objectives', in *Measurement and Evaluation in Teaching.* Collier Macmillan.
Hogben, J. (1972) 'The behavioural approach—some problems and some dangers', in *Journal of Curriculum Studies*, **4.**
Kibler, R.J., et al. (1981) *Objectives for Instruction and Evaluation.* Allyn & Bacon.
Kneller, G. (1972) 'Behavioural objectives? No!', in *Educational Leadership.*

Krathwohl, N. (ed.) (1964) *Taxonomy of Educational Objectives: Handbook II—the Affective Domain.* Longmans.

Macdonald, J. (1965) 'Myths about instruction', in *Educational Leadership,* 7.

Macdonald-Ross, M. (1973) 'Behavioural objectives—a critical review', in *Instructional Science,* 2.

Mager, R.F. (1984) *Goal Analysis.* Pitman.

Mager, R.F. (1984) *Preparing Instructional Objectives.* Pitman.

Popham, W.J., & Baker, E.L. (1970) *Establishing Instructional Goals.* Prentice-Hall.

Rowntree, D. (1973) 'Which objectives are the most worthwhile?', in *Aspects of Educational Technology.* Pitman.

Ryba, R., & Drake, K. (1974) 'Towards a taxonomy of educational objectives for economics?', in *Curriculum Development for Economics,* ed. Whitehead, D. Heinemann.

Tyler, R. (1949) *Basic Principles of Curriculum and Instruction.* U. of Chicago Press.

Tyler, R. (1964) 'Some persistent questions on the defining of objectives', in *Defining Educational Objectives,* ed. Lindvall, C. U. of Pittsburgh.

Vargas, J. (1972) *Writing worthwhile behavioural objectives.* Harper & Row.

Chapter 9

Beard, R. (1974) *Objectives in Higher Education.* SRHE.

Belbin, E. et al. (1984) 'Analysing the learning process', in *How do I Learn?* FEU. DES.

Bloom, B.S. (ed.) (1956) *Taxonomy of Educational Objectives: Handbook I—the Cognitive Domain.* Longmans.

Bloom, B.S., et al. (1981) 'Strategies and sources for developing educational objectives', in *Evaluation to Improve Learning.* McGraw-Hill.

Bobbitt, F. (1924) *How to Make a Curriculum.* Norton.

Delandsheere, V. (1977) 'On refining educational objectives', in *Evaluation in Education,* ed. Choppin, B.H., & Postlethwaite, H. Holt.

Dembo, M.H. (1981) 'Instructional objectives', in *Teaching for Learning.* Goodyear.

Duchastel, P.C., & Brown, B.R. (1957) 'Incidental and Relevant Learning with Instructional Objectives', in *Journal of Educational Psychology,* **66.**

Ebel, R. (1979) *Essentials of Educational Measurement.* Prentice-Hall.

Enever, L., & Harlen, W. (1972) *With Objectives in Mind.* Macdonald.

Gagné, R. (1983) *The Conditions of Learning.* Holt, Rinehart and Winston.

Gronlund, N.E. (1978) *Stating Objectives for Classroom Instruction.* Macmillan.

Harrow, A.J. (1972) *A taxonomy of the psychomotor domain.* McKay.

Kibler, R.J., et al. (1981) *Objectives for Instruction and Evaluation.* Allyn & Bacon.

Knox, R. (1949) *Trials of a Translator.* Sheed & Ward.

Krathwohl, D.R., & Payne, D.A. (1971) 'The nature and definition of educational objectives, and strategies for their assessment', in *Educational Measurement,* ed. Thorndike, R.L. American Council on Education.

Noll, V.H., et al. (1979) 'Objectives as the basis of all good measurement', in *Introduction to Educational Measurement.* Houghton Mifflin.

Popham, W.J. (1973) *Criterion-referenced instruction.* Fearon.

Scheffler, I. (1965) *Conditions of Knowledge—an Introduction to Epistemology and Education*. Scott, Foresman.

Simpson, E.J. (1966) *The Classification of Educational Objectives*. U. of Illinois.

Sockett, H., & Pring, R. (1971) 'Bloom's Taxonomy—a Philosophical Critique', in *Cambridge Journal of Education*, **1, 2**.

Sullivan, H. (1969) 'Objectives, evaluation and improved learner achievement', in *American Educational Research Monographs on Curriculum Evaluation*. Rand McNally.

Tuckman, B.W. (1975) 'The what and why of taxonomies', in *Measuring Educational Outcomes*. Harcourt Brace Jovanovich.

Tyler, R. (1974) 'Assisting educational achievment in the affective domain', in *Measurement in Education*, **3**.

Chapter 10

Baume, A., & Jones, B. (1974) *Education by Objectives*. NELP Press.

Bedeian, A.G. & Glueck, W.F. (1983) *Management*. Holt, Rinehart and Winston.

Davies, I.K. (1971) *The Management of Learning*. McGraw-Hill.

Davies, I.K. (1981) 'Instructional Concerns', in *Instructional Technique*, McGraw-Hill.

Dessler, G. (1982) *Organisation and Management*. Reston.

Dick, W., & Carey, L. (1978) *The Systematic Design of Instruction*. Scott, Foresman.

Gage, N.L. (1977) *The Scientific Basis of the Art of Teaching*. Teachers' College Press, USA.

Gagné, R. (1974) 'Planning instruction', in *Essentials of Learning for Instruction*. Dryden.

Gagné, R., & Briggs, L.J. (1979) *Principles of Instructional Design*. Holt, Rinehart and Winston.

Haimann, T., & Scott, W.G. (1978) *Managing the Modern Organisation*. Houghton Mifflin.

Hampton, D.R. (1982) *Contemporary Management*. McGraw-Hill.

Handy, C.B. (1981) *Understanding Organisations*. Penguin.

Kemp, J.E. (1971) *Instructional Design*. Fearon.

Koontz, H., et al. (1982) *Essentials of Management*. McGraw-Hill.

Kozman, R.B., et al. (1978) *Instructional Technology in Higher Education*. Educational Technology Publications.

Miller, R.D. (1963) 'Task descriptions and analysis', in *Psychological principles in system development*. Holt, Rinehart and Winston.

Milton, C.R. (1981) *Human Behaviour in Organisations*. Prentice-Hall.

Mondy, C., et al. (1983) Management—concepts and practices. Allyn & Bacon.

Popham, E.L., et al. (1975) *A Teaching-Learning System for Business Education*. McGraw-Hill.

Posner, G.J., & Rudinsky, A.N. (1978) *Course Design*. Longman.

Saylor, J.G., et al. (1981) *Curriculum Planning for Better Teaching and Learning*. Holt, Rinehart and Winston.

Stoner, J.A. (1982) *Management*. Prentice-Hall.

Tanner, D., & Tanner, L. (1980) *Curriculum Development Theory into Practice.* Macmillan.

Tosi, H.L., & Carroll, S.J. (1982) *Management.* Wiley.

Weil, M., & Joyce, B. (1982) *Information Processing Models of Teaching.* Prentice-Hall.

Chapter 11

Atkinson, R.C., & Shiffrin, R.M. (1968) 'Human memory', in *The Psychology of Learning and Motivation.* Academic Press.

Broadbent, D.E. (1958) *Perception and Communication.* Pergamon.

Cofer, C. (ed.) (1976) *The Structure of Human Memory.* W.H. Freeman.

Crick, F.H. (1979) 'Thinking about the brain', in *Scientific American*, **3.**

Donahoe, J.W., & Wessells, M.G. (1980) *Learning, Language and Memory.* Harper & Row.

Ellis, H. (1965) *The Transfer of Learning.* Macmillan.

Gagné, R. (1983) *The Conditions of Learning.* Holt, Rinehart and Winston.

Garcia, J. (1966) 'Relation of cue to consequences in avoidance learning', in *Psychonomic Science*, **4.**

Gerard, R. (1953) 'The memory', in *Scientific American*, **2.**

Geschwind, N. (1979) 'Specialisation of the human brain', in *Scientific American*, **3.**

Gregory, R.L. (1984) 'Limits of memory', in *Mind in Science.* Peregrine.

Gruneberg, M., & Morris, P. (1978) *Aspects of Memory.* Methuen.

Harlow, H. (1949) 'The formation of learning sets', in *Psychological Review*, **56.**

Hebb, D. (1949) *The Organisation of Behaviour.* Wiley.

Houston, J.P. (1981) *Fundamentals of Learning and Memory.* Academic Press.

James, W. (1890) *Principles of Psychology.* Holt.

Kandel, E.R. (1979) 'Small systems of neurons', in *Scientific American*, **3.**

Klatzky, R.L. (1979) *Human Memory.* W.H. Freeman.

Levitt, R.A. (1981) *Physiological Psychology.* Holt, Rinehart and Winston.

Luria, A.R. (1973) *The Working Brain.* Penguin.

Miller, G.A. (1956) 'The magical number $7\pm$', in *Psychological Review*, **63.**

Milner, P. (1961) *Current trends in psychological theory.* U. of Pittsburgh.

Neisser, U. (1982) *Memory observed.* W.H. Freeman.

Norman, D.A. (1982) *Learning and Memory.* W.H. Freeman.

Norman, D.A., & Rumelhart, D. (eds.) (1970) *Models of Human Memory.* Academic Press.

Osgood, C.E. (1953) *Method and theory in experimental psychology.* OUP.

Popper, K.R., & Eccles, J.C. (1979) *The Self and Its Brain.* Springer.

Russell, P. (1979) *The Brain Book.* Routledge & Kegan Paul.

Seligman, M. (1970) 'On the generality of the laws of learning', in *Psychological Review*, **77.**

Smith, K. (1966) *Cybernetic Principles of Learning and Educational Design.* Holt, Rinehart and Winston.

Stein, D.G., & Rosen, J.J. (1974) *Learning and Memory.* Macmillan.

Stephens, J. & Evans (1973) *Development and Classroom Learning.* Holt, Rinehart and Winston.

Thorndike, E., & Woodworth, R. (1901) 'The influence of improvement in one mental function upon the efficiency of other functions', in *Psychological Review,* **8.**

Trusted, J. (1979) *The Logic of Scientific Inference.* Macmillan.

Waugh, N.C., & Norman, D.A. (1965) 'Primary memory', in *Psychological Review,* **72.**

Wingfield, A., & Byrnes, D.L. (1981) *The Psychology of Human Memory.* Academic Press.

Chapter 12

Ard, B.N. (1975) 'Should all counsellors be classroom teachers?', in *Counselling and Psychotherapy,* ed. Ard, B.N. Science and Behaviour Books.

Ausubel, D., et al. (1978) *Educational Psychology—a Cognitive View.* Holt, Rinehart and Winston.

Bentley, J.C. (1968) *The Counsellor's Role.* Houghton Mifflin.

Cleugh, M. (1971) *Discipline and Morale in School and College.* Tavistock.

Dewey, J. (1910) *How We Think.* Heath.

Festinger, L. (1964) *Conflict, Decision and Dissonance.* Stanford U. Press.

Haire, M. (1975) *Modern Organisation Theory.* Krieger.

Hamblin, D.H. (1980) *The Teacher and Counselling.* Blackwell.

Jones, L.H. & Page, D. (1983) 'Punishment—its use and abuse', in *Education and Training,* **2.**

Lewis, E. (1976) *The Psychology of Counselling.* Holt, Rinehart and Winston.

Parker, C.A. (1968) *Counselling Theories and Counsellor Education.* Houghton Mifflin.

Remarque, E.M. (1931) *The Road Back* (trans. Wheen, A.W.). Little, Brown.

Schertzer, B., & Stone, S.C. (1980) *Fundamentals of Counselling.* Houghton Mifflin.

Simon, H. (1969) *The Science of the Artificial.* MIT Press.

Wadd, K. (1979) 'Good relationships with students', in *Journal of Further and Higher Education,* **2.**

Williamson, E.G. (1975) 'The fusion of discipline and counselling in the educative process', in *Counselling and Psychotherapy,* ed. Ard, B.N. Science and Behaviour Books.

Chapter 13

Ashman, S., & George, A. (1982) *Study and Learn.* Heinemann.

Baker, E.I. (1975) *A Guide to Study.* BACIE.

Belbin, E. et al. (1984) *How do I Learn,* FEU. DES.

Bragstad, B.J., & Stumpf, S.M. (1982) *A Guidebook for Teaching Study Skills and Motivation.* Allyn & Bacon.

Buzan, T. (1974) *Use Your Head.* BBC.

Cassie, W.F., & Constantine, C. (1979) *Student's Guide to Success.* Macmillan.

Fraenkel, J.R. (1980) 'Helping students to think for themselves', in *Helping Students Think and Value.* Prentice-Hall.

Freeman, R. (1982) *Mastering Study Skills.* Macmillan.

Gagné R. (1983) *The Conditions of Learning.* Holt, Rinehart and Winston.

Gibbs, G. (1981) *Teaching Students to Learn.* Open University Press.

Hills, P.J., & Barlow, H. (1980) *Effective Study Skills.* Pan.
Ladas, S.H. (1980) 'Notetaking in Lectures—an information-processing approach', in *Educational Psychologist,* **15.**
Mace, C. (1973) *The Psychology of Study.* Penguin.
Maddox, H. (1979) *How to Study.* Pan.
Main, A. (1980) *Encouraging Effective Learning.* Scottish Academic Press.
O'Neil, H.F. (ed.) (1978) *Learning Strategies.* Academic Press.
Parsons, C. (1980) *How to Study Effectively.* Arrow.
Pauk, W. (1974) *How to Study in College.* Houghton Mifflin.
Robinson, F.P. (1970) *Effective Study.* Harper & Row.
Rowntree, D. (1970) *Learn How to Study.* Macdonald.
Wingfield, A., & Byrnes, D.L. (1981) *The Psychology of Human Memory.* Academic Press.

Chapter 14

Apps, W. (1978) *Problems in Continuing Education.* McGraw-Hill.
Battleday, S. et al. (1984) 'Communication skills in adult education', in *Education and Training.* May.
Bischof, L.J. (1969) *Adult Psychology.* Harper & Row.
Cleugh, M.F. (1973) *Educating Older People.* Tavistock.
Combs, A., & Snygg, D. (1959) *Individual Behaviour.* Harper & Row.
Dickinson, G. (1973) *Teaching Adults.* New Press.
Howe, M.J. (1978) *Adult Learning.* Wiley.
Kidd, J.R. (1975) *How Adults Learn.* Association Press.
Lumsden, D.B., & Sherron, R.H. (1975) *Experimental Studies in Adult Learning and Memory.* Wiley.
Powers, W.T. (1974) *Behaviour—the Control of Perception.* Wildwood House.
Rogers, J. (1977) *Adults Learning.* Open University.
Rogers, J. (ed.) (1977) *Adults in Education.* BBC.
Ruddock, R. (1972) *Sociological Perspectives on Adult Education.* U. of Manchester.
Schiff, W. (1980) *Perception—an applied approach.* Houghton Mifflin.
Smith, R., et al. (1970) *Handbook of Adult Education.* Macmillan.
Stephens, M.D., & Roderick, G.W. (1974) *Teaching Techniques in Adult Education.* David & Charles.
Thorndike, E. (1928) *Adult Learning.* Macmillan.
Verduin, J.R., et al. (1978) *Adults Teaching Adults.* Learning Concepts.

Chapter 15

Bigge, M.L. (1983) *Learning Theories for Teachers.* Harper & Row.
Brophy, J.E. (1979) 'Teacher behaviour and its effects', in *Journal of Educational Psychology,* **71.**
Brown, G.A. (1975) *Microteaching.* Methuen.
Carin, A., & Sund, R.B. (1978) *Creative Questioning.* Merrill.
Davies, I.K. (1971) *The Management of Learning.* McGraw-Hill.
Davies, I.K. (1981) *Instructional Technique.* McGraw-Hill.
De Young, R., & Glenn, M. (1981) 'Developing Critical Thinkers through the Art of Questioning', in *Journal of Business Education,* Oct.

Faraday, M. (1967) *Advice to a Lecturer*. The Royal Institution.
Felker, P.P., & Dapna, R.A. (1975) 'Effects of question type on problem-solving ability', in *Journal of Educational Psychology,* **67.**
Flanders, N.A. (1970) *Analysing teacher behaviour.* Addison Wesley.
Gagné, R. (1974) *Essentials of Learning for Instruction.* Dryden.
Gagné, R. (1983) *The Conditions of Learning.* Holt, Rinehart and Winston.
Highet, G. (1982) *The art of teaching.* Methuen.
Hunter, M.C. (1971) 'The Teaching Process', in *The Teacher's Handbook.* Scott, Foresman.
Kissock, C., & Iyortsuun, P. (1982) *A Guide to Questioning.* Macmillan.
Lancaster, O.E. (1979) *Effective Teaching and Learning.* Gordon & Beach.
Lin Yutang, ed. (1966) *The Wisdom of Confucius.* Random House.
Porter, G., & Friday, J. (1974) *Advice to Lecturers—an anthology from the writings of Michael Faraday and Lawrence Bragg.* The Royal Institution.
Sanders, N.M. (1966) *Classroom Questions—What Kinds?* Harper & Row.
Walklin, L. (1982) *Instructional Techniques and Practice.* Thornes.
Yorke, D. (1981) *Patterns of Teaching.* CET.

Chapter 16

Adams, J. (1968) 'A Closed-Loop Theory of Motor Learning', in *Psychological Bulletin,* **70.**
Ammons, R. (1956) 'Effects of Knowledge on Performance', in *Journal of General Psychology,* **64.**
Annett, J., & Kay, H. (1956) 'Skilled Performance', in *Occupational Psychology,* **30.**
Ausubel, D., et al. (1978) *Educational Psychology—a Cognitive View.* Holt, Rinehart and Winston.
Bartlett, F.C. (1974) 'The measurement of human skill', in *British Medical Journal,* **1.**
Belbin, E., & M. (1969) *The Discovery Method in Training.* HMSO.
Belbin, E., et al. (1984) *How Do I Learn?* FEU. DES.
Crossman, E. (1964) 'Information processes in human skills', in *British Medical Bulletin,* **20.**
Davies, I.K. (1981) *Instructional Technique.* McGraw-Hill.
Demaree, R. (1979) *Development of Training Equipment Planning Information.* Wiley.
Edney, P. (1972) *A Systems Analysis of Training.* Pitman.
Fitts, P. (1965) 'Factors in complex skill training', in *Training Research and Education,* ed. Glaser, R. Wiley.
Fitts, P., & Posner, M. (1967) *Human Performance.* Brooks-Cole.
Gagné, R. (1974) *Essentials of Learning for Instruction.* Dryden.
Gagné, R. (1983) *The Conditions of Learning.* Holt, Rinehart and Winston.
Harms, H. (1972) *Methods of Teaching Business and Distributive Education.* South-Western Publishing.
Holding, D. (1965) *Principles of Training.* Pergamon.
Howarth, L. (1981) *The Structure of Psychology.* Allen & Unwin.
Keller, F.S. (1954) *Papers in Psychology.* Doubleday.
Legge, D. (ed.) (1970) *Selected Readings in Skills.* Penguin.
Lessenberry, D. (1967) *Practices and Preferences in Teaching Typewriting.* South-Western Publishing.

Miller, G., et al. (1960) *Plans and the Structure of Behaviour.* Holt, Rinehart and Winston.

Miller, J. (ed.) (1983) *States of Mind.* BBC.

Miller, J.G. (1960) 'Input overload and psychopathology', in *American Journal of Psychiatry,* **116.**

Miller, R. (1965) 'Analysis and Specification of Behaviour for Training', in *Training Research and Education,* ed. Glaser, R. Wiley.

Okon, W. (1980) 'Formation of the unity of personality', in *Diversity and Unity in Education,* ed. Holmes, B. Allen & Unwin.

Oxendine, J.B. (1978) *Psychology of Motor Learning.* McGraw-Hill.

Singer, R. (ed.) (1972) *Readings in Motor Learning.* Lea.

Smith, K.U. (1966) *Cybernetic Principles of Learning and Educational Design.* Holt, Rinehart & Winston.

Stammers, R., & Patrick, J. (1975) *The Psychology of Training.* Methuen.

Thorndike, E.L. (1935) *The Psychology of Wants, Interests and Attitudes.* Appleton, Century.

Walklin, L. (1982) *Instructional Techniques and Practice.* Thornes.

Wanous, S., & Russon, A. (1972) *Philosophy and Psychology of Teaching Business Subjects.* South-Western Publishing.

Welford, A. (1968) *Fundamentals of Skill.* Methuen.

Winfield, I. (1979) *Learning to Teach Practical Skills.* Kogan Page.

Wright, D. (ed.) (1978) *Introducing Psychology.* Penguin.

Chapter 17

Abercrombie, M.L.J. (1960) *The Anatomy of Judgment.* Hutchinson.

Argyle, M., & Kendon, J. (1967) 'The experimental analysis of social performance', in *Communication in Face to Face Interaction,* ed. Laver, J., & Hutcheson, S. Penguin.

Bligh, D. (1972) *What's the Use of Lectures?* Penguin.

Bloom, B. (1953) 'Thought processes in lectures and discussions', in *Journal of General Education,* **7.**

Bostrom, R.N., & Bryant, C.L. (1980) 'Factors in the retention of information presented orally', in *Western Journal of Speech Communication,* **44.**

Broadwell, M.M. (1980) *Lecture Method of Instruction.* Educational & Technical Publications.

Brown, G.A. (1978) *Lecturing and Explaining.* Methuen.

Cooper, B. (1967) 'Evaluating the effectiveness of lectures', in *University Quarterly,* **21.**

Darwin, F., ed. (1958) *Autobiography of Charles Darwin.* Constable.

Davies, I.K. (1981) *Instructional Technique.* McGraw-Hill.

Faraday, M. (1967) *Advice to a Lecturer.* The Royal Institution.

Goolkasian, P. (1979) 'Memory for lectures', in *Journal of Educational Psychology,* **71.**

Green, E.B. (1928) 'Relative effectiveness of the lecture and individual readings as methods of college teaching', in *Genetic Psychology Monographs,* **4.**

Hartley, J. (1967) 'Some observations on the efficiency of lecturing', in *Educational Review,* **20.**

Hartley, J., & Marshall, S. (1974) 'On notes and note-taking', in *University Quarterly,* **28.**

Hinde, R. (ed.) (1972) *Nonverbal communication.* Cambridge University Press.

Howe, M.J. (1970) 'Using students' notes', in *Journal of Educational Research.* **64.**

Kintsch, W. (1977) 'Recognition Memory', in *Journal of Experimental Psychology,* **3.**

Maqsud, M. (1980) 'Effects of personal lecture notes on recall', in *British Journal of Educational Psychology,* **50.**

Mason, A. (1983) *Understanding Academic Lectures.* Prentice-Hall.

McLeish, J. (1968) *The Lecture Method.* Cambridge Institute of Education.

Morawetz, T. (1980) *Wittgenstein and Knowledge.* Humanities Press.

Osborne, C. (1979) *The Life of a Poet—W.H. Auden.* Eyre Methuen.

Popper, K. (1966) 'Two Kinds of Definitions', in *The Open Society and Its Enemies.* Routledge & Kegan Paul.

Porter, G., & Friday, J. (1978) *Advice to Lecturers—an anthology from the writings of Michael Faraday and Lawrence Bragg.* The Royal Institution.

Powell, L.S. (1970) *Lecturing to Large Groups.* BACIE.

Powell, L.S. (1980) *Lecturing.* Pitman.

Russell, B. (1975) *Autobiography,* Allen & Unwin.

Sommer, R. (1969) *Personal Space.* Prentice-Hall.

Verner, A., & Dickinson, T. (1968) 'The lecture—an analysis and review of research', in *Adult Education,* **17.**

Watson, O., & Graves, T. (1973) 'Quantitative research in proxemic behaviour', in *Social Encounters,* ed. Argyle, M. Penguin.

Weiland, A. (1979) 'Immediate and delayed recall of lecture material', in *Journal of Educational Research,* **72.**

Wolvin, A.D., & Cookley, C.G. (1982) *Listening.* Brown.

Yorke, D. (1981) *Patterns of Teaching.* CET.

Chapter 18

Abercrombie, M.L.J. (1960) *The Anatomy of Judgment.* Hutchison.

Cooper, C. (1979) *Learning from Others in Groups.* Associated Business Press.

Davies, I.K. (1981) *Instructional Technique.* McGraw-Hill.

Elgood, C. (1974) 'How to get the most out of case studies', in *Industrial and Commercial Training,* **6.**

Neeley, S.E., & Pringle, C.D. (1983) 'An innovative technique for improving case method courses', in *Journal of Business Education,* **10.**

Paterson, R. (1970) 'The concept of discussion', in *Studies in Adult Education,* **2.**

Seale, C. (1980) 'Two views of discussion groups', in *Journal of Further and Higher Education,* **1.**

Seale, C., & Canning, J. (1978). 'The analysis of a discussion and seminar group', in *Journal of Further and Higher Education,* **2.**

Todd, F. (1979) 'Talking and learning', in *Journal of Further and Higher Education,* **2.**

Yorke, D.M. (1981) *Patterns of Teaching.* CET.

298 *Teaching in further education*

Chapter 19

Blair, M., & Woodward, R. (1970) *Team Teaching in Action*. Houghton Mifflin.
Freeman, J. (1969) *Team Teaching in Britain*. Ward Lock.
Howland, K., et al. (1974) 'Team teaching in business studies', in *The Technical Journal*, December.
Joyner, T. (1977) 'Team teaching in physics at a college of further education', in *Vocational Aspects of Education*, **29**.
Lovell, K. (1967) *Team Teaching*. U. of Leeds.
Mansell, J. (1975) 'Team teaching in further education', in *Educational Research*, **17**.
Taylor, M. (ed.) (1974) *Team teaching experiments*. NFER.
Trump, J.L. (1966) 'Team teaching', in *Visual Education*, November.
Warwick, D. (1971) *Team Teaching*. U.L.P.
Van der Eyken, W. (1974) *The Open University Opens*. Routledge.
Yorke, D.M. (1981) 'Team teaching', in *Patterns of Teaching*. CET.

Chapter 20

Brown, J.S., & Sleeman, D. (1982) *Intelligent Tutoring Systems*. Academic Press.
Coburn, P., et al. (1982) *Practical Guide to Computers in Education*. Addison-Wesley.
Ellingham, D. (1982) *Managing the Computer in the Classroom*. CET.
Evans, C. (1983) *The Mighty Micro*. Gollancz.
Fox, J. (1984) 'Computer-assisted vocabulary learning' in *ELT Journal*, **1**.
Gilbert, T. (1978) 'How writing programmed instruction can develop teaching skills', in *Journal of Higher and Further Education*, **1**.
Green, E. (1962) *The Learning Process and Programmed Instruction*. Holt, Rinehart and Winston.
Hartley, J. (ed.) (1972) *Strategies for Programmed Instruction*. Butterworth.
Hartley, R. (1982) 'A cool look at computer-aided learning', in *Educational Computing*, **5**.
Hawkridge, D. (1983) *New Informational Technology in Education*. Croom Helm.
Hills, P.J. (1982) *Trends in Information Transfer*. Pinter.
Kay, H., et al. (1968) *Teaching Machines and Programmed Instruction*. Penguin.
Kenning, M.J. (1983) *Introduction to Computer Assisted Language Teaching*. OUP.
Lecarme, O., & Lewis, R. (eds.) (1975) *Computers in Education*. North-Holland Publishing Co.
Maddison, J. (1983) *Education in the Microelectronic Era*. Open University.
Mager, R. (1960) *Preparing Programs for Programmed Instruction*. Fearon.
O'Shea, T., & Self, J. (1983) *Learning and Teaching with Computers*. Harvester Press.
Rich, E. (1983) *Artificial Intelligence*. McGraw-Hill.
Rowley, J.E. (1980) *Computers for Libraries*. Bingley.

Skinner, B.F. (1953) *Science and Human Behaviour.* Macmillan.
Skinner, B.F. (1954) 'The science of learning and the art of teaching', in *Harvard Educational Review,* **24.**
Skinner, B.F. (1961) 'Why we need teaching machines', in *Cumulative Record.* Appleton.
Stonier, T. (1981) 'Changes in Western society—educational implications', in *Recurrent Education and Lifelong Learning,* ed. Schuller, T., & Megarry, J. Kogan Page.
Talyzina, N. (1981) *The Psychology of Learning.* Progress Publishers.

Chapter 21

Allen, S.A. (1979) *A Manager's Guide to Audiovisuals.* McGraw-Hill.
Anderson, R. (1980) *Selecting and Developing Media for Instruction.* Van Nostrand Reinhold.
Billows, F.L. (1980) 'Visual aids to language learning', in *The Techniques of Language Learning.* Longman.
Brook, D., & Race, P. (1978) *Educational Technology in a Changing World.* Kogan Page.
Brown, J., et al. (1978) *AV Instruction—technology, media and methods.* McGraw-Hill.
Campbell, J. (1984) 'The bottom and top of memory', in *Grammatical Man.* Pelican.
Coggle, P.A. (1970) 'The role of the language laboratory in post O-level studies', in *Post O-level in Modern Languages,* ed. Russell, C.V. Pergamon.
Corder, S.P. (1974) *The Visual Element in Language Teaching.* Longman.
Dakin, J. (1973) *The language laboratory and language learning.* Longman.
Erickson, C.W., & Curl, D.H. (1972) *Fundamentals of teaching with audio-visual technology.* Macmillan.
Fisch, A.L. (1972) 'The trigger film technique', in *Improving College and University Teaching,* **20.**
Gagné, R. (1983) *The Conditions of Learning.* Holt, Rinehart and Winston.
Gerlach, V., & Ely, D. (1978) *Teaching and Media—A Systematic Approach.* Prentice-Hall.
Gilbert, J.K. et al. (1979) *Research in Educational Technology.* CET.
Hartley, J., & Fuller, H.C. (1971) 'Using slides in lectures', in *Visual Education,* Aug.
Heidt, E.V. (1978) *Instructional Media and the Individual Learner.* Kogan Page.
Hilgard, E.R., & Bower, G.H. (1981) *Theories of Learning.* Prentice-Hall.
Kemp, J.E. (1975) *Planning and Producing Audio-Visual Materials.* Harper & Row.
Levie, W.H., & Dickie, K.E. (1973) 'The analysis and application of media', in *Handbook of Research on Teaching,* ed. Travers, R. Rand McNally.
Minor, E., & Frye, H.R. (1977) *Techniques for producing visual instructional media.* McGraw-Hill.
Page, C.F., & Kitching, J. (1981) *Technical Aids to Teaching in Higher Education.* U. of Surrey.
Paivio, A. (1971) *Imagery and verbal process.* Holt, Rinehart and Winston.

Parke, T.H. (1982) 'Integrating the Language Laboratory', in *British Journal of Language Teaching*, **1**.

Powell, L. (1981) *A Guide to the Use of Visual Aids*. BACIE.

Rivers, W.M. (1981) 'Technology and Language Learning Centres', in *Teaching Foreign Language Skills*. U. of Chicago Press.

Romiszowski, A. (1974) *The Selection and Use of Instructional Media—a Systems Approach*. Wiley.

Sieve, M. (1978) *Selecting Instructional Media*. Colorado.

Stack, E.M. (1971) *The Language Laboratory and Modern Language Teaching*. OUP.

Chapter 22

Ausubel, D.P. et al. (1978) *Cognitive Psychology—A Cognitive View*, Holt, Rinehart and Winston.

Bruner, J. (1965) *The Process of Education*. Harvard U. Press.

Burns, E. (1979) *The development, use and abuse of tests*. Thomas.

Chase, C.I. (1979) 'The impact of achievement expectations and handwriting quality on scoring essay tests', in *Journal of Educational Measurement*, **16**.

Coffman, W.E. (1971) 'Essay questions', in *Educational Measurement*, ed. Thorndike, R.L. American Council on Education.

Davies, I.K. (1981) 'Assessment techniques', in *Instructional Technique*. McGraw-Hill.

Ebel, R.L. (1979) 'Essay tests', in *Essentials of Educational Measurement*. Prentice-Hall.

Glaser, R., & Nitko, A.J. (1971) 'Measurement in learning and instruction', in *Educational Measurement*, ed. Thorndike, R.L. American Council on Education.

Gronlund, N.E. (1981) *Measurement and Evaluation in Teaching*. Collier Macmillan.

Heywood, J. (1977) *Assessment in Higher Education*. Wiley.

Ingram, G.F. (1980) *Fundamentals of Educational Assessment*. Van Nostrand.

Lewis, D.G. (1974) *Assessment in Education*. ULP.

Mager, R.F. (1984) *Measuring Instructional Results*. Pitman.

Rowntree, D. (1977) *Assessing Students*. Harper & Row.

Shaw, D. (1974) *Examination and Assessment Methods*. RAF School of Education.

TenBrink, T.D. (1974) *Evaluation—a practical guide for teachers*. McGraw-Hill.

Thyne, J. (1974) *Principles of Examining*. ULP.

Tuckman, B.W. (1975) *Measuring Educational Outcomes*. Harcourt Brace Jovanovich.

Tyler, L.E., & Walsh, W.B. (1979) *Tests and Measurement*. Prentice-Hall.

Ward, C. (1980) *Designing a Scheme of Assessment*. Thornes.

Ward, C. (1981) *Preparing and Using Constructed-Answer Questions*. Thornes.

Worthen, B.R., & Sanders, J.R. (1972) *Educational Evaluation—theory and practice*. Jones.

Yorke, D.M. (1981) 'Project work', in *Patterns of Teaching*. CET.

Chapter 23

Ausubel, D.P. et al. (1978) *Educational Psychology—A Cognitive View*. Holt, Rinehart and Winston.

Baker, F.B. (1977) 'Advances in item analysis', in *Review of Educational Research*, **41**.

Bloom, B.S., et al. (1981) 'Item writing and item selection', in *Evaluation to Improve Learning*. McGraw-Hill.

Choppin, B. (1975) 'Guessing the answer on objective tests', in *British Journal of Educational Psychology*, **45**.

City & Guilds. (1970, updated 1984) *Objective Testing*. City & Guilds Institute.

Denova, C. (1980) *Test Construction for Training Evaluation*. Van Nostrand Reinhold.

Ebel, R. (1970) 'The case for true-false test items', in *The School Review*, **78**.

Ebel, R. (1979) 'Multiple-choice test items', in *Essentials of Educational Measurement*. Prentice-Hall.

Gronlund, N.E. (1977) *Constructing Achievement Tests*. Prentice-Hall.

Gronlund, N.E. (1981) 'Constructing objective test items', in *Measurement and Evaluation in Teaching*. Macmillan.

Houts, P.L. (ed.) (1977) *The Myth of Measurability*. Hart.

Hudson, B. (ed.) (1973) 'Objective tests', in *Assessment Techniques—an Introduction*. Methuen.

Kibler, R., *et al.* (1981) *Objectives for Instruction and Evaluation*. Allyn & Bacon.

Mehrens, W.A., & Lehman, I.J. (1978) *Measurement and Evaluation in Education and Psychology*. Holt, Rinehart and Winston.

Rust, W.B. (1973) *Objective Testing in Training and Education*. Pitman.

Scammell, D.P., & Tracy, D.B. (1980) 'Multiple Choice Tests', in *Testing and Measurement in the Classroom*. Houghton Mifflin.

Tuckman, B.W. (1975) 'Constructing a test', in *Measuring Educational Outcomes*. Harcourt Brace Jovanovich.

Turnbull, W. (1956) 'Item analysis', in *Journal of Educational Psychology*, **37**.

Vernon, P. (1956) *The Measurement of Abilities*. ULP.

Ward, C. (1981) *Preparing and Using Objective Questions*. Thornes.

Wesman, A. (1976) 'Writing the test item', in *Educational Measurement*, ed. Thorndike, R.L. American Council on Education.

Index